THE ART OF THE POSSIBLE

Javad Hassan

An Autobiography
Edited, Co-Written, And Produced By

Sanjeev Loomba

Author Of *The Ninth Gear*
Speaker And Transformationalist
In Strategy And Leadership

Incorporating Extensive Biographical
Material And Research From A Biography Script
As Of 6 January 2024

W&M

THE ART OF THE POSSIBLE

Javad Hassan
Edited By Sanjeev Loomba

First published in August 2024

W&M Publishing

ISBN 978-1-917265-17-1 Hbk

Contents

I Dedicate This Book

To my father, Nagoor Rawther, and my mother, Begum Khadijoo:

From whom, I learned resilience even in adversity, creative entrepreneurship, adaptability, courage, hard work, and the importance of family values.

To my wife, Sabiha:

You have been my rock and steadfast soul mate. Your inspiration, support, and encouragement have been invaluable in all my endeavors. You have enriched my life both socially and culturally.

To my brother, Jehangir:

You shaped the dream of establishing the first offshore manufacturing unit in our homeland. As the anchor of our growth at NeST Technologies and SFO in Kerala, your efforts have made me proud.

To my daughters, Naureen and Hafiza:

You have brought me immense joy and pride through your brilliant and accomplished careers.

Your patience and support during my busiest times have meant the world to me.

Acknowledgments

To all my team members and business associates:

Your dedication and loyalty have been instrumental throughout my professional journey.

Thank you for your unwavering support and hard work.

Foreword: Andre de Moller

The story of Javad K. Hassan is a classic saga of innovation, determination and relentless commitment to excellence. For example, from his time as a young engineer with IBM, to his rise as a senior executive at AMP, and even his ultimate successful jaunt as an entrepreneur, Javad has lived life as a maverick — a renegade who forged his own path, and one who constantly pushed against, and directly challenged conventional wisdom.

Javad has had a hugely successful professional career, smashing through glass ceiling after glass ceiling.

After joining IBM as a simple engineer, he excelled so much the company could not ignore him for long. His work in semiconductor research set him up for senior leadership roles and opened the door for further generations of immigrant executives in corporate America. Stories from IBM and AMP highlight Javad's zeal for innovation, his aggressive push for radical new developments in fiber optics, and his creation of many profitable business initiatives.

But it is his second life as an entrepreneur that Javad has had his greatest effect. With the help of younger brother N. Jehangir, Javad helped Kerala find its place on the global electronic manufacturing map. This pursuit was a big initiative - it was not just a business but a journey where he wanted to give back to his community and provide a multitude of people with opportunities. Thanks to their endeavors, they could create a prosperous technology ecosystem all across Kerala and generate an electric change in the entire community.

This is Javad's legacy for the ages to come - his commitment to empowerment and transformation in his entrepreneurial journey, not just results and monetary success.

Throughout his career, Javad would be guided by two principles: *have passion* and *be willing to do the work*.

These values shone through in all areas of his life, from his working successes to his personal beliefs. This commitment to mastering his surroundings and not taking undisciplined risks meant he stayed a solid, cautious, effective leader in both the corporate and entrepreneurial arenas.

Javad's style of leadership inspires and empowers everyone around him. He believes in empowering his people to make decisions and providing sufficient backing so that they can learn from their mistakes. This not only helped cultivate a culture that embraced innovation and accountability but also defined his identity as a visionary leader who knew how to believe in the potential of his team members.

When we look back at Javad's path, it is also the story of overcoming difficulties and creating the future.

The positive impact he has had as an entrepreneur has not only reshuffled industries but also left his influence on the communities and for the generations to come. Javad has remained eternally the trailblazer.

Javad's life teaches essential lessons for budding entrepreneurs and upcoming leaders. From his story, we can learn that the key to success is perseverance, making your own way in doing what you believe in, and, of course, always giving back to the community. This goes to show that success is not only a testament to one's personal accomplishments but also a reflection of the difference one makes to others.

Within the pages of this autobiography, you will discover the phenomenal journey of a man who refused to accept limitations, challenged the norms, raised standards of achievement, and built a formidable legacy in the world. Javad K. Hassan's story is a shining example for those who seek to create an impact and achieve incredible heights of success.

Andre de Moller
Barrister at Law

A Special Tribute By Sabiha To Her Husband, Javad

In the realm of human experience, few stories are as captivating as the journey of a singular individual. The pages that follow recount the extraordinary life of my husband, whose path has been one of determination, resilience, and unwavering integrity.

From humble beginnings, he has carved out a life marked by grand and personal achievements.

His life has been a testament to the power of hard work, the courage to embrace challenges, and the grace to endure life's inevitable trials and tribulations. His story reminds us that one's impact is not measured solely by accolades but by the lives touched along the way.

As you read this autobiography, you will come to know that his values are deeply rooted in family, community, and a desire to make the world a better place.

His journey is a mosaic of moments, some filled with triumph and others with tribulations – but through it all, his spirit has remained steadfast.

It is my hope that this book will offer you a glimpse into the heart and mind of a remarkable individual. May you find inspiration in his story and discover a renewed sense of purpose in your own journey.

As we embark on this journey through my husband's life, I would like to leave you with the wisdom of two great philosophers— Rumi and Plato.

Rumi said, 'Let the beauty of what you love be what you do.'

My husband wielded his influence with humility and grace throughout his life, using it to uplift others and create a legacy of positive change. Plato offered insights into the measure of a man in what he does with power. May these quotes inspire you as they have inspired us to live a life of integrity and love.

Sabiha

How To Get the Best From This Book
An Introductory Message
From The Co-writing Editor

Dear Reader

This book captures the enigmatic Dr Javad Hassan's character, philosophy, and cardinal traits, which led him to impressive zeniths of achievement. It is told through myriad cases and situations he encountered, each one analyzed to provide you with the thinking, approach, and methods to apply in your own professional journey.

More than just an autobiography, this book is a practical manual, a toolkit, and a guide for entrepreneurs and industry leaders—both aspiring and established. As you delve into its pages, you will be captivated, entertained, and astounded by the practical applicability of his methods in your own work or business, regardless of your field.

It has been a joy for me to co-write it with Dr Javad, and I invite you to approach it not just as a story of an immensely successful man and definitely not as a historical account of his life and work but as a fascinating insight into what drives this level of success. At every step of the read, reflect on how those ideas can influence your own future accomplishments.

Having led corporations myself, and then brought transformational outcomes for companies and individuals, Dr Javad's story resonated hugely with me and inspired me to work on this project.

My mega respect for him made me extract his message for you and, in each section, provide clear advice and guidance, brought to life by cross-referencing these nuggets to the stories and cases described in each phase of his brilliant professional life.

The Structure Of The Book

Moving away from a strictly chronological flow we begin the story with Dr Javad's big professional curtain raiser as he enters, innovates, and rises meteorically at IBM (Section 1).

Next comes his leadership career at AMP, full of strategic creativity (Section 2).

Then follows his prolific entrepreneurial odyssey as a serial business creator, building a business empire that continues to be in full swing today (Section 3).

We go back and explore his early life (pre-IBM) and how it shaped the corporate leader and business that magnate he became (Sections 6 and 7).

There are two more vital Sections in the middle—first, a set of captivating interviews with seven colleagues who open up fascinating insights into Dr Javad's nature and success drivers, with invaluable lessons to be learned.

Then three interviews with Dr Javad himself, where he speaks candidly about situations, his philosophy, and transformational events (Section 4).

Section 5 describes how a supportive soul mate can help propel your trajectory, accelerating excellent outcomes. This Section is the story of Sabiha and Dr Javad.

Three Further Pointers
To Enhance Your Encounter With This Book

- The book contains a lot of history and detailed facts. The facts themselves only serve as a context for the learning points and case studies. The latter are key aspects, so please don't get lost in the details but look at the inferences and lessons from them.

- As the case studies and story are set in an era alien to most of you, you may find the facts archaic or even not understand them, e.g., tape drives etc. However, at that time, this was cutting-edge technology – so please don't get bogged down by the relevance or otherwise of the stories, products, or technology – the lessons learned are as applicable today as they were then. Please focus on these illuminated nuggets of wisdom that are practical and immensely relevant today.

- The lessons learned may appear repetitive, but this is intentional. After all, it's the simplicity and sharp focus on the few points of success that made him so successful. But please read them all – You may find the point repeated, but the context in which it is expressed will be new and open up fresh perspectives and utility each time and with every story.

I wish you a happy reading and an enormously successful career.

Sanjeev Loomba
Author of 'The Ninth Gear'
Speaker and Transformationalist in Strategy
and Leadership Pioneer of Valuepreneurship

The Whole Story In A Nutshell
A Prelude To My Autobiography

The Genesis Of A Visionary Leader
What People Often Describe Me As

Every remarkable journey begins with a single step. For me, Javad Hassan, that first step was not just a stride into the corporate world but a leap into a lifetime of innovation, leadership, and unyielding determination. This autobiography chronicles my fascinating evolution from a simple engineer to a corporate leader and then to a serial entrepreneur who built a business empire, leaving an indelible mark on the industry and inspiring countless future leaders. I say this with humbleness and gratitude.

From Junior Engineer To Corporate Leadership:
My IBM Years

My journey began with a clear sense that I was destined for something beyond the conventional norms of my upbringing. As the eldest of eight children, I learned responsibility early on, viewing it not as a burden but as an honor. This instilled in me a strong sense of duty and purpose, driving my ambitions throughout my life. My fascination with technology and innovation was not merely about the allure of new gadgets but stemmed from a deeper belief in the transformative power of technology to turn the mundane into the extraordinary.

After earning a master's degree in 1968 from the University of Bridgeport, I stood at a critical crossroads. Despite the safe and respectful path of returning to India, I chose to pursue my dream of joining IBM, a leading technology company at the forefront of the technological revolution.

Joining IBM in the fall of 1968 marked a significant milestone in my career. IBM represented the pinnacle of success for any technology professional at the time. Despite my excitement, I faced the reality of being an outsider in a predominantly white, American corporate environment. My distinct appearance, accent, and background made me stand out, presenting both challenges and opportunities. Determined to earn respect through my work, I focused on demonstrating my capabilities and leadership.

My time at IBM was marked by ground-breaking innovations. I contributed to semiconductor technology, developing an automated wafer-handling system that revolutionized the industry and earned me numerous patents and awards. This period of intense professional development was also one of personal growth, as I honed my leadership skills and strategic thinking. These experiences at IBM were instrumental in shaping my professional ethos and my approach to life.

Several factors drove my success at IBM. First and foremost was my insatiable curiosity and passion for innovation. I was constantly seeking new ways to solve problems and improve processes. This relentless pursuit of excellence was not just about achieving technical milestones but about making a meaningful impact on the industry and the world.

Another driving force was my resilience in the face of adversity. Being an outsider in a new country and a new corporate culture presented numerous challenges. However, I viewed these obstacles as opportunities for growth and learning. My determination to prove myself and my belief in the power of perseverance kept me going through the toughest times.

Moreover, I was driven by a deep-seated desire to create value and make a difference. My work at IBM was not just a job; it was a calling. I believed that technology had the potential to transform lives, and I was committed to pushing the boundaries of what was possible.

The Corporate VP Turns Entrepreneurial On AMP Soil

Leaving IBM, where I had risen to a senior director, was a bold and daring move. The offer from AMP presented a unique opportunity to break new ground. This decision was not just a change of employer; it was a leap into an entirely different organizational culture and geographical location.

At AMP, I faced significant cultural and organizational challenges. My background did not align with the company's traditional practices, and my attempt to break the ice with humor fell flat. However, I approached the challenge with humility and a readiness to learn. I gradually won the trust and cooperation of my new colleagues by being supportive, encouraging open communication, and showing respect for the company's traditions.

My determination and positive outlook, honed through my experiences at IBM, helped me navigate the daily obstacles I faced.

My strategic vision was to transform AMP from a connector company into a leader in interconnection technologies and solutions. This involved significant restructuring and the creation of the Global Interconnect Systems Business (GISB). By focusing on innovation and strategic mergers and partnerships, I positioned AMP to compete in the rapidly evolving technological landscape. My approach involved not just reorganizing structures but also fostering a culture of innovation and continuous improvement within the company.

One of my proudest achievements at AMP was pioneering the concept of outsourcing. Recognizing the limitations of localized operations, I advocated for a broader, global approach, laying the foundation for what would become a standard practice in manufacturing and technology. This vision of leveraging global talent was a significant step in driving innovation and efficiency.

Several factors drove my success at AMP. One was my ability to adapt to new environments and embrace change. Moving from a well-established company like IBM to a new and different corporate culture required flexibility and an open mind. My willingness to learn and adapt was crucial in navigating this transition.

Another driving force was my strategic thinking and vision. I was not content with maintaining the status quo; I was always looking for ways to improve and innovate. My ability to see the big picture and develop a strategic plan for the future was instrumental in transforming AMP into a leader in interconnection technologies. Moreover, I was driven by a desire to make a difference. I believed that AMP had the potential to be a global leader, and I was committed to making that vision a reality. My passion for innovation and my belief in the power of technology to transform lives kept me focused and motivated.

My Entrepreneurial Odyssey: From Small Beginnings To Established Business Leader

My entrepreneurial journey is deeply rooted in my family's history and values. My grandfather and maternal uncle were significant exporters of lemon grass to Europe and America, laying the foundation for my lifelong dream of becoming an entrepreneur. My family viewed entrepreneurship as more than just a way to make a living; it was a way of life.

My entrepreneurial journey began with small, yet significant ventures. In 1962, while still an apprentice at Hindustan Machine Tools, I started a casting company from my home. This venture focused on investment casting and was my first practical application of entrepreneurial principles. It was a small but significant step in my journey, teaching me the importance of first-hand experience and know-how.

During my tenure at IBM, I started a business producing grandfather clocks made of teak wood, combining German watchmaking precision with Indian woodworking craftsmanship. This venture was close to my heart because it represented a fusion of respect for traditional craftsmanship and a passion for creative innovation.

In the early 1980s, I established Nagoor Trading Corporation to market spices from my father's estate. This initiative increased production and found better markets for their spices, teaching me the importance of understanding global markets and building solid supply chains.

My significant investment in Processor Systems (India) Private Limited marked my entry into the world of technology and software development. This dual role of corporate employment and entrepreneurship taught me valuable lessons in managing risks and ensuring sustainability. My involvement in Processor Systems demonstrated my belief in the potential of technology to drive innovation and create significant value.

My entrepreneurial journey took a significant turn when I moved to Quakertown, a small town north of Philadelphia. Leaving the comfort and security of a salaried job at the age of 58—a time when many contemplate retirement—was a significant decision. Driven by my entrepreneurial spirit, I was determined to pursue my dreams.

Under my leadership, AM Communications entered a new era of growth and innovation. The establishment of the Global Interconnect Systems Business (GISB) was a significant step in broadening AMP's product portfolio. By focusing on innovation and strategic mergers and partnerships, I positioned AMP to compete in the rapidly evolving technological landscape.

One of the most pivotal moments in my career was navigating the financial crisis of 1997 and the subsequent market crash.

Steering AM Communications through the rough waters of economic downturn and financial difficulty was not just a professional challenge but a personal trial, demanding financial deftness and the courage to thrive under pressure. This period reinforced my belief in resilience and strategic thinking.

Reviving AM Communications required recovering customer confidence, stabilizing finances, and charting a strong strategic direction. By leveraging strategic partnerships and focusing on innovation, we transformed AM Communications into a major player in the broadband industry.

Several factors drove my success as an entrepreneur. One was my relentless pursuit of innovation. I was constantly seeking new opportunities and exploring new ideas. This drive for continuous improvement and my willingness to take risks were crucial in building successful ventures.

Another driving force was my resilience and determination. Entrepreneurship is fraught with challenges and setbacks, but I viewed these obstacles as opportunities for growth and learning. My ability to bounce back from failures and keep pushing forward was instrumental in my success.

Moreover, I was driven by a desire to make a meaningful impact. I believed that my ventures had the potential to create significant value and improve lives. This sense of purpose kept me focused and motivated, even in the face of adversity.

My Beliefs And Philosophy

Throughout my career, my beliefs and philosophy have guided my actions and decisions. I believe in the transformative power of technology and innovation to improve lives and create value. This belief has been the driving force behind my relentless pursuit of excellence and my commitment to pushing the boundaries of what is possible.

One of my guiding philosophies can be encapsulated in the '5 Ps': *Passion, Patience, Persistence, Perseverance,* and *Practice.* These principles have been instrumental in my approach to life and business.

- **Passion:** Passion is the fuel that drives success. It is the inner fire that keeps you going, even in the face of challenges and setbacks. My passion for technology and innovation has been the driving force behind my achievements.

- **Patience:** Success does not come overnight. It requires time, effort, and patience. I have learned to stay the course and trust the process, knowing that perseverance will eventually pay off.

- **Persistence:** Persistence is the key to overcoming obstacles. It is the determination to keep going, even when the odds are against you. My persistence has helped me navigate numerous challenges and achieve my goals.

- **Perseverance:** Perseverance is the ability to stay focused and committed, even in the face of adversity. It is the unwavering dedication to your vision and goals. My perseverance has been crucial in my journey from a junior engineer to a successful entrepreneur.

- **Practice:** Practice really does make perfect. Continuous learning and improvement are essential for success. I have always been committed to honing my skills and expanding my knowledge, ensuring that I am always prepared for new opportunities and challenges.

These principles have guided my actions and decisions, helping me achieve my goals and make a meaningful impact. They have been the foundation of my success and will continue to guide me in my future endeavors.

Final Words Before We Dive In

Reflecting on my journey, several key lessons stand out for aspiring entrepreneurs and future leaders. Embrace curiosity and continuous learning; drive and passion define your potential, not your background. Challenge the status quo; innovative ideas often face resistance, but persistence and vision can turn skepticism into success. Build strong teams; surround yourself with capable individuals who share your vision and complement your strengths. Focus on solving problems; aim to improve existing processes and technologies.

My story is more than just an autobiography; it is a roadmap for anyone with the ambition to make their mark on the world. My journey from a corporate leader to a serial entrepreneur is a testament to the power of vision, hard work, and unwavering positivity. As you delve into the chapters that follow, may you find inspiration, guidance, and the courage to embark on your own extraordinary journey.

Section 1

From Junior Engineer
To Corporate Leadership
My IBM Years Of Innovation
And Meteoric Rise

A Maverick By Design Contesting Norms

As a child, I did not fit the mold. Where I was from, the expectations were to get an education, get a job, and follow the prescribed path. However, my interests and fascinations were firing in many directions, well beyond what was being taught in school.

Even in my early years, I felt a distinct calling. It wasn't a rebellion against the norm but a quiet understanding that I was destined for something different. This is the beginning of my story, the tale of how I set out on a path that was uniquely mine.

At a very young age, I knew that my life would not be limited by the conventional norms that stifle the ambitions of people around me. Having spent some of my childhood being the eldest of eight, six girls and one boy, my father taught me a strong sense of responsibility. He compared me to a train engine who leads the family and pulls them through. The burden of all that responsibility should have borne me down, but instead, it fueled me with strength and a sense of purpose. My duty to family was always in my nature, and taking care of them was more of an honor than a chore.

Fascinated By Innovation

I am bitten by the bug of all things tech related and not just because of the cool factor but because of the way in which technology can take the mundane and turn it into the extraordinary. I realized then that innovation was more than just an abstract thing, innovation was real and it was exciting.

I loved creating other things for the sheer joy of writing, not the praise or the acceptance. My focus was on making products and ideas happen – *quickly* – and without loose targets or goals around them.

And then, I follow the stream of inspiration and intuition instead.

Yet, my love for tech and innovation was not just about the hardware, and the software; it was an expression of my greatest values. The sense of being able to create, in terms of building something out of nothing, was directly related to my core sense that there are always alternative pathways that can lead to better outcomes. To me technology, at its core, was *magic*. The *magic* that could bring the world to one platform, or open doors into worlds previously unknown in a few words and a click. I saw every technological leap forward as a way of getting closer to a world where technology actually did meet some of those early promises, a device that gave individuals and communities alike power. It was no longer just about developing or utilizing new devices; it was about dreaming up a future in which technology wasn't just a way to escape or compete, but a way to live more fully and connect more meaningfully. Was that about seeing greater than the obvious, that as aloof as a worldwide move however connective enough to raise humanity. I embedded this love for innovation in my identity and it became a vector pointing me in a direction of a search not just for profoundness, but for profoundness that serves a better good.

My brother, Jehangir, always quotes me as his *mentor* and *life maker*. This goes beyond siblings — even within our circle, I have been able to help settle my nephews providing them with jobs and livelihoods. Turning the last page in a manuscript and seeing them carve out their place in the world is the quiet proof of the picture I had in my head of where we could end up.

Choosing The Path: Challenges And Big Decisions

After graduating with a Master's Degree from the University of Bridgeport in the hot summers of 1968, I sat at a crossroads. I had some big choices to make, some that would change my family's life, too.

In our small town of Aluva, India, in the backyard I grew up in, my father, Nagoor Rawther, had a simple wish for me—*to one day come back and apply my learning to our people.* I respected his conservative views but had a different path in mind: my father-in-law, N.A. Noor Muhammad, the catalyst behind my educational venture in the USA, saw a different future for me, for which I was immensely grateful.

When I assessed my situation and options in my final semester, a number of choices opened up. The first was to honor my roots by going back to India and landing a job in some brand-name company or government department. That was the safe bet, after satisfying my father, and I would have a future to look forward to earning.

The Pull Of Academia

The other route was up the ivory tower – a Ph.D. in Psychology. D. from a top-notch school like MIT or Stanford University.

The idea of being able to add to the pool of existing human knowledge sounded cool to me. However, the thought of such an exhausting doctoral program made me question whether I was ready to dedicate myself to years of academic work when, honestly, my love for practical innovation powered my inspiration more than the theory side of things.

A Steppingstone At Bullard

A third alternative was to stay with Bullard Machine Tools Co., which I had been with for the past year. They applauded my work, and a rapid promotion was getting closer. But my work with Bullard always felt like a means to an end, and I wanted something grander to gnaw on. I knew there was more for me out there.

Dreaming Of IBM

But the big dream was to join IBM. This could change everything for IBM workers. I could live a good life for my three-year-old daughter, who was with her grandparents in Somalia, and I could also take care of my family back in Aluva. By the time I got the job at IBM, I was going all out for my career. I didn't know if it would work out, but I had to try.

In the late 1960s, joining IBM was a dream for any professional in America's technology sector.

The Interview That Transformed Everything

I recall my interview at IBM's Fishkill plant, which was a little over an hour away from my university. I was principally interviewed by one person, George Micklus, Senior Associate Engineer. He was very understanding, caring, and reassuring. I left optimistic then, and a couple of days later, I received the job.

It was a memory I will always cherish.

Against All Odds: The Wins And The Pitfalls

I was the odd man out at IBM. I wasn't part of the ranks of the WASP upper-crust management level, nor did I blend in with working-class America in the plants and machine rooms; I was an anomaly. My skin color, accent, and race were easily recognizable, which set me apart, but this also motivated me to earn the respect of those whom I supervised and those who supervised me.

Micklus, being an immigrant, was the first to offer me comfort in a foreign land among unknown faces. Some were less so. But the sweet taste of victory was even greater for overcoming such obstacles.

Cutting-Edge Environment Full Of Inspiration

Joining IBM in the fall of 1968 was a milestone for me. IBM was a massive corporation leading the technological age globally. If you were in tech, you were meant to be there. At this time, IBM was generating $5.34 billion per year and was one of the biggest U.S. corporations—larger than most car and oil companies.

IBM traces its origins to 1911, when the Computing-Tabulating-Recording Company (CTR) was formed and later morphed into IBM in 1924. The business became huge, churning out equipment that companies and the government relied on to help store information. IBM replaced the Social Security system in the U.S., a massive project that had been created in 1936.

The East Fishkill campus for IBM was a place full of smart people and new ideas. How cool it was to work in a team taking all the new and advanced technology. I learned a ton about enterprise and working on large projects. People like George Micklus not only tuned me into engineering but also mentored me in leadership and having a big-picture vision.

Adaptable And Open To Challenges

As I matured into my role at IBM, the world was rapidly evolving, and I found myself in the center of a tech revolution. There was never a question of IBM's dominance in mainframe computers, to the extent that the industry was commonly described, tongue firmly in cheek, as *IBM and the Seven Dwarfs*. This was hard work, but these were some of the most satisfying challenges of my career.

I like to think back on the path that brought me here, and all the choices that once felt so crucial are now chapters in a sweeping story. As the first son of a Kerala family that revelled in tradition and who went out in the world to learn, I had now begun to make a difference in the technology that would define the future.

My tenure at IBM was not a job; it was a chapter of an ongoing journey that began even before I arrived in the United States. It was filled with courage, a sprinkling of doubt, and lots of hard work, all in service of my vision for opportunities and drive to create technology and innovation.

An Unusual Path
Without Compromising Responsibility

My success at IBM helped me fulfil the promise to my family. My daughter who had been waiting for me in Mogadishu was now growing up under the bright lights of America. My extended family in Aluva, whom I had left behind to pursue career opportunities, now benefited from my endeavors. But balancing the two has always been a significant theme in my life's work.

Thinking back upon my father's vision, I realize that my road may have taken an unusual turn. Still, it did not conflict with his wishes—nor was it separate from them. He had not seen me become the civil servant or government engineer he had hoped for. Still, I contributed to social progress through innovation and technology leadership. Perhaps my own path was stitched into a cloth he had not imagined—but it respected his wishes for me.

Beyond my innovations and the family I've supported, my driving force is the belief that expectations should not limit life. While I delighted in responsibilities, I pursued innovation after innovation and turned to creating both responsible and unconventional paths.

Three Vital Lessons Learned

Looking back on those years, I learned three vital lessons.

- First, life is tough, and you must keep going, even when things go wrong.
- Second, you have to be willing to change and try something new.
- Third, having a clear vision of what you want to achieve is essential.

Staying honest with oneself and keeping to the principles that have guided one's path is driven by a blend of duty, curiosity, and relentless pursuit of one's beliefs.

Leverage Your Environment:
Use It To Boost Your Success

My time at IBM was instrumental in shaping the professional I have become. Working on a team that created tools for making semiconductor chips allowed me to collaborate with some of the best engineers and scientists in the industry. More importantly, if one insists on overcoming steep odds, IBM is where my successful career started.

- Every decision and every challenge add another piece to your journey. The road will only sometimes be smooth, but the rewards are worth the trouble. Keep on advancing – never forget your dreams.

- Embrace the uncertainty, take risks, and trust in yourself.

- Keep pushing ahead towards success, but also remember to savor travel's joys and profit from every experience in life.

- Submit your capabilities to your enthusiasm, and let it guide you on the road ahead. The most thrilling adventures start with a leap of faith into the unknown.

- Don't let perceived boundaries limit you or the judgment of others decide what you can achieve. Remember that your fate is in your own hands.

- The only limitations are those that you create for yourself. Keep driving forward, breaking barriers, and striving for ever-higher goals. Never settle for less than your best.

In life, we often encounter challenges that seem insurmountable. But we discover our true strength and resilience in these moments of difficulty. Embrace the struggle, for it will make you into the person you are meant to be. Looking back on your journey, each obstacle will be a steppingstone toward success.

From Gunga Din To Pioneer: An Unexpected Entrant

Late in the 1960s, I stood at the once-famous East Fishkill IBM plant in New York. Now, I could feel its old-fashioned industrial aura surrounding me again. This was an unfamiliar world to me. It starkly resembled the old traditional world. It was, for all intents and purposes, the American aristocracy. At the same time, the machine rooms were the precincts of the underprivileged white workers, African Americans, and immigrants. Then there was me, an anomaly who didn't fit either group.

My bronze skin and thick accent set me apart. But I would go on to be an example of survival, of innovation fueled by difference. My experiences illustrate that sometimes, your uniqueness can be just what makes you unique to get ahead.

Surmounting Adversity

In many ways, adversity is what steers us to grow up. I saw barriers everywhere when I took up my position in front of the machine. The beginning was the most challenging period. I remember the awkward glances in hallways, the whispers behind my back, and even some outright hostility. There were moments when it all seemed far too much to bear. Yet deep inside myself lay a quiet tenaciousness, born of the dreams I nurtured and ideals I stood for. Knowing that to clear away these obstacles, I must use all rejections and biases as fodder to help me grow.

I faced every challenge and turned it into an exercise in endurance and adaptation. I devoured all the learning I could grab. In the noisy machine rooms, where the atmosphere could be intimidating, I sharpened my skills and let my abilities speak for themselves. As I became more familiar with this crowded terrain, unexpected allies rallied around me.

They began to see beyond my accent and skin color, recognizing the value I offered work. They were all colleagues of mine. Looking back, the hardships I'd gone through were not just obstacles: *they were switches and fuel for turning on my own sense of excellence.* My trials gave me a profound appreciation for diversity and how powerful it can be to affirm our individual identities. Conquering adversity wasn't just about defeating the odds, it was changing the very essence of those problems into steppingstones toward new horizons.

The Powerful Value Of Diversity

Imagine being an alien in a world dominated by people of their own nationality and culture. Not only is your appearance different, but so is your accent. Amidst all this, I found one person who did understand. A second-level manager named Micklus, an immigrant himself saw my difficulties clearly. His background made it possible for him to get past my accent and skin color and judge the work from his innate quality as an evaluator and mentor.

The first time I reported to work, an Irish American technician, Leroy Tamney, greeted me with what one writer described derogatorily as *Gunga Din.* But even though I stood my ground and refused to be insulted by him, I let my work speak for itself. Years later, in the early 1980s, Tamney sought my counsel to get his medical premium reimbursed by IBM. I helped him out.

I was willing to forgo the anger of the past.

Bearing No Grudges Welcome Every Individual

I have come across many personalities; some are supportive, and others are not. I decided to treat those instances patiently and not let grudges take root. This approach reflected a general belief in my mind about people — that given time and understanding, anyone could change. Also, there were times when dealing peacefully with adversaries brought improbable alliances and mutual respect. By choosing to take no offense at small slights, I freed my heart from the chains and grudges of bitterness. It was then that every incident offered a learning opportunity, and each interaction taught me something fresh. I could only find strength in unity and compassion. People like Micklus, and in the end even Leroy, through their example, showed that given truly heartfelt effort and openness, people from different cultures can combine to produce things worthwhile. On those occasions when I achieved such union, unbiased by grudge or hostility, the absolute immensity of human collaborative power was displayed to me. My life is proof of the enormous benefit of seeing challenges and individuals as partners on a journey to improve understanding and innovate rather than defeating adversarial enemies.

Forgiveness At The Forefront Of Leadership

I have always felt this to be a prime factor of good leadership. It also served as a guiding principle for me as I moved in and out through the complexities of human relations on that challenging and fragrant industrial plain. The more I encountered prejudice early on, the less I believed in carrying grudges. Living with an anger one cannot resolve is like carrying around a weight that makes it hard to move forward. Anger is an awful reaction that can establish negative habits for life. But, if eradicated, it will often leave behind most desirable peace and freedom.

Forgiveness, therefore, became a hallmark of my way of doing things after I went out to embrace the world. This attitude clarified that leaders should remain removed from personal disputes and only then feel a sense of enlightenment. It also built solid, diverse teams free of past animosities by spreading tolerance and communication rather than dissension. From my journey as a marginal voice to a pioneering leader in the Silicon Age, forgiveness was more than just an act of kindness - it was a conscious decision that drove innovation and new collaboration in science and technology.

My Identity: What's In A Name?

Guy Rabbat, who co-worked with me at IBM during the 1970s (one of Lebanese and Syrian descent), once observed on one occasion that *We all feel as if we do not belong.*

My unusual name, 'Javad Hassan', intrigued him, and it was a deviation from the routine. To blend in better with my surroundings, I had anglicized my name to 'Jay Hassan'. This was a common practice in those days for Indian Americans. It was an attempt to bridge cultural gaps and testify to my adaptability and determination to thrive in alien surroundings.

Adapting Oneself To Put People At Ease

From the start, I realized that if one desires to build entirely new relationships and working conditions that naturally encourage people to achieve those objectives together, then one must also create an atmosphere in which everyone around feels comfortable. This meant not just changing my name; it needed an acute sense of what others need and how they feel.

In practice, it often meant clearly effective but relatively trivial adjustments. For instance, when I spoke with someone who did not like to talk much, I assumed a gentle and encouraging attitude to create the conditions for them to vent their opinions. Faced with a more assertive nature, however, I felt I had to make my point quickly and clearly, given their urge for efficiency and decisiveness, while still maintaining an atmosphere of mutual respect and understanding by treating them equally in all cases.

Having lived with cultural differences from a young age, I could easily flow in and out of cultures freely. Knowing that members from various backgrounds might have differing styles and preferences in communication, I accepted these differences instead of trying to force all into uniformity. Our business environment was richer for this practice, and it helped to enrich our encounters. With the attempt to constantly adapt my approach to suit those around me, I facilitated relationships that were not only pleasant but very meaningful – a perfect illustration of what a harmonious and diverse workplace should be.

The Way To Excellence: Fired By Innovation

My work at IBM was unique. For instance, at that time, I was in a team developing tools to manufacture semiconductor chips. Semiconductor chips control and manage the flow of electric current in computers and other electronic devices. During this period in its history, IBM was the largest manufacturer of chips worldwide, churning out more than any other maker of computer chips combined.

A vital tool in semiconductor operation was the radio frequency (rf) sputtering machine, which protected semiconductor devices from contamination with silicon dioxide. This process was essential for isolating and passivating the metal lines within semiconductor devices. At that time, most of the equipment in IBM's semiconductor factories was designed and developed in-house.

I played a pivotal role in this development, working closely with technicians like Tamney. Silicon dioxide is deposited on semiconductor devices through the *rf* sputtering machine, an important tool in semiconductor processing. It was vital when isolating or passivating the metal lines within semiconductor devices. Everything in IBM's semiconductor factories was primarily designed, developed, and even fabricated in-house. I played a crucial role in its development, working together with technicians like Tamney. In retrospect, I see that my work had a far-reaching influence on how people fabricate semiconductor chips. I was the first before giants like Applied Materials, Inc. became industry leaders.

A Look At The Future

Nowadays, companies like Applied Materials, Inc., founded in 1967, dominate the market for industrial equipment used by chipmakers, with revenues in the billions. However, in the 1960s and early 1970s, IBM relied on in-house engineering teams to design and develop their semiconductor manufacturing equipment. During this period, my performance was outstanding, showing inherent originality and practical ability.

Flourishing Beyond Innovation: Lessons In Endurance

My experience has taught me that success in life is about much more than mere technology and invention alone. It involves endurance, the capacity to adapt to adversity, and a dogged determination to move forward, come what may. So:

1. **Embrace diversity:** Think of your unique perspective as a strength, not a liability.

2. **Make Alliances with people:** Value relationships that provide guidance and support.

3. **Overcome setbacks to the best of your ability:** Remain professional and dignified even when faced with adversity.

4. **Strive to create Excellence:** Dedicate yourself to hard work and the pursuit of the best.

5. **Be Compassionate:** Even towards people who may have wronged you.

From Misfit To Pioneer: A Tale Of Endurance

From East Fishkill to IBM's corporate headquarters in Armonk, my experience reminds you that success belongs to the adaptable and tenacious. From misfit to pioneer has been my transformation, building a legacy of innovation and endurance.

In the end, no one can determine their fate by where they were born and raised. Being different is the engine of progress, and distinguished potential is the only guarantee of success in one's choice of occupation. Keep focused on your goal and always keep trying.

Crafting A Corporate Pathway At IBM
Fast Promotions At IBM – Flying Into Tucson

I got my first promotion at IBM within a year of joining the company, moving up to first-line manager in what is generally considered the foundational step toward senior management. This initial recognition was due to the pure potential for hard work that my superiors saw in me. The earliest years saw no let-up in learning and innovation as I threaded my way through the complex and swift-moving world of technology.

IBM was a well-structured and organized business with four management levels at the grass-roots level, managing different functions and teams. By the mid-1970s, I had reached the position of fourth-level manager at IBM. This represented a significant leap, considering I had been aiming to perfect my skills as an engineer.

Challenges And Breakthroughs

I faced unprecedented challenges along the management road at IBM and made some wonderful discoveries. One of the hardest problems was also the most interesting; constantly, balancing between meeting my unit's expectations and focusing on what should be planned for our organization overall. Every day brought new difficulties: coordinating between departments, assigning people to the right task, or dealing with inevitable conflicts among any group of people.

Yet it was precisely these very difficulties that led me to grow most deeply.

I brought about a critical breakthrough when I learned how to exploit each team member's unique strengths. Focusing on understanding individual talents better instead of imposing a one-size-fits-all approach has made me better at it. With this shift, productivity increased, and we saw better results in the long term. Still, the office also became a more harmonious place to work in general. Besides, as time passed, the notion of failure shifted from being a disruptive setback to an opportunity to learn and grow. Each defeat was a guidepost to help me find better, more effective strategies.

Putting myself in my employees' shoes and learning from past mistakes made this transformation possible. Nevertheless, it was a long and arduous journey paved with traps at every turn. Through the pain of repeated blows, I could encounter what constitutes leadership.

Deploying The Engine Of Innovation

For any budding young engineer or scientist, the IBM group was an ecosystem supportive of and conducive to innovation. We had all the most modern tools available in our work and were always encouraged to create. The company's patent department applied for patents on our creations, so I was no exception.

In 1973, my first significant invention was a new system that moves semiconductor wafers from inside and outside vacuum chambers in perfect balance. This radically new design, developed jointly with Alfred Mack and Michael Wojtaszek, doubled the efficiency of handling wafers under vacuum. This was an automated wafer handling system and brought with it a profound effect. Not only did it streamline a critical step in semiconductor manufacturing, but it set new benchmarks in both efficiency and accuracy. The team was invigorated by the recognition and excellent results from our efforts. The late-night marathons of brainstorming and prototype testing had given rise to rewards beyond our wildest dreams. The team received a massive boost from this success; everyone felt great with a sense of common goal and creativity to match. It was not just about fixing a technical problem; it involved pushing the envelope of what was possible. I recall a profound sense of accomplishment at that time--not only for myself but also for my colleagues, who had all made contributions to the project. Our success hammered home the value of collaboration and what can be achieved when working together closely.

That automated wafer-handling system was just a start. Strengthened by this success, I put even more effort into pushing IBM to use innovative methods. Every subsequent project focused not only on immediate difficulties but also on seeking new areas for development and looking far into the future. It was this change of attitude that made the difference and kept us ahead in a fast-moving technology world.

As I spent more years at IBM, each new challenge was met with a spirit of unswerving curiosity and resolve. Every project had the scope to make a big difference. Through these efforts, I fully realized the power of creativity. Whether it was developing better processes or coming up with revolutionary technology, the core of our work was always the same: to be new, better, and inspiring.

Recognition And Reward: A Decade Of Genius

Innovation was accepted as my hallmark at IBM. Over the next nine years, II received 13 more patents, each a testament to the creativity and teamwork that characterized IBM. The company honored me with several awards, including its first *Innovation Achievement Award* in December 1974 and an *Outstanding Innovation Award* for developing electron beam technology. These awards constituted a marker in my career and expressed the strength I derived from hard work and unwavering commitment. As my career at IBM progressed, although the job required much more than innovation skills, I received still further rewards.

In February 1978, I was awarded the *Outstanding Innovation Award* for the *New Fluid Mechanics Wafer Orientor*, my fifth prize in recognition of creativity. This period was one of relentless drive and immense accomplishments in semiconductor technology to the point of never being satisfied with what had already been done. Every breakthrough, each patent, was a solution to some intricate problem and further advanced the industry. In fact, my successful career at IBM was largely due to hard work — an attitude of *'The Art of the Possible'* that activates creative flow.

Each Breakthrough Provides A Platform For Another

In December 1974, when I received the first innovation achievement award of my career, it was a critical point. This recognition did not just give my resume a shot in the arm; it was an approving nod on all the endless hours, the tireless pursuit of superior quality, and the endless dedication I had poured into my job.

The award proved that, after all, my vision still stood firm. Accolades for my contributions to electron beam technology and the fluid mechanic's wafer oriented suddenly opened up vast new opportunities that would have / worked out bright futures for IBM. These accolades were significant milestones in themselves and served as springboards to still greater opportunities. Invitations to join more complex projects and collaborate with the leading figures in our business followed these victories. Such cooperative working practice produced an atmosphere of knowledge sharing and mutual respect. This collective wisdom became the basis for our many breakthroughs in technology.

However, the ripple effect of the accolades did not stop there; my personal growth was also heavily influenced. The recognition pointed out the lasting importance of persistence, resilience, and adaptability.

It taught me that reverses and failures are never an end but rather an inevitable part of making any breakthrough.

Each setback I faced and every obstacle that I could overcome tempered my approach to problem-solving and helped me settle on my life goal.

Eventually, the recognition I received had a knock-on effect on my colleagues. Watching our team's hard work and creativity come to fruition provided motivation that made us strive even higher. It helped us form an atmosphere of innovation and perfection in which every staff member felt positively obliged to do their part and contribute something good. Recognition of our contributions. It brought collective pride and reinforced the value of teamwork in our efforts.

Moreover, the awards served as an inspiration to upcoming young engineers and scientists at IBM. They showed that outstanding achievements lie within reach with hard work and a continuous search for fresh solutions. But they also encouraged them to reach out beyond traditional thinking patterns of the moment and to push the envelope of technical possibilities. That made the enduring mark of what took place at IBM, as far as my career was concerned. It was about innovation in practice – of innovation by teams working together and of the pervading desire to learn more. It was about laying down the foundation work that would carry forward trends in the industry. It inspired new generation engineers and scientists to go fit and be bold in their creativity and innovation.

Climbing To The Top:
The Journey To The Lab Director's Chair

In 1978, around a decade into my IBM career, I became Acting Lab Director at East Fishkill Laboratory, the semiconductor lab of IBM. This lab was a gargantuan campus with more than 3 million square feet of floor space and housed a total of 1,500 technicians and engineers. It was also an integral part of IBM's research into semiconductors. As director, I had overall control over both programs and engineering new methods--my reports going off initially to Dr. Paul Low, and then indirectly by way of Jack D. Kuehler who loomed large at IBM.

The East Fishkill plant was not just a place of work but also a think tank with research and production facilities. Work there kept IBM semiconductors at the cutting edge of technology. In fact, everything that was done in chip production came from East Fishkill: high-density chips, conductor materials like copper interconnects, and CPUs looking like supercomputers.

Jack Kuehler's guidance was invaluable to me. It was his vision and support that brought about my growth and development as a leader. He saw ability in me, encouraging every further effort until one day, I looked back and found myself standing where I stand today.

Flying with Kuehler's scheme, my career took inspiration; he started out as an associate engineer but eventually rose to one of the most influential IBM executives. His confidence in my abilities gave me new self-assurance and pushed me towards success with great force.

Those hitherto unheard-of promotions were not something I had actually anticipated. They were the reward for having worked hard and showed that culture expresses and reinforces abilities: you have to push limits if you want to reach them.

Upon taking the position, I felt the enormous weight of

responsibility that came with it. To lead such a crucial department at the company required technical expertise combined with strong leadership skills and dedication towards promoting cooperation.

Reporting directly to Dr. Paul Low, I expanded my duties to oversee all engineering and programming activities. But in order to do justice to this promotion, I had to combine the skills of handling many high-stakes projects with attention to the long-term direction of semiconductor technology during its future at IBM.

The support and cooperation I received from colleagues and mentors were crucial during this transition. The collective trust shown in me expressed their faith in my ability and demonstrated that persistence and continual learning are key to career success.

In this position, I was able to forge new directions in technology and was able to pass on to teams of people I led, a new fervor for excellence. My path to the Lab Director's chair has been one marked by the importance of taking on constraints whose achievement all but seemed impossible then seeing them as challenges today. It's essence lay in every step forward not just carrying out my day job but taking another step toward realizing an even greater vision of innovation and excellence.

Ultimately, this swift promotion was a testament to the teamwork required to push the boundaries of technological possibility. It also served as a powerful reminder that with commitment, collaboration and daring to try new approaches to innovation such quick rise through the ranks within an organization like IBM could be achieved by anyone who dared to dream big and work hard enough for it to become reality.

From The Field To The Château At Armonk:
The Corporate Leap

In the early 1980s, I started feeling uneasy about the future of my work in semiconductor lab. Having already spent over a decade up and down the various departments of semiconductor chip design and production. And it wasn't just within design. I had accumulated so much experience from management to the actual manufacturing of chips that I knew this industry inside out.

My ambition led me to look for new challenges and opportunities. I decided that moving up to corporate headquarters in Armonk seemed a logical next step for my professional career in managerial progression. Armonk was the nerve center of IBM, the power base. This is where IBM top executives made decisions and main headquarters were located.

In 1982, I approached Bob 'Boe' Evans, IBM's Vice President for Worldwide Engineering, Programming, and Technology. He was very supportive and offered me a position as Director of Corporate Engineering and Technology. This new position meant a wider range of responsibilities—encompassing all types of IBM technology—than just semiconductor chips.

But my boss, Dr. Low, advised against it, warning that my leaving Kuehler's wing might hamper my future. Low's counsel had much in the management field behind it; he was sure that transferring to this other division would hold out better growth opportunities. After all, Kuehler himself, for his part, was on his way up inside IBM. However, despite his warnings and urging to expand my horizons, I went through with my plan. I declared, *'I am nobody's man. I am my own man.'*

'My Own Man': Listening To Opinions But Making My Own Decisions

I have realized the importance of respecting the opinions of others. Therefore, I also realized I could not allow others' words to spoil my fortune. The spoken word of Dr. Low and a number of mentors played a valuable role in my life, encouraging me to grow and change perspectives. But what happens if I rely almost entirely on their judgments to the exclusion of my own inner ones? The decision to move to Armonk reflected that, in my own mind, I was turning point. It wasn't a reaction against the mentorship. Reading articles and taking classes prepared me in both directions, yet I understood that this was crossing a major threshold into independentism and confidence in my decisions. Charting my own path as a leader meant that, while appreciative of the wisdom imparted to me, I also realized an obligation to stand by my beliefs and make choices which resonated with who I am and what matters most in life.

Being my own man necessitated assuming responsibility for the decisions I took, both those big victories and face-in-the-mud failures. It was about having bravery in following what felt right, though it meant moving away from other people's expectations. The manner of survival formulated my road ahead. On the other hand, it stood as a long lesson in pacing respect for other people's views while keeping faith in the needle of one's own innermost compass. That was what my move to Armonk meant. It did not just mean switching jobs; it became an acknowledgment that in confidence and self-belief, there is strength.

Recognize Your Path And Stay True To Your Passion

In 1982, I joined corporate headquarters at Armonk as the Director of Corporate Engineering Technology Worldwide. This opened up a whole new world of possibilities for me. I could go outside my own semiconductor domain and into areas such as tape drives, disk drives, mainframe computers or wherever IBM was a leader in technology. The range of technologies I was exposed to was both exhilarating and confusing. Each brand presented its own set of issues, and each wanted an altogether different approach to creativity and problem-solving.

When I landed the job at Armonk as Director of Corporate Engineering Technology Worldwide marked a major transition in my life. As I walked into corporate headquarters, I felt the ebb and flow of emotions. On one hand I was excited about new challenges and opportunities; on the other I couldn't help feeling sad at leaving behind East Fishkill's buzzing labs. I had grown very attached to an intimate team there. It was a time of significant personal growth and self-examination.

Though the position greatly broadened my horizons, I found it lacked the excitement of a line job. I missed my hands-on technical work so much that after being deeply involved with it for years on end, felt somewhat isolated from all the cutting-edge new technologies driving IBM's growth.

At first my responsibility was to oversee the firm's worldwide technological advance. I had to keep abreast of the latest technological trends developed around each regional market that we were targeting, and work with various departments so that everything happened together.

However, the initial excitement soon began to wane when I realized that this role was one of primarily strategic planning rather than direct hands-on work as had been so instrumental to my upbringing. I wanted to be back close to all the action and feel hands-on with what kind of engineering was being done. I was involved in problem-solving at close quarters and could see immediate results from my labor. It was this realization more than ever which clarified that what I really loved about engineering lay primarily in its practical aspects, not high-order strategy as demanded by an Armonk job.

Armonk taught me some important lessons about corporate politics. It served as a reminder of the need to match career moves with one's own strengths and passions. Despite having left Kuehler's embrace, I was resolved to stick with my own course of growth and innovation. It also taught me something about the need for flexibility and adaptability in one's career: although Armonk was not what I had expected, it gave me a broader perspective on IBM's operations and strategic aims.

Recognizing this, I sought advice from Jack Bertram, a respected IBM figure known for his acumen and strategic thinking. In our talks, Jack helped me understand the benefit of aligning personal aspirations with professional roles. He urged me to use my extensive experience and not shy away from seeking assignments that reflected my true passion for engineering.

Courage To Reset Your Path

I was determined to reconnect with my true passion. For advice, I sought out mentors and colleagues for opinions and thoughts. With Kuehler himself, (the very mentor I was so reluctant to leave behind): I examined the dilemma he pointed out that, in such situations we should understand clearly: one must make tough choices and have the courage to change direction if one is remain true to one's passion. He urged me to reflect deeply on what had been the most rewarding elements of my career as a guide to what kind of opportunities to pursue in the future. With this more solid direction in mind, I made the pivotal decision to transition back into a hands-on engineering role. It was not a case of return to what I had known but rather doing work that was joyous and stirred my creativity. It struck me that I felt a sense of achievement from directly solving hard problems that could not be achieved through high-level planning. Taking a new post was not a matter of regressing. Instead, it was tactical redirection, and also an affirmation that I intended personally as well as professionally to be true to myself. Thus, I learned from this experience that career satisfaction is inseparable from passion. Should the steps you take up the corporate ladder fail to nurture your enthusiasm and curiosity then just going forward isn't enough. Staying true to one's inner voice and letting one's career be guided by it requires courage. Yet this path led me to make more meaningful contributions and thus find, in the end, a fuller life. This journey underscored the need at any cost to remain true to your own path in life, instead of yielding to external pressures and letting them dictate your course of action. Shaped by Kuehler's advice, I sought a new role that balanced leadership with my passion for engineering This not only enabled me to encourage and mentor aspiring engineers; it allowed support for my unfulfilled technological research interests. The change not only reinvigorated my professional journey but also stiffened my resolve to always stay behind what I love and then take the path towards it.

'Nothing Goes To Waste.'

Armonk gave me much more than a time of professional reassessment; it also provided an opportunity for deep personal growth. From this period of life, one of the most valuable things I learned was how important it is to listen— *to yourself as well as others.* Deciding to contact Jack and trying out a new path in my life gave me a vital lesson that I would always keep in mind: *Trust your instincts.*

This kind of thinking had a big impact on my leadership style.

At Armonk, leadership meant achieving a balance between vision and compassion. I had to learn to encourage those around me without neglecting their personalities or stance on things. Equilibrium is essential in any political context, particularly with powers at stake. It was here that I polished my negotiation and communication skills, and also the knack for setting up people who will be useful to your career in the future.

Moreover, cultural contact at IBM's worldwide head office brought me new perspectives on global trends in engineering and market demands. It opened up for me an overall view of IBM's operations, which was extremely valuable indeed. However, the call to return to hands-on engineering was considerable, and I resolved to answer it.

Happily, Back To My Roots As An Engineer

With Jack Bertram, I began looking for a job that would take me back to the grassroots of engineering. It was a delicate process: transitioning from a high-powered corporate job to more technical levels without appearing to be taking a step back.

The chance came in the form of leading a ground breaking project within IBM's emerging technologies division. This was pioneering work, the vanguard of tomorrow's computing solutions. It would position me alongside cutting-edge advancement and at the same time draw on my technical know-how to drive projects with real impact.

A Leader Inspired By His Own Team

Working with a group of dynamic, talented people such as these was inspiring beyond belief. Every one of them brought his own angle and overweening determination to transcend what had been regarded as limits. These were not just colleagues, people in their own right who looked beyond the world as it is and could be. Their ingenuity sparked off new ideas and their innovative ways of approaching problems upset the weighty dead hand of tradition.

The team positively crackled with energy. Brainstorming sessions would turn into fiery debates, with ideas shooting in all directions; and at those times I felt really alive. The common enthusiasm that ran like a thread through us all was a force multiplier, helping to drive us to targets which had seemed almost unattainable to begin with. Their dedication and ingenuity rubbed off on all, raising everyone's morale and standards.

This period of teamwork once again reconfirmed my faith in the power of an energetic, creative, and pioneering group. With each man's enthusiasm feeding into the collective ambition and mingling creativity with technical expertise, our accomplishments were not just possible; they were amazing.

Know Your Strengths And Resource Your Gaps
I Am A Starter But I Deploy Strong Finishers

Leveraging the power of a strong team means that I could focus on my strongest aspect which is the generation of ideas and projects. As the projects evolve and get into a lot of detail my mind moves swiftly to new ones. I could even say I get bored of the detail, not that I don't give it importance otherwise the end result would not be there. However, this is the phase where I rely on experts and good people who can follow through, implement, and carry forward to brilliant completion.

Valuable Insights: From My Experience To Your Success

Lessons Learned And Advice
For Aspiring Entrepreneurs/Leaders

When I look back on my journey, I am now aware that resilience, adaptability, and continuous learning are no less significant to success than opportunity itself. My rise at IBM was due to technical expertise, readiness to tackle new challenges, and the advice of genuinely great mentors. I now offer the following insights to would-be entrepreneurs and future leaders:

- **Embrace Innovation:** Always look for new ways to solve problems and ways to make things even better. Innovation is the foundation stone of progress. In my own career this pursuit of innovation flowered into significant breakthroughs and success. You must keep on being curious, hungry for new thoughts. This is what can bring you to the edge of what's been done before.

- **Value Mentorship:** Listen to those who have trod the path before you. Their advice is invaluable. My mentors, such as Jack D. Kuehler and John E. Bertram played key roles in my career development. They gave me the technical expertise as well as strategic guidance to find a way through the complex corporate terrain of those times.

- **Stay Resilient:** Challenges and setbacks are food for growth. Take these experiences to move forward. When I decided to move, Armonk provided both challenges and lessons in corporate strategy-adaptability and management. Resilience is seeing opportunities in obstacles and pursuing goals without relenting.

- **Adapt and Grow:** Long-term success demands adapting to new roles and settings. My career at IBM was a series of transfers, each with its own set of problems and things to learn.
  It was that adaptability that allowed me to grow well in Armonk and over at East Fishkill: this ability to change locations and try my hand wherever needed.

- **Follow Your Passion:** Make your career choices in accordance with what you like doing best--align. Passion makes you driven and able to succeed. My passion for engineering and innovation took me into jobs (roles) where I could do real work. It's important to identify what you are passionate about and then stick closely to it. This will carry your career through to great achievement and satisfaction.

My progression at IBM, from a young engineer to a senior leader at the forefront of the semiconductor industry, is all thanks to the power of creative innovation, brilliant mentorship, and persistence. And as you begin shaping your own paths, make every challenge a chance for growth. I have followed these principles since my IBM tenure and applied them to my business ventures.

From the East Coast To Tucson:
A Journey Of Growth And Technological Revolution

My professional career started on the East Coast, a region that is well known for its vigorous high-tech. By the time I graduated from college I had already spent sixteen years at one of the most prestigious and innovative companies in all IT, IBM. That period in my life was marked by intense self-education, tough challenges, and meeting many kinds of people who interested me. IBM gave me a place and a means to improve my technical skills and put me in an environment of unique intellectual vigor and forward-thinking characters.

The Eastern U.S. was necessary for my career development. The proximity to major education and research centers created fertile ground for invention. In this thriving environment, I met Jack Bertram, a giant in his field. Jack, affectionately known as "Blackjack," enjoyed a global reputation for his highly effective yet unconventional administrative style. His importance to my professional career is invaluable.

As the head of the IBM General Systems Division, Jack was a mentor who could identify upcoming leaders in an era of its own. His belief in me gave me the confidence to confront more and more complex problems. Jack's nickname, 'Blackjack', was from his imposing presence and his unorthodox methods, which often went against mainstream thinking but yielded remarkable results. His leadership was a combination of strict discipline and creative problem-solving, so he was universally respected within IBM. Jack was for me much more than just a mentor; he was a guiding force who shaped the pattern of my early career and helped me steer a course through the meandering world of corporate America. His wisdom and his support were critical to my growth, and much of my success in later life can be traced back to things I learned from him. For me, Jack was a big model. His leadership was different from anything I had ever seen before.

Jack could balance strict discipline with almost poetic creativity, motivating his team to challenge the boundaries of the possible. His ability to find potential in people and ideas that others saw as limits was downright inspirational. Yet there wasn't a hint of condescension in his high expectations. That's incredibly empowering for a person and their abilities. Jack's mentorship was hands-on; he gladly rolled up his sleeves, diving right into the nitty-gritty of a project along with his team. This generated a strong sense of unity and showed that genuine leadership consists of serving others and raising them. His far-sighted vision and readiness to take calculated risks taught me to think beyond conventional limits and to approach problems with an innovative mindset. These lessons became the basis of my leadership style and have continued to define my career path years after leaving IBM. However, the attraction of running a major plant again and returning to a 'production' line position where I could directly influence product development harmoniously intermingled with the promise of innovation was too much to resist.'

Jack Bertram, Guiding Light Beacon Of Change

The influence Jack Bertram had on IBM and the wider tech industry is well-known. He joined IBM in 1958, a time when it was enjoying great technological advances. As soon as Jack came on scene, he quickly rose through the ranks and was made vice president by 1973. His leadership showed most impressively in the Advanced Computer System (ACS) project, a pioneering effort aimed at revolutionizing computer technology. Jack's forward-looking thinking and pursuit of excellence were key to the project's success. During my stint as East Fishkill's lab director, I had the pleasure of working closely with Jack. We had a lot in common, from our fondness for cigars to our passionate love for technology and innovation. Our conversation usually centered around our personal and career dreams. Jack's faith in my potential and his sage advice had a great influence on my career at IBM. Jack didn't *mentor* me in only a professional capacity; he also provided personal help. What I especially admired and tried to follow was his skill in combining a high-pressured career with a wholesome home life.

His mentorship gave me a rounder meaning of success: the two aspects of career and personal wellness were both necessary for a professional. What an impact Jack made on my career! His legacy inspires me to this very day. In 1983, I had to make a significant change in my career: after Jack Bertram, who now led IBM's Data Systems Division, invited me to take over the Tucson Development Lab, I accepted. This was a major commitment since the lab was a significant IBM facility, and the role combined substantial leadership with strategic planning. The prospect of such a major change was both exciting and scary. Leaving the known environment of the East Coast and venturing into the totally unfamiliar realm Tucson offered posed a great challenge but also a strong attraction. However, the chance to manage a major facility and return directly to product development and innovation was too attractive to turn down. Taking on this position meant a leap of faith and readiness to accept uncertainty. It was no mean task shifting from familiar routines and networks on the East Coast to the new and unfamiliar environment of Tucson. Yet I looked forward to the potential for expansion and the challenge of leading a dynamic team in a state-of-the-art facility.

The move to Tucson was an entirely new chapter in my professional life, one full of possibilities for innovation and the opportunity to make a major contribution to IBM's future. Embracing change and the unknown has always been vital for personal and professional growth. Moving to Tucson exemplified this principle. Stepping into a new environment, with its challenges and dynamics, required an open mind and willingness to adapt. Accepting the uncertainty allowed me to discover strengths I never knew I had and stretch my capabilities in ways that would never have occurred had I been confined to my comfort zone.

The move was far more than just a change of scene: it was a transformative journey that broadened my horizons and deepened my appreciation for leadership and innovation.

In Tucson, my exposure to diverse viewpoints and ways of doing things opened up fresh ideas, which translated into inventive solutions. The unfamiliar territory of the West created a spirit of exploration and hardiness that pervaded our work at the Development Lab. We were able to channel this spirit to break through the barriers of what was possible, pioneering new technologies and processes. By embracing change and the unknown, I discovered that the boundaries of what is possible for me were not just expanded, they were redefined. This experience strengthened my faith that real innovation usually emerges when we dare to go beyond the beaten track and immerse ourselves in new, unexplored areas. The unknown can be hard to take, but it is also invariably rewarding. It forces us to confront our fears and prejudices, form new relationships, and adapt at a rapid pace.

Through such pain, we open up endless heights for growth, creativity, and success. In this way, the move to Tucson convinced me that by embracing change with curiosity and courage, we not only go through the unknown but also discover the hidden potential within ourselves and our organization.

Acceptance Of Change And Exploration Of New Opportunities

1984 was a time of great change at IBM. Replacing John R. Opel in this capacity, John F. Akers took over as CEO of the company. At the same time, Thomas J. Watson retired. He was a giant figure at IBM for over a quarter of a century and was dubbed Mr. IBM. One major change for me during this period was the retirement of my mentor, Bob Evans. Within the company, everything shifts. This period was especially significant as I was just beginning to accept my change of scene to Tucson. Emigrating my family from the humid and rainy East Coast to the Arizona desert with its endless sunshine rates as quite an adjustment. In contrast to our former surroundings, the new house we bought in Skyline Country Club Estates had rolling green golf courses and a desert background. We felt at peace with our relocation here, which we needed after such big changes.

Despite a few initial problems, settling in Tucson feels like beginning a new life. The local community were most hospitable and welcomed our family with warmth.

To embrace this fresh start with both, an open mind and resilience, I had to develop those qualities meaningfully in my new role.

These changes were a reminder that success often comes from stepping out of the comfort zone and trying new, even daunting, things. Giving in to fear is like giving up to failure.

Forget the Box - *There Is No Box!*

In my new role, I was determined to create an environment where people not only thought with open minds and outside the traditional boundaries but were expected to do so. I used to tell my team, 'Don't just think outside the box – *there is no box.*' This kind of mindset was essential for fostering genuine innovation. With 'the box' missing its constraints and limiting beliefs, problem-solving techniques emerged with ease.

In our everyday conversations, avoiding opaque or overly technical theories helped to eliminate abstract problems. Instead, we concentrated on clear, practical steps that were action oriented. This made it easy for everyone to offer ideas and solutions.

We implemented the maxim that *'there is no box'* as not only a guiding principle for our projects, but also a reframing of the way we looked at our own potential. It allowed a broad range of ideas to be welcomed before we moved into one area or another. And in so doing, we found that creativity did not belong exclusively within fixed boundaries but flourished best when freed from all preconceptions.

Taking The Reigns – Leading Tucson Lab

Stepping up to lead the Tucson Development Lab was one of my biggest milestones. It was set up in 1980 as a test site for new technologies. There were over 4,000 people working there, all skilled employees. The basic tasks that fell to me involved providing leadership both in terms of strategic direction and responsible governance for this lab. One of the lab's principal projects, which started early on, was developing the 3480 cartridge tape drive systems, a vital attempt by IBM to take data storage technology into its very own era by replacing reel-to-reel tape drives.

At the Tucson lab, I needed to have a combination of technical expertise, strategic vision, and good managerial skills. The development of the 3480 Tape Drive Systems was a difficult and testing job that required careful planning, innovative thinking, and effective teamwork. This project's ultimate success not only further advanced data storage technology but also consolidated IBM's position as a leader in the field. It was a matter of profound satisfaction which underlined the value of teamwork and showed that cultivating a culture of innovation can bear fruits.

The 3480 Cartridge Tape Drive: A Revolution In Data Storage

The introduction of the 3480 Magnetic Tape Subsystem in 1984 was a milestone in the history of both IBM and the tech industry as a whole. This compact, efficient system completely changed data storage, providing unprecedented amounts of capacity and reliability. The 3480 tape drive was a product of cutting-edge engineering and innovative design. It met the growing requirements for high-capacity data storage solutions in an increasingly digital world.

There is no doubt that the development of the 3480 tape drive was the result of collaboration and innovation. From extensive research to rigorous testing and the combined efforts of a team with high technical skills, it is also a testament to teamwork.

The launch of the system marks a significant milestone in my working career, as well being something for me to draw great satisfaction from. It is also witness to unwavering support from my mentor Jack Bertram, who played an above-all role in making this project succeed.

The 3480 Cartridge Tape Drive's success did not just happen. If anything, it was the result of a rigorous process: collaboration, perseverance, and determination to transcend the ordinary. For each difficulty faced, we were not only determined to overcome it but to do so in an extraordinary way. The team's dedication to excellence served as a launchpad for their landmark achievements. No matter how small, every milestone was an occasion of joy, and we celebrated it and felt joy in mutual success and cooperation.

During the development phase, I never failed to realize the enormous responsibility we bore. Our mission was not just manufacturing a product or a future way of information storage and retrieval; it was shaping the landscape itself. This consciousness strengthened my commitment to this cause, and constant reflection on its potential made me realize that our results might well affect millions of lives worldwide in fields like education, industry, etc. Furthermore, late nights, many long discussions, and bouts of doubt were all part and parcel of that collective energy and work.

Whether the 3480 Cartridge Tape Drive will remain in use or not is uncertain. What seems most certain, however, is that it has become a classic piece of work for all mankind. Vision, educational training, and teamwork have made it a valuable advancement for the future. It also taught us that amidst all this, there can be surprising results. Innovation in the face of doubt doesn't necessarily bring disaster; extraordinary outcomes are also possible, with a spirit of continuous trial and not giving up.

IBM not only managed to strengthen its own place as a front-runner in the industry but also took everyone on board for the journey.

A Legacy And Valuable Learning

Reflecting on the journey of the 3480 Tape Cartridge Drive, what comes to mind are a number of key lessons learned. These lessons would influence my outlook on leadership and innovation for years to come.

One of the first and most important lessons is the impact that a clear, appealing vision can make. It provides guidance for teams and encouragement in the uphill battle against disorder and uncertainty. The 3480 project idea was lofty, but it was precisely this aspiration that brought the team together.

Equally important was the recognition that the environment which encourages curiosity and experimentation is also one in which innovation can flourish. Both successes and failures were seen as opportunities to learn. The incremental progress each time brought us closer to a breakthrough. This way of thinking has helped shape the lens through which we view events in life and find ways to transform obstacles into opportunities. This mindset led us to be proactive and flexible when we were faced with rapid change, something that today's IT world is constantly faced with.

The journey reinforced my faith in leadership. True leaders inspire, promote growth and lay the groundwork for individuals to live up to their abilities. Looking back on the 3480 project, I have nothing but gratitude for such a talented team and for all the wisdom gained along the way. This legacy goes beyond the technical achievements of the 3480 Cartridge Tape Drive. It clearly demonstrated to the team that anything can be achieved when people join forces with a common purpose.

Looking Back And Moving Forward

The years spent leading the Tucson Development Lab were some of the most challenging and rewarding of my career. There I learned 'big' ideas about leadership, innovation and resilience. It was a period that saw great personal growth as well as the solidifying of my opinions on today's quick-change technology scene.

While I look back at my career path flitting from East Coast office to Tucson Development Lab, then beyond. I'm full of gratitude for the opportunities and insights that have made me what I am. The call from Tucson was a turning point, which led to new beginnings and remarkable achievements. It was a passage full of uncertainty, determination and pursuit of excellence - lessons that were constantly exerted. We can but hope to achieve these same qualities in our own lives as we face new challenges and opportunities.

Valuable Insights: From My Experience To Your Success

Here, I share with you some valuable insights which have helped me immensely, and I believe that they might also prove beneficial for you:

- **Accept change and take advantage of the opportunities it brings.** For me, this meant a big move to Tucson, where, although life changed a lot in many ways, it allowed for personal growth and professional development.

- **Look for teachers and learn from the best.** My own career owes so much to the mentoring I received from Jack Bertram. Build strong relationships with experienced people, and a wealth of opportunities will open up for you.

- **Be creative and stay abreast of developments in your field.** It was the 3480 tape drive that really brought home the power of innovation. A rapid industry needs to be adaptable at all times.

- **You must balance your work and your life.** Despite a career which takes lots of time and thought, you cant neglect to put together some kind of happy family life too--the two really go hand in hand.

- **Exercise financial prudence by saving and investing.** In this way you give yourself financial stability as well as freedom for later years.

Leaving Tucson

I transferred back to IBM's Armonk headquarters in the summer of 1987. Thus, after three and a half years as the head of the laboratory, it was another anticipated change.

James Marley: A Turning Point

In 1986 I, met the newly elected president of AMP Inc., a leading Pennsylvania-based connector company called James Marley. After earning my degrees in aeronautical and mechanical engineering, I began working at IBM's Tucson facility in 1963. AMP, a user of mainframe computers, had a lot to do with my career development as well.

Excellent Timing

James Marley was tall and robust, with great personal charm. That immediately appealed to me. And in no time at all, he had won my confidence completely. Marley reminded me of executives such as Bob Evans, Bertram, and Keuhler - men all prominently associated with IBM – yet there was a degree of approachability about this man which set him apart.

Our first discussions, covering a range of topics in connection to rapid developments occurring in the computing industry, both new and old, were stimulating and enlightening.

Marley was greatly impressed by my extremely knowledgeable and insightful analyses, combined with an ability to expand on them in detail. This was a period of major changes for the industry, with companies such as Apple and Microsoft emerging as new powers that would challenge IBM's pre-eminent position at the time. Marley's visit helped me to see that I had been fortunate with timing. IBM's mainframe computers had long held sway in the market, but personal computers were just arriving on the scene, so everything was now up for grabs. There were newcomer companies with great ambition, like Apple and Microsoft, which put out innovative products capable to change the industry. We discussed these trends and I gave him my thoughts on the potentials and challenges ahead. Marley seemed keenly interested in what I had to say partly because of my nearly two decades of experience in product development across different IBM facilities.

Serendipity? No. Pull Of Nature? Yes!

But is it really fair to say that Marley's visit to IBM was pure serendipity? I don't think so. While coincidences do happen, I don't believe that there is a motivating force behind them. And even if there were such a force, I wouldn't think of it in that way at all. It can be dangerous since we may just sit here and hope for things that may never happen. But if you exert genuine focus, passion, and hard work, there is a pull in nature that opens paths you never thought of. Thus, many plans are botched because they are over-designed compared to what was expected. They lead to disappointment and then loss of heart. Just be free, let your determination carve a path, like water carving the best course for a stream, flowing naturally with great force. This is why I feel Marley's visit was no serendipity but a path that opened up through my determination and unrestrained flow of work.

Dinner With Marley: A Turning Point

In 1987, Marley visited Tucson once more, and I had the privilege of entertaining him for dinner in my home. We sat down to a spread of Indian food and drinks, chatting easily about football, hunting, and other social subjects. Then the conversation flowed naturally into more relevant areas such as technology and especially the whole concept of outsourcing: He immediately became interested in this new idea, which was still a mere fledgling back then in name if not for reality. Marley was intrigued when I expounded upon my dream to tap into the huge reservoirs of capable and cheap engineers in countries like India and China. This was during the late 1980s, a time when those two nations' economies had just begun to wake up, and their GNP was a mere fraction of where it is today and the economic giants they have become.

The dinner was perfect, filled with laughter, stories, and shared memories. We talked about our work and family affairs, effectively blurring the line between professional and personal life. I found him extremely interesting, well-intentioned, and amicable. He became more enthused the further our discussions went. Marley epitomized the concept of curiosity as we had lunch outside in freezing weather two days later.

Pivotal Moment

It was the summer of 1989, and the world was beginning to awaken to something called outsourcing. Marley was fascinated by the alternatives and to learn about how a company might use the skills of engineers in India or China to its advantage.

I saw this conversation as a turning point which planted the seed of a significant career change for me.

Marley's Proposal

At the dinner, I mentioned to Marley that I was awaiting a transfer back to IBM's headquarters in Armonk. Without a moment's hesitation, Marley proposed me for a top executive position at AMP in Harrisburg. He explained the opportunity: AMP was looking for someone who could strategically broaden its scope beyond connectors and offer fresh ideas and a strong vision that the company needed. He felt that within me, there existed the potential to make this change itself. AMP was a turning point in my career, making it possible for me to leave IBM, where, at the age of 48, I needed to spread my wings in a newer environment. My last eight years at IBM as director were quite static, and at AMP as a senior executive, I would be in a strong decision-making role. It was compelling.

AMP, though smaller than IBM, gave me the chance to become the spearhead of innovation and diversification. Marley's faith in my abilities and his vision for AMP were perfectly aligned with my own aspirations. Not only did I participate in shaping a company's future, but I would now have the opportunity to initiate new technological frontiers.

Balancing The Scales

For nearly 25 years, IBM has been my professional domicile. Through many opportunities it has provided me to grow professionally and personally, this company has woven directly into my very fabric, providing me with the most cherished memories. From computer engineer to senior director, it has been a journey rich in experiences and learning. Under IBM's roof lived such bright stars as Bob Evans, the father of System/360. Every project and position I took at IBM gave me insights that have become part of the tech landscape.

While I treasured this experience, IBM's hierarchical structure and the intensely competitive nature of its upper echelons meant that my future progress would be much slower. A group of influencing mentors is imperative if you want promotions; it's very hard to get ahead by yourself alone inside IBM. Although I had the respect and affection of its employees and subordinates, promotion from director to senior vice president cannot be achieved merely on the strength of past achievements.

One also needs political mentors with clout who are prepared to stand fast behind you so that your most daring ideas may take root and blossom.

Evaluating AMP: Opportunities And Challenges

While the prospect of moving to a small concern like AMP initially seemed like a demotion, it also opened new doors that IBM could never provide. As the world's largest manufacturer of connectors, AMP wanted to diversify its product line and enter new technical terrain. So, this ambition perfectly fitted with my strengths and vision. Marley's offer included the guarantee of substantial decision-making power and a direct line to headquarters, which meant that my work would immediately impact both visibly for the better.

At IBM, I was part of an extremely large, intricate organization. This frequently meant that achieving new ideas would often require negotiating the complex labyrinth of bureaucracy. Even its smaller size promised a more flexible vantage point from which fresh ideas might be expounded on. This possible swiftness of the organism and hence the immediacy of real benefits was most appealing.

Professional Growth And New Directions

The switch to AMP also meant I was stepping into parts of a role different from anything I had done before. At IBM, one main thread was running through my activities: computing technology with its component areas. In a broad sense, these areas comprised almost everything I had done up to then. However, I saw my switch to AMP as an opportunity to expand into new fields and different technological areas. Working with new technologies like fiber optics was very exciting and held out the possibility of contributing to areas that were ripe for the new industrial revolution.

Moreover, there had been a relationship developing with Marley which was an important factor in my decision. His unyielding efforts and sincere appreciation of my talent were both encouraging. Marley saw me as someone who could lead change and innovation at AMP; his vision for the company was in line with what I wanted. The idea of working in close cooperation with a leader who valued his own particular kinds of insight as well as those offered by his subordinates and was committed to using both for the good of all concerned within an organization still growing rapidly was an exciting appeal.

Personal Considerations

At a personal level, the choice to go away from IBM was no easier. Thus, my family and I had constructed our lives around the stability and opportunities provided by IBM. The company's name and the benefits of being part of such a prestigious organization were not to be dismissed lightly. However, I had come to a time when personal development and professional satisfaction were increasing my rankings in importance consecutively; IBM had probably seen its best days as far as personal influence went. Stagnation at IBM would have been a risk I could ill afford. Moreover, the timing of Marley's offer matched a stage of soul-searching concerning my long-term goals.

I was 48 years old, a time when decisions about my career had a special impact feeling. If I didn't take advantage of that window and get into leadership positions as soon as possible, then later on, maybe even never--due to my age, it might be impossible to do so. AMP's desire to make a big impact and fear of missed opportunities forced me to think deeply about what employers should be.

The Big Decision

Marley pursued me incessantly, and after considering it for some time, I agreed to interview for the post of Head of Technology at VP-level AMP. The interviewing procedure with company board members went smoothly, and I was also confident in its result. Marley told me there would be no trouble persuading the board to let me join.

The interview itself was arduous but illuminating, offering me an insight into facets of AMP's workings, problems, and strategic aims I had never before contemplated. I outlined how I saw AMP diversifying and opening up the use of new technologies to keep ahead of things. The board members were receptive and impressed by my perspective and strategic thinking. Such good feedback only served to confirm my decision to join AMP.

After carefully weighing the pros and cons, the decision to join AMP became clear. The opportunities for professional growth, the chance to work closely with Marley, and the discovery of new frontiers in technology were enough reasons to break away from IBM's security. I chose to face the uncertainties and challenges head-on for two reasons.

First, I believed such a move would bring me greater fulfillment and success. Second, it represented a chance to grow.

Cutting free from IBM and setting out to explore AMP was at heart a matter of faith. It was hard to leave behind what you know in favor of the unknown. But it was that decision that was most truly founded upon a clear sense of where I wanted to go in life and upon my determination never to stop growing or changing. The fact that everyone from Guy Rabbat to Marley himself showed endless faith in my abilities and urged me on gave me the confidence to take this major change in direction.

When I think back on it now, this choice shows itself in the clearest light as a crucial moment for me along my professional career path. Thanks to this change, I could enjoy new possibilities, use the skills I had gained in new ways, and set a foundation for fulfilling AMP's growth and diversification ambitions. The insights gained in this period were to be my guidance in the years ahead as a leader and innovator.

A New Beginning – The Transition To AMP

Moving to AMP was a major career transition for me. IBM had been a good place for me to learn. There, I gained experience in a number of different technologies. The fresh perspective and challenges AMP provided were also completely different. Being a leading connectors and applied development, AMP had much to offer me. During the time when fiber optics emerged as an emerging technology, yet another new area for my learning, the company moved in this direction. As a result, I had to change my way of thinking when I moved to AMP from IBM.

In a giant institution like IBM, with its rules and hierarchy, it was very different from AMP. With fewer people, things move faster at AMP, and decisions were made more quickly.

There were no long procedures waiting for approvals of initiatives, so innovative ideas could be put into practice right away. I found the physical environment at AMP refreshing. This gave me more effective leverage to move things forward and make changes.

Welcome New Challenges

The shift from IBM to AMP posed challenges for me. It involved leaving a well-established role at IBM and making a fresh start. However, because AMP was smaller in scale, there was also more freedom and speed in decision-making. As I actively participated in the company's diversification push and sought to inject new ideas into it, I found this both pleasurable and productive.

My first project at AMP was to explore and lead the revolutionary fiber optics technology. We recognized that this could be used to change communication altogether in the future, and accordingly, there were three new product developments in a very short time.

I worked closely with R&D to develop products that could position AMP as an emerging leader in fiber optics. The team's spirit of cooperation and pure hard work made a real impression on us, and together, we reached a lot of landmarks that would serve as a brilliant path for AMP's future.

Valuable Insights: From My Experience To Your Success

Lessons Learned in Adaptability and Vision

When I look back on this winding path, certain pivotal moments stand out:

- **Adaptability:** Embrace the new world and new opportunities. It will greatly promote your personal as well as professional growth.

- **Vision:** Clear vision, the confidence to pursue it and success. My thoughts on outsourcing and using the global talents were premature, but I believed in their possibility anyway. In this way, I was able to make a really meaningful contribution to AMP strategic planning.

- **Flexibility:** To transition from a big corporation into one smaller and with its set of demands required me to be flexible in both approach and style.

- **Relationship Building:** If you have strong relationships, like I did with Marley, can present new opportunities for you.

- **Continuous Learning:** Keeping up with the latest developments in one's industry is a necessity if you are going to prosper over the long run.

- **Mentorship:** The value of mentorship cannot be overestimated. Find mentors who can teach you wisdom and offer encouragement.

For Future Entrepreneurs And Leaders

My story has often served aspiring young businessmen and future industry leaders. Building strong relationships, like the one I had with Marley, can open all sorts of doors later. In addition, continuous learning and 'ears to the ground' are important if you're going to succeed long term.

For young leaders, the value of mentorship can hardly be over-emphasized. Throughout my career I benefited greatly from the guidance and support of mentors who believed in my potential and brought valuable insights. As you traverse your career paths, seek out mentors who will be able to offer advice and encouragement.

Risk Taking

In conclusion, my meeting with James Marley and subsequent transition into AMP was a transformative period in my career. It taught me valuable lessons about flexibility, vision, and the necessity to seize opportunities. I urge you to take risky decisions as you move forward with your career, to deal with brand new challenges stoically and always see yourself as extending and innovating. Just like my journey, yours will be full of unexpected opportunities and valuable learning experiences.

It took perseverance, strategic thinking, and a willingness to adapt for me to successfully navigate such a large career transition and make concrete inputs toward the development and diversification of AMP. I hope my experiences will serve as an inspiration to you, showing that with determination and an open mind, you can achieve remarkable success and leave a lasting impression in your chosen area.

Returning To The East Coast With Changes And Uncertainties -The Desire To Make Higher Ground At IBM

It was the late 1980s when I got back to Armonk. I felt anxious and excited at the same time. Although I had an offer from AMP, I wanted something beyond that--a higher-level position in IBM's vast network. I was aiming for the top echelons of the IBM hierarchy, a position that had once seemed easily attainable but now seemed just out of reach. Instead of moving into a big house, I stayed in a small apartment in White Plains. I was in the midst of change, weighing my options and trying to see which of them would give me the best career.

Dr. Paul Low's Words Seemed Prophetic

After I got back, my situation unfolded exactly how Paul Low, who used to be my boss at East Fishkill Laboratory, had outlined. Changes had swept through IBM. Bob Evans, my mentor in Armonk, had also left IBM in 1984, the year I went to Tucson. Bob's departure created a big vacuum. The absence was deeply felt. In April 1986, Jack Bertram, the person who relocated me to Tucson, died at the age of 58. He was serving Information Systems Technology Group as a Senior Vice President then. His untimely death was a harsh reminder of how life and career can so easily slip away.

Meanwhile, Jack Kuehler, in 1985 took charge of worldwide development and U.S. manufacturing. He became a board member by 1986, and in 1987 was made an executive vice president. By early 1988, he was the vice chairman of the board and a member of its executive committee. Eventually, he went on to serve as IBM's president in 1989, succeeding John Akers. Dr. Low himself had risen to vice president and general manager of technology products.

As I saw all these changes take place, I felt like an orphan in the corporate landscape without a mentor or advocate at my side. Even so, I refused to give up. I decided to make one last bid for a VP position, for I felt I had earned it.

When I returned to the East Coast, everything seemed familiar and yet different entirely. From the very halls of IBM headquarters, permeated with an air of innovation and cutting-edge technology, I was always inspired. However, it was not possible to get instructions from people like Bob Evans or Jack Bertram. These two people had so deeply affected my career path that their absence just left me feeling empty. Nonetheless, their teachings still guided me about integrity, innovation, and the relentless pursuit of excellence.

A Bold Attempt At Promotion

Back from a family trip to India in 1988 summer, I asked John F. Akers for a meeting. John F. Akers, former U.S. Navy fighter pilot, came to IBM as a sales trainee in 1960 and moved around his sales districts. He had been president since 1982 and CEO since 1985. During his time at the helm of IBM, however, the company was on the wane. It was slowly being pushed out of position by companies like Microsoft or Intel. The highly charged atmosphere at IBM consisted of both insecurity and a sense of impending doom.

Ranging from resolved to uncertain, my feelings when I met Akers were mixed. Keenly, I listed my experience and successes at IBM: managing the Fishkill laboratory, turning the storage business around in Tucson, and driving innovation. Dressed in his customary blue suit, he was amenable to speak, listening politely. But he would not make promises. 'Keep your head down for two years, Jay. Later, we'll raise you up', he said. His response, a foregone conclusion, marked a turning point. With it my 20-year career with IBM came to an end.

Nevertheless, this burst of introspective clarity brought me tremendous joy. The interview turned into a long talk. Approaching Akers was not a natural decision. It was fraught with the risk of failure and that he may simply refuse. It was only belief in my chances and a love for innovation that drove me forward. The conversation was a dance between crowing over my gains and navigating through corporate politics in IBM. The outcome of this exchange re-energized and cleansed my mind. Not just the end of a book, but it was the beginning of a new chapter. The understanding that my IBM years were about to be behind me filled me with fear, mingled with joy and apprehension.

Speaking The Truth To Power: A Radical Proposal

Taking a deep breath, I told him, "John, I am out of here, but before I leave, I have some unsolicited advice for you: You need to lose 25 percent of the people here because it's a complete impossibility to get anything done due to all the red tape. At every level of management, there are layers upon layers of review. Creative people are at the bottom, and this won't work for you. If you fire 25 percent of the people, you will have much more room to maneuver."

He was opposed to my idea. Akers pointed out IBM's long-standing policy of "no layoffs." By the middle 1980s it was one of the few Fortune 1000 companies to follow suit. 'Well in that case you might as well suggest that they all go play golf,' I said. 'Let them be on the payroll but not bother turning up to work. At least others can get things done.'

Leaving Akers's office, I felt as though a huge weight had been lifted off my shoulders. All the difficulties of the last few years were over. When the offer came for the AMP job, I decided to take it at once.

The decision to speak to the Akers frankly was not made lightly. The culture of IBM was deeply established, and it was almost heretical to suggest such a radical change. But my frustration with this bureaucracy's inertia had finally reached its peak. The layers of management stifled creativity and innovation, things I cherished most. My conversation with Akers was a final attempt to inject some urgency and help change the organization, which never happened.

I planned to leave.

In Defiance of Logic: Throw Caution To The Wind

Jim Marley, AMP's chairman, called a few days later. 'Jay, we've had board approval for you to come,' he said.

Swallowing hard, I shook my head. 'Jim, I asked my computer three questions. First, I am at IBM, a big technology company, and I am coming to AMP, a much smaller company. The whole screen just turned red. Second, I'm in New York, and now I'm going to Harrisburg, red again. Third, I'm moving from a hi-tech company to a connector company. It turned red... *again.*'

Marley could sense my disappointment. But I stopped him by saying, 'Jim, I have decided to throw the computer out and come along with you on this adventure!'

This was not a decision I arrived at lightly. I had to weigh the pros and cons: the comfort of the known versus the attractive challenge of the new. The thought of moving to Harrisburg at first seemed daunting; I was used to a Big Apple way of life. Then came the promise of starting anew with AMP, which was exhilarating. This move marked another chapter in my life, filled with anticipation and a renewed sense of purpose.

Quitting IBM for a less well-established company like AMP

was a leap of faith. But the supreme sense of accomplishment in being able to achieve from totally new circumstances gave me real excitement. AMP offered an opportunity to begin again; its business valued both innovation and flexibility. Because AMP was small, I could influence change directly and see the quick feedback of new ideas being put into practice.

There were challenging aspects of moving to Harrisburg. Firstly, settling down in a place that was far but felt so much smaller and getting used to an alien organization's way of things was not easy. But then, challenges are also chances for development. Smaller communities mean close connections and greater cooperation, such as at work. AMP was about to undergo a great leap forward, and I took firm determination to make contributions to the success of AMP.

If You Can't Solve The Blockage – *Make The Jump!*

After leaving IBM, the company's fortunes continued to decline under Akers' stewardship. By 1992, IBM was US$5 billion in the red, causing Akers to institute a voluntary retirement program. In early 1993, Akers was gone, forced into retirement. At the same time, his successor Louis V. Gerstner Jr. initiated a colossal reorganization which slashed tens of thousands of jobs, including those at my old stomping ground, East Fishkill.

In looking back over my career with IBM and my departure from the company, I feel that events and conditions both played a major role in my tenure there. If I had gone along with Jack Kuehler, perhaps I might now be vice president or division president of IBM. But in 1988, nothing of that sort seemed possible to me, so I left.

Leaving IBM was a bittersweet experience. It had been my professional "home," a place where I had grown and achieved much. But it was also a place where I felt that my potential was being muffled by bureaucratic rules and a refusal to change. In the end, my decision to leave was about finding an atmosphere of innovation and creativity that would welcome me.

Following my departure, developments at IBM confirmed some of my apprehensions. The company's continuation of old policies and inertia against change led directly to its decline. Watching from the sidelines, I felt a combination of relief and sadness. I had hoped for a different outcome, one in which IBM had enough potential to change flexibly and become part of a truly new technology landscape which was fast taking shape.

Valuable Insights: From My Experience To Your Success

The Entrepreneurial Spirit: Lessons For Future Leaders/ Entrepreneurs

1. **Persistence and Resilience.** During my stint at IBM, it was these two traits of persistence that characterized my entire experience there. Although buffeted by setbacks, I kept my eyes open for opportunities and promoted myself. In the face of obstacles, it is important to maintain one's ground and continue to go ahead. The road to success can be bumpy, but being resilient makes obstacles turn into stepping stones. On my IBM journey, persistence, and resilience have always stood by me. Whether dealing with the intricacies of a large company or making the transition to a new job, these essential attributes helped me stay focused on achieving my objectives. They taught me that setbacks are temporary; they often lead to fresh paths and new opportunities.

2. **Innovation and Adaptability.** Change and innovation must be embraced. My move to AMP–while I had my misgivings–brought about new opportunities for growth. Whatever field we are in, adapting to new circumstances and incorporating the latest advances is essential. Remaining open to change can yield surprising and rewarding results. Innovation was the leitmotif of my career. At IBM, I had the chance

to work on state-of-the-art projects and pioneer technological advances. Transfer to AMP enabled me to put this knowledge into practice in a whole new setting, fostering creativity and problem solving. Being adaptable was my strength, and it has enabled me to thrive in different places.

3. **Speaking Truth to Power.** Don't let the status quo dictate to you. My conversation with Akers, though highly unconventional, simply told him what he couldn't ignore. Constructive criticism, delivered thoughtfully, can make great strides in promoting innovative open-mindedness and bringing about substantial change. Put Value success in success and your heart, and everybody will join your cause. To speak truth to power needs courage, sincerity, and conviction. My conversation with the head of IBM was conducted out of a deep-seated desire to see the company achieve success. While my proposals were bold, they derived from a serious need for change. With opposition in front and a sense of right behind it. This experience taught me how valuable it is for a person to express their beliefs.

4. **Be Mentored and Advocated.** It's valuable to have a mentor advocate. My journey has been shaped by mentors such as Bob Evans and Jack Bertram. Seek mentors who can guide and support you. Their insights and support will help you along the complex path of your own career goals. Mentorship was crucial to my career. Bob Evans and Jack Bertram were not only my colleagues but the guiding light in my work. Their confidence in my abilities gave me the courage to take on ambitious projects future leaders must seek out mentors--and also become them.

5. **Challenge comfort zones for new opportunities.** In some cases, leaving a familiar environment can bring growth and new experiences. My departure from IBM for AMP was a significant turning point. Don't be afraid to invite change. Cautious risks bring rich rewards. Embracing new opportunities often means moving out of your comfort zone. My leaving IBM for AMP was a big step, but it led to both personal

and professional growth. Taking calculated risks led me further afield. Each fresh experience lent me still more valuable lessons and insights.

6. **Personal Growth and Self-Discovery.** Throughout my professional journey, I have been able to feel the significance of self-discovery and self-perfection. Every test, every choice, shapes human temperament and spirit.

I advise you to come into your journey with an open mind, with a readiness to experience new things. Personal growth is an ongoing process. Every encounter, whether good or bad, has something to give towards your growth and development. Reflect back on your experiences, try to learn from them and as a result you can be a more solid, resilient self. This journey of self-discovery is really very personal. Each decision, challenge, and triumph has helped me to grow. I learned to trust my intuition, value my experiences, and keep a clear, open mind for new things. As a result of this introspection, I started understanding my strong-points and where I was lacking in ability. Consequently, it's how I came to develop the habit of continuous improvement.

Pearls For Future Leaders/Entrepreneurs

To all of you who hope to become entrepreneurs and future leaders: Every challenge will serve as an opportunity for your growth. Persevere and remain innovative; never wait to say what you think.

Seek your own mentors, be flexible, and always remain open to new possibilities.

You are unique, and your journey will be unique, with its ups and downs. However, with courage, today's innovation, and willingness to learn, you can travel the complex landscape of business and come out on top in your own way.

Thank you for joining me on this introspective journey. I hope my story inspires you to pursue your ideal with determination and courage.

So, as you embark on your own journey, remember: *the process is just as important as the destination itself.* Cherish each moment, learn from each experience, and always stand by your own convictions. In time, your unique experience will be a testimony to resilience, originality and leadership.

In summation, although my journey from IBM to AMP – and beyond -- has seen struggles and difficulties, it has also been marked by growth and golden lessons. I was inspired to chase after my dreams with passion and determination. I pursued change, sought out teachers, and never hesitated to tell the truth.

Your journey lies out there uncharted.

Cultivate *'The Art of the Possible'.*

Section 2

The Corporate VP
Turns Entrepreneurial On AMP Soil
High Octane Creativity At AMP
Setting The Pace For My Future Business

A Preview To My AMP Experience

Life is a series of challenges and opportunities, but we may not immediately realize how these shape our path. My move from IBM to AMP is a stirring testament to the strength of my determination, the courage to stand up for one's convictions and a relentless drive aimed at attaining goals. As a corporate leader, my story is not solely one of individual triumph It is also the story of an entire organization standing behind its beliefs and carrying out its work with integrity and vision.

Embracing Change: A Leap Into The Unknown

The decision to leave IBM, a company where I had grown my skills and worked my way up from a simple engineer to senior director, seemed like temerity born of frustration. Yet, I viewed the offer made by AMP as an opportunity. This job offered me the chance to break fresh ground and lead a company in a whole new area with rich traditions. The transition from IBM to AMP was not only a change of employer, but it also meant moving to an entirely different organizational culture and geographical location. Changing environments in this way was a trial that I was ready to meet head on.

Determination And Courage

When I first came before AMP's board, it was clear that someone with my background did not mesh well with the company's traditional practices. My opening jocular remark that I came to this country on a 707 rather than the Mayflower fell on deaf ears.

This remark symbolized the cultural oppositions that I would have to learn to bridge, but it was also a lesson in humility and the importance of cultural adaptation with respect.

One of the most important dimensions of my tenure at AMP was building relationships with my new colleagues. The top managers, nearly all company men, had all spent the entirety of their careers at AMP. My arrival was seen as an interruption in that well-established order and I met with considerable resistance. However, I approached this latest challenge with respect and a readiness to learn. By being supportive and caring to my team and colleagues and encouraging open communication, I gradually won their trust and cooperation.

Emotional Resilience: Staying Power In Adversity

Getting through the cultural and organizational obstacles of AMP was a big emotional burden. There were times of doubt and frustration, but my determination and faith in my goal focus kept me fighting on. In my experiences at IBM, I had learned the importance of persistence and keeping a positive outlook even when you're under tremendous pressure. Every day there were new obstacles at AMP, and every day offered opportunities for learning and growth. I had confidence in the knowledge that I would be making positive contributions to AMP's ultimate success.

Celebrating Small Wins

During my time at AMP, it was my habit to celebrate small successes. Each small step forward, however inconsequential it might seem, was in fact a sign of where we were going and helped to lift team morale. These small victories served to build a sense of unity among the staff and the company purpose behind our work.

As a message for potential entrepreneurs and emerging business leaders, my experiences at AMP have some important teachings:

- **Greet Change With Open Arms and Adaptability:** Transitioning from IBM to AMP involved major cultural as well as organizational adjustments, This experience taught me the importance of being flexible and open towards novel environments.

- **Humility and Learning from Mistakes:** My crack at a gag during the first meeting with the board represented, amongst other things, a lesson in humility and a reminder that you must keep the audience in mind. Humility and the capacity to learn from blunders are crucial for growth as an individual.

- **Perseverance in the Face of Adversity:** Encountering hostility and negative attitudes of others could have derailed my cause. But I never lost heart and stayed focused on achieving real results. Having clear goals and an unquenchable spirit is vital for surmounting obstacles.

- **The Value of Diversity and Inclusion:** As a person of colour among AMP's top executives, I contributed a unique way for the company to think. With a corporate culture in which all types of people participate, you go largely further and more richly.

- **Continuous Growth and Innovation:** My time at AMP was notable for technological advances and constant innovation. Continuous learning and gathering new knowledge are necessary to keep ahead in an ever-changing marketplace.

In Conclusion

My transition from IBM to AMP is a story of perseverance, courage, and determination in pursuit of decisive objectives. It vividly demonstrates that if you stand by your principles and think through situations carefully before drawing any conclusions, the results will be certain over time. For the generation of up-and-coming business leaders, the lesson is to always embrace change, as pushing ahead and growing with it form perseverance when faced with adversity. Consider diversity a virtue, and it is necessary to constantly enrich yourself with new knowledge.

By striving to fulfill these directives, management successes w ill not only follow personnel achievements but also bring benefits to those organizations and the people in them.

The AMP SAGA

A Courageous Switch: IBM To AMP

Towards the close of 1980s, came a crucial moment in my career. I was presented as one of AMP's newest vice presidents by its Company President, James E. Marley. He had spent months working to persuade me to join AMP, and he even persuaded the board to offer me $600,000 USD in a signing bonus in the form of a loan. For AMP, this was an audacious move. In its 47-year history, the company had never brought anyone in at such a senior level from outside. With this move, I relocated from Tucson, Arizona, to Harrisburg, Pennsylvania, both geographically and sociologically. This was a big change indeed.

However, in terms of organization, the change from IBM to AMP was not merely change of employer. It had far more profound implications for ethos and atmosphere. Enterprises like IBM were where I learned my own skills from scratch and climbed up through their corporate hierarchies, growing in knowledge about both technology and also leadership. While Breaking with IBM, at whose head office it was I had only recently arrived in Armonk, New York, was a wrenching experience, the pull of AMP proved irresistible.

As I stood there about to speak to the board, I could not help but notice the landscape-size painting of U.A. Whitaker, the company's founder and its first native of Christianity in Asia. I began by saying thanks to Marley: I knew this decision had required a great deal of trust from him. The contrast between the backgrounds of these home-office personnel and that of myself, their new president, was immediately appallingly clear. I tried to lighten things up with a joke: 'Some of your ancestors may have arrived in this country on the Mayflower. I didn't come that way; I landed on a 707 at Idlewild airport.'

But it didn't go over as well as I had thought. Remarks were largely negative, and I saw that what I had looked on as a bid to make them laugh may have merely made me out for a braggart.

Later, when I thought about this incident, it struck me as simply an act of hubris. I would never do so today.

Understanding AMP:
At The Outset – Know Your Environment

Aero Marine Products, or AMP, was established in 1941 during World War II in Elizabeth, New Jersey. Mechanical and electrical engineer U.A. Whitaker, MIT-trained, started the company to produce lots of wiring connecting terminals used in aircraft and on ships. Two years later, in 1943, AMP moved its core operations to Harrisburg, Pennsylvania. The goal was to hire workers from its highly-trained German American community and not become ensnarled in union labor problems there.

Post-war, the company relabelled itself AMP Incorporated and went public during the 1950s. Flush with cash, AMP took control of the connector industry, particularly cars. By the mid-1980s, AMP had settled down. It grew a lot bigger, until in 1987, the year before I entered its employ, AMP was doing revenues of $1.3 billion and was 171st in Fortune magazine's annual list of America's biggest 500 firms. It employed 22,000 people, all over the world through affiliated enterprises.

My decision to join AMP was largely the result of the company's age-old tradition and the outsize part played by it in manufacturing. I was optimistic about my ability to lead the company's engineering and technology divisions and to create another legend of innovation. However, there were potential difficulties: 'There would definitely be resistance from inside.'

Navigating A New World – Keep An Open Mind

When I arrived in Harrisburg, I was keenly aware of the cultural differences. Though I had spent most of my career in more diverse and progressive environments, Harrisburg was like a slap in the face. I jokingly called it 'Alabama in the Middle.' From the first day, I found that the people there were all basically of one race. This was not a negative evaluation but a recognition of reality.

However, despite these initial observations I began to approach my new job with a mind wide open and an enthusiastic attitude. I knew that meeting the needs of the local community would be vital to my success, embracing its culture essential for me to deliver real results. While remaining true to my principles and visions, I was determined to integrate into this new environment.

Building Relationships – Crucial To Success

For one, I needed to relate to my new colleagues. Most of the top managers at AMP are 'company men' who have spent their whole lives with the firm. These include such luminaries as Chairman and CEO Walter F. Raab and Vice-Chairman Harold A. McInnes. My appointment was thought to be something of a sea change and faced internal resistance.

In resisting the normal pattern, my predecessor, Joseph P. Sweeney, is a prime example of this. Sweeney had been with AMP since 1955, and here I was seen as a force of chaos to the established order. I was the unwelcome storm that he had foretold.

When news of my arrival broke, senior engineer Bret Matz related something he had heard from Sweeney. Matz, who came from the local area and had joined AMP while completing his engineering degree, remembered asking Sweeney against me, 'What does it mean? Is he coming to take over your position?' Sweeney's answer was clear: 'He won't take my job.'

Then this conversation highlighted the resistance I would encounter.

Nevertheless, I made a point of treating my new colleagues with respect and trying to learn from them instead. I could appreciate their apprehensions and address these fears through open channels of communication and collaboration. It was essential to demonstrate that I had no intention of replacing or overshadowing anyone but to work with others to push AMP forward.

He did succeed in overcoming the attitude of resentment AMP employees held towards him. Meantime, other employees at AMP felt unable to accept the board's decision on this matter. With such a substantial price tag, there had never been another case where AMP would offer an outsider its compensation. The feeling that their own efforts and those of their compatriots had gone unrecognized created a huge sense of injustice among workers here. While I refunded the bonus eventually, I believed I had every right to keep it. Looking at it in a different way, rather than as grumbling, I treated this attitude of resentment as an opportunity to prove myself. Actions speak louder than words, and I concentrated on producing results of merit. By showing my commitment to AMP's well-being, I hoped to establish an atmosphere in which colleagues would trust and respect me.

Emotional Resilience

To navigate the challenge of AMP, it requires a heavy emotional load. Although there were times of self-doubt and frustration, was always convinced that I could make a positive contribution to AMP. At IBM, I acquired a sense of perseverance and learned that having an optimistic attitude is important when you have people breathing down your neck.

Every day brought new difficulties but also new opportunities for learning and growth. With the support of my family, I felt confident that I had found the right path.

My professional journey was not just about advancing my personal career but also to contribute meaning towards an organization with such great history and an even more brilliant future before finding Common Ground.

One of my most effective strategies was to find common ground with my colleagues. Despite our differences, we all wanted to see AMP succeed. By concentrating on this shared objective, we were able to get over our initial disagreements and work together with efficiency.

I made a deliberate effort to understand the viewpoints of my colleagues and to align our goals. This meant actively listening, showing empathy, and occasionally modifying my approach when it was needed. Eventually, these efforts began to pay off, and I established strong, collaborative relationships with my team.

Guide Yourself With Every Gain – No Matter How Small

Throughout their journey I made it a point to celebrate small victories. Every inch of progress that was made, no matter how scanty, served as a testament to the development we were experiencing. These small successes encouraged even tighter unity within our team.

Regardless of whether it was successfully launching a new product, improving a manufacturing process, or obtaining positive feedback from a colleague, these wins were important in keeping up moral and showing that our toil was not in vain.

Lessons Learnt And Personal Growth At AMP

I have found several very important lessons that I think are applicable to both aspiring entrepreneurs and business leaders today.

Embrace Change and Adaptation

When I moved from IBM to AMP, I had to make a big cultural adjustment. This change of job experience gave me the understanding how adaptable people can be and a chance to acquire new characteristics. A good leader must be able to get used as though nothing has happened in completely foreign surroundings, while negotiating hurdles every bit as high.' Adapt to Harrisburg and the corporate culture at AMP was a test of endurance and flexibility.

Humility and Learning from Mistakes

That little joke in my first AMP board meeting certainly pulled me down a peg. It brought it home to me how laughter sounded to people outside of my immediate surroundings.

Humility, or the ability to learn from your errors, is half the battle won for personal growth. But doing this means you should always remember where you are grounded in relation to what everything looks like around you. In particular, I remember the reality of this moment of perseverance in the face of adversity. I faced resistance and hostility during my time at AMP, but I persevered. Attending to hardware and my expertise led to the development of technological innovations within the group. Sticking in there when the going gets tough is a lesson every leader should learn from. After overcoming the initial chilliness, which came as some small relief.

The Value of Diversity and Inclusion

My experience demonstrates the importance of diversity and inclusivity in business. As the sole person of colour among AMP's top leadership team, I brought a unique perspective which was fruitful for the development and innovation of the company.

Embracing diversity can create a richer and more dynamic corporate culture. The broader representation and greater inclusion I called for at AMP could never be clearer than my never once seeing a single another enormously tall Black person on the management team had to be.

Continuous growth and innovation

During my years at AMP, a number of technological advances and innovation programmes were led by me. With my IBM background, my skills and vision were able to thrust AMP forward into an increasingly competitive market. Innovation and success follow from both accumulating experience and constantly seeking new knowledge. It was essential that AMP be in a position to nurture innovation and learning.

Innovating for the Future

Once I was in charge, AMP expanded its product range and streamlined manufacturing processes, making it one of the world's major connector suppliers. The stamina with which I was able to draw on past experience and put it to work in a new environment is a clear indication of this. My own course serves to testify that even one person can have a crucial impact on an organization faced with daunting obstacles.

One of the nicest aspects of my job was being able to see just how real the benefits of our technological innovations are. Line expansions at all five of our product families and further refining of our manufacturing process contributed to AMP's reputation for excellence in electrical and electronic connection devices. Dare I say it was a tenure grounded firmly in the conviction that there are always new things technology can help us do?

The Cultural Revolution And Industry Trends

When I was at AMP, the technological horizon was changing very rapidly. The late 1980s and early 1990s saw several important advances in electronics and manufacturing first start briefing to take place. The rise of personal computers, the arrival of telecommunications at an advanced level, and globalization in the field of manufacturing all offered both challenges and opportunities.

To navigate these changes in industry dynamics, we needed to understand future trends in technology underlying every move and what impact this would bring on AMP operations. My days at IBM had taught me to anticipate these changes. At AMP, focused on getting our technological capabilities in line with those changes and trends emerging elsewhere.

We heavily invested in research and development within the company, fostering a culture of innovation. Our goal was to not just keep up with the industry but to lead it. We sought to develop products that were not only cutting-edge but also lined up with the future needs of our customers. This forward-looking effort helped to cement AMP's position as an industry leader.

Build A Resilient And Innovative Team Creating Together And Collaborating

Building and nurturing a team that is both resilient and innovative was a significant part of my job at AMP. To achieve this required creating an atmosphere where new ideas could flourish and employees were encouraged to break through limits, seeing what could be possible and not held back by obstacles.

The focus was on establishing a culture of cooperation and ongoing growth in learning. Cross-functional teams were brought together to work, with their respective expertise combined that flowering into an environment of invention. This approach not only improved the product development process for our business but also helped build a united and motivated staff.

One of the main things I did was to set up innovation laboratories within the company. Here, new ideas and technologies could be developed in safety and numbers -- with people trying out different ways to solve problems, rot chewing on old thoughts simply due to those constraints. All told this initiative played a pivotal role in forming an ethos of creativity for today's crew.

For Aspiring Entrepreneurs And Future Leaders

When I made the move from IBM to AMP, it was not just a step forward in my career; more importantly, this reflected ongoing self-development and took its form as change-maker for the whole outfit. The key lessons from my experience could be summed up simply as follows:

- **Fearless of Change:** Being able to adapt is vital in learning new environments, tackling obstacles and ridding oneself of organizational hold backs.

- **Learn from Mistakes:** Humility towards oneself and one's actions is a prerequisite for personal and professional growth.

- **Perseverance:** Even resistance can be overcome; grit and determination enable you to accomplish your aims.

- **Diversity is Strength:** The many different angles that life can offer lead to a deeper understanding, knowledge, better innovations, and ultimately greater organization.

- **Continuous Learning:** These enable past experiences to be used, then provide further growth through picking up any new information or knowledge that comes one way without bias against subsequent sources in each case. What I can say to young entrepreneurs is derived from my own experience: believe that by changing, learning from errors, and valuing diversity your life will reach the state of your choice.

Evolve To Open Path: A New Era For AMP

AMP had grown steadily for decades based on its reputation for reliable products and top-shelf customer service. It was satisfied with its way of working, even if occasional economic disasters did hit. Time was a little slower at AMP, favoring company cultural politics over rapid advancement. The employees were mainly connectivity industry experts and circuit board design engineers who would put their hearts into work. But all this was about to change when I took over as general manager."

I was used to a totally different culture at IBM. At IBM, working things out and fast was the rule. Being one's, own pioneer was indispensable for survival and not something exceptional. When I served as director and vice president of IBM, I worked with creative geniuses the likes of Jack Kuehler, Jack Bertram, and Bob Evans. These people were not only very talented, but they were also very passionate about their work. Through their own drive to succeed, this deeply imprinted upon my much later process (and innovation) approaches whether I was consciously aware or not.

When I came to AMP, I knew I had to bring that kind of proactive, forward-thinking attitude into the company. My philosophy was simple: keep on innovating. Never stop striving for perfection.

I felt that complacency was the enemy of progress, and this belief became deeply ingrained in my work style. Right from the start, made it quite clear that I was here as a disruptive force to move things around-to shake up and challenge the fixed order of things all the time. I knew that approach would upset those who had grown comfortable with the old ways, and they certainly did resist change. However, I was determined to take the section under my care and turn it into something different and, if possible, revolutionize the entire company. I was there to offer no olive branches to those clinging on and battling to the end.

Instead, I concentrated on promoting advances in technology at every opportunity and breathing a spirit of efficiency throughout the organization.

My personal philosophy derived from the idea that every day presents an opportunity to improve and advance. Thomas Edison once said, "There is always a better way to do something; find it." That spirit drove me to seek constantly for improvements in what we were trying to accomplish; and it encouraged others around me embrace similar thinking.

Pressing The Right Buttons: Inaction Is No Option

Back when I first joined AMP, one of the first things I had to do was to get Bret Matz over and let him give me a presentation on the line of business for his department, an engineer who had worked under my predecessor Sweeney. Matz was eager to impress his new boss, and he put together an elaborate presentation complete with translucent foils and transparencies because Microsoft PowerPoint wasn't around back then. Yet I just couldn't help but interrupt him once he started his presentation. I recklessly asked him for an overview of the whole thing. Matz, who had devoted much effort to making his visual material, continued to use slides. Frustrated, I asked. 'You just want me to go through your entire presentation then?'

That first encounter didn't go well for Matz, but it cemented an understanding. My idea was about sparing people useless multi-hour presentations I demanded actionable answers; results. Matz and his colleagues soon realized I was not following the old Sweeney model in the slightest.

Although Sweeney's approach had its merit, it didn't gel with my vision of an organization that focuses on outputs. He concentrated on basic research and getting patents and then left others to productize the research.

Sweeney was pursuing an old model, where the R&D department was off on its own and all-too-frequently produced products that nobody wanted to buy. Their mission was invention, not necessarily profit. On the other hand, I was more concerned with an integrated approach, which seemed more appropriate. All employees contributed to the profitability line in some manner. My dream was to establish an organization of products, not a research post. The budget for various research teams in my division was cleared before I took over, but I made it clear from the outset that this was to produce marketable products.

My first job was to identify who in the company makes things that can be sold and who is mere overhead. Despite resistance from the start, this method became the established way of scaling back what the company spent on staff or operations while maintaining commercially viable product development. As they saw it, they were being proper guardians of business conduct and the sacred values of AMP. My approach must, therefore, be resisted with every bone in their bodies, as much as possible without risking dismissal. Impatient of excuses, I held all of my team accountable when things went wrong.

My philosophy was based on the twin tenets of responsibility and achievement. I believed that true innovation could only happen when each person sought their own level of excellence and then urged others to try for something better. This was not a widely held view at the time, but it was essential in changing ways that superficially seemed unchangeable.

Riding Out The Resistance

Influential figures were opposed to my vision and I had to adopt creative solutions for them. One of these figures was Dimitry G. Grabbe, a brilliant scientist on the Board of Research and Technology at AMP. Given his many contributions, including some 500 patents worldwide Grabbe was untouchable. So, in this instance, the AMP Fellowship was born. Modeled after IBM's own fellowship, it reserved heights of engineering and scientific research for Grabbe, where exact results are not necessarily required every single day.

The AMP Fellowship was not only a strategic move but also an expression of my own belief in recognizing and rewarding talent. My personal philosophy has always been to respect and treasure those people who contribute greatly to an organization's development, even if their work has to change. This is how I dealt with opposition while making sure that the best people in these fields felt they were being taken care of.

Although I met with considerable objections at first, Jim Marley who was president of AMP was on my side. Marley had come to AMP in 1963 and liked me; he understood what I was trying to do. In fact, he brought me in for the very thing you see here today-changing AMP into a forward-trendy interactive company.

Marley's support was everything. It brought to mind a lesson I had learned at IBM: the importance of having a 'rabbi' in upper management who supports and publicizes your concepts. At AMP, that was Marley. This allowed me to press ahead with my plans, secure in the knowledge that I had a friend at the top of the organization.

Interrelated Solutions – Clear Vision

When I looked at the products AMP made, I could see that the company was still thinking in the mindset of the mid-20th century. This technology could be rendered obsolete very quickly. Although they controlled an important portion of worldwide connector output, AMP's dominance was being threatened by changing technology. If it wanted to survive, AMP had to change its way of thinking and create a new image for itself as a 21st-century company.

AMP used to concentrate on passive components, but I believed there was potential to develop new areas such as fibre optics technology. This looked like it would be the wave of future telecommunications industry development. It was relatively easy to make connectors, but electronics trended toward more integrated solutions. In other words, future products were those that connected devices across different platforms and networks.

The first requirement for changing AMP was to have a division advocating my dream of connected products. Building this service and finding people with ability in a conservative business was difficult. With Marley's assistance, I set up a technology board to support my independence. The key was to extract substantial parts of AMP from the connector business.

A big problem was finding the right people. Hiring employees from outside AMP was not an option, so I set up the Statue of Liberty project, named after the poem 'The New Colossus' by Emma Lazarus. I sucked up underperforming people from the departments and from elsewhere in the company in an attempt to turn them into useful people. This stratagem allowed us to form a team that could drive the transformation of the company.

My own philosophy at this time was capitalized on the belief that everyone has untapped capacity. I often recalled a statement made by Michelangelo that "I saw the angel in the marble and carved until I set him free." Uncovering talent and cultivating it within the organization became natural extensions of this idea, making neglected individuals into productive team members.

Birth Of A New Division

One of the earliest departments I visited was the fiber optics department, which hadn't been doing well. In need of direction but capable of development, this department was where Bret Matz had got his start. We needed someone with Bill Stape's abilities and connections, although he had fallen from favor. Against this background, Stape was appointed as part of the Liberty Statue program to redeem his career and contribute towards our vision.

Fiber optics technology was a keystone in my AMP strategy. In the whole United States of America only a handful of companies were working energetically on this promising technology. AMP hoped to turn out connectors and cable assemblies of fiber optics devices, and on this basis we planned our future. But in actual fact, it was necessary to raise our technical level if we were to profit by this venture. There was only one way: acquisition. I persuaded Marley and the board that this was unavoidable.

But buying up companies was not just for technological purposes; it also created overall benefit. By incorporating new companies and their persons of ability, AMP could breed a more open and creative attitude throughout the company.

According to my creed, different ways of thinking and experience are all important: many new ideas and ways of thinking come from the collision of different countries. I champion this idea for business.

R&D Relevance – A New Philosophy

My time with AMP saw a transformation in business philosophy. We had been primarily research and development. From the IBM we learned how important it is for a company to stay ahead of its rivals – not only through research but also by marketing any new findings as products. IBM's attitude was, in fact, the one I was trying to impress on AMP.

I undertook a comprehensive review of both AMP's existing projects and its personnel, from those who could directly contribute to product development and those who sold. I re-set the positions to contribute better to AMP's business advancement. This led to some disagreement, particularly among long-established staff accustomed to doing things the old way.

However, it was my firm belief that if AMP was to progress smoothly, it had to be product centered. That was to say the budget for research should be increased, and more important still, research must serve the needs of markets. This philosophy ran counter to the traditional view that R&D should operate independently of business objectives. In my opinion, R&D is part and parcel and, indeed, an indispensable part of company strategy. To generate sales in the market, development must translate directly into revenue and market share.

The Importance Of Influential Allies

In any company environment, having the backing of major executives is important. In IBM, the hard way was found to be important about having a 'rabbi' - some person in senior leadership who speaks up for you. At AMP, it was Jim Marley who offered this help. Marley saw to understand my vision and then provided crucial backing for implementing change.

Marley's support was not simply personal approval but a practical alliance that allowed me to put through substantial changes. With his support, I was able to move ahead without fear and take big decisions, carrying the confidence that there was someone high above to back me up. This relationship compounds the need for solidarity within an organization seeking substantial change.

Leverage Acquisitions For Growth

One of the strategies I pursued at AMP was leveraging acquisitions to move business forward. While internal development was important, I knew that acquiring companies with expertise in new technologies of the future could help us along.

Take the fiber optics department. That was a key part of my vision for AMP but we had to get some new people and technology in here to make it flourish. I persuaded Marley and the board that buying companies working on pioneering research in fiber optics was a necessity if we wanted any hope at all. This approach allowed us both quickly to expand our capabilities as a company and to put innovative technologies from the leading edge into our products.

Acquisitions weren't just about broadening our technical portfolio but also obvious; they brought in new people and expertise. By integrating fresh companies and their skills, we could create a more active, inventive climate within AMP.

Vision And Innovation

Thinking back over my time at AMP, I have learned several lessons. Furthermore, being able to communicate a clear vision is crucial. Change is unsettling, but a well-articulated vision can gain support and impel progress.

Moreover, the significance of having strong internal support within the organization cannot be overstressed.

Jim Marley and allies were crucial to my capacity for making big changes. Deciding to innovate takes not only fresh ideas but also the willingness to disrupt well-established norms. This frequently leads to opposition and hard decisions. Through my experiences at AMP, I was reminded over and again of the necessity for resilience and adaptability in the face of difficulty. For aspiring entrepreneurs and future captains of industry, vision, resilience, and the ability to think strategically are essential. You can't just keep things as they are; go looking for new opportunities in every corner of reality. Gather around you people who share your vision and do not be afraid to make bold moves. Innovation is a lonely journey yet richly rewarding. By welcoming change and building an innovative culture, you can change not just a single company but a whole industry. During my time at AMP, I was taught the value of persistence, adaptability, and the power of a clear vision. As you take up your own entrepreneurial journey, step by step, please remember that success hinges on being able to inspire and lead others in working towards a common goal.

Deploy Visionaries: Getting Kapany On Board

In 1990, I set out on a life-changing journey that would enmesh my own path with another visionary, Narinder Singh Kapany. Known as the 'Father of Fiber Optics', Kapany's contributions to the early development of this revolutionary technology were monumental. A native of Moga, Punjab, who was born in 1926, he shared my Indian nationality but resided 1,800 miles further north in Aluva than I did. Kapany's unceasing advocacy of fiber optics had already made possible subsequent cooperation between us. His work from 1955 to 1965, which included 46 scientific papers and a classic book on fiber optics, formed the foundation of this entire field.

Kapany had been working to sell his company, Kaptron, which he formed in 1973, to Corning, Inc., a glass and ceramics technology company. But neither side trusted the other party again. This chance was seized by me: AMP acquired Kaptron at the end of 1990, opening up a bright future for our revitalized new friend. It was a strategic decision to bring Kapany on board as a part of the AMP core which greatly bolstered our research capacity and market positioning.

In his memoir, *'The Man Who Bent Light'*, Kapany recalls the joy and fulfillment he got from AMP. He engaged in research and taught young engineers, satisfied in his dual role as learner and innovator. His arrival was a great boon. Not only did it put AMP in the forefront of fiber optics research, it also meshed well with my business philosophy of combining technology with true cooperation as the way to industrial success. I believed that significant advances came from bringing together wide-ranging strengths and maintaining an atmosphere of teaching plus continuous learning.

A profession could bring us together. But it should not be the thing that keeps the friendship going. There would be many times when people with experience in different spheres of life drift apart. Our friendship could withstand these changes and stay strong because we both understood each other's needs—an interest in innovation for its own sake rather than as a means of survival. In 1998, when I purchased a condo in London from Kapany, it was near Hyde Park, a beacon reflecting our boundless bond. His influence on my path was large and his light will continue to guide me forever. Kapany died in December 2020. Although a shock to many, he left behind timeless contributions in the world of fiber optics.

Outsourcing To India: A Strategic Move With Profound Implications – Seeing The Potential

Before I arrived in Harrisburg one year prior to my joining AMP the company had set up operations in Asia. They had subsidiaries in South Korea, Taiwan, and Singapore. However, at that time, there was one major country left off it's list and that was India. In other words, this was a little detail which could not escape my attention. Being a great believer in the potential of Indian engineers, I felt this was significant neglect on their part. India-that great breeding ground of engineers- was truly a gold mine waiting to be mined. I was sure of it and had numerous earlier experiences only backed up what I said.

The Catalyst For Change

After joining AMP, one day the company received a large order for sophisticated printed circuit board assemblies (PCBA). If a new unit was set up or the work given to another U.S. manufacturer, it would have eaten into our profit margins. At that time China, still not the great manufacturing powerhouse it exists even today, was also not an option. As an alternative I suggested India. This was more than a business decision. It was a kind of faith in the skills of my own people.

Family Bond Combines With Business Acumen

My brother, N. Jehangir, who had entered into contract manufacturing, was the ideal partner for this enterprise. Jehangir had already tried his hand at various professions, from marketing pharmaceutical products to selling coconut oil manufactured by our mother's factory. His entrepreneurial spirit and adaptability made him the perfect collaborator for this undertaking.

Jehangir established Sun Fiber Optics in the Cochin Export Processing Zone (CEPZ), a zone promoted by the government to encourage exports. The zone provided an uninterrupted supply of electricity and streamlined regulatory processes. This was crucial for manufacturing operations and exports to be efficient. Our mother, M.M. Khadijoo, performed the opening ceremony, a mark of how much this endeavor generated from our family's own resources. This was the start of a successful cooperation, with Sun Fiber Optics producing high-quality products for AMP. The success of this move ratified my belief in the potential of India and set the stage for further activity in that part of the world.

Navigating Political And Cultural Landscapes

Outsourcing to India had its difficulties. A lot of insight had to be applied with regard to political and cultural landscapes.

In the early 1990s, India was introducing economic reforms under Prime Minister P. V. Narasimha Rao and Finance Minister Dr. Manmohan Singh.

These sought to liberalize the country's economy by inviting foreign investment and removing bureaucratic obstacles. However, change occurred gradually, and it was of vital importance to understand the local regulatory environment.

Cultural Adaptation and Integration

These differences of culture determined how we understood the challenge. The hierarchy of the Indian work culture, and its respect for authority, contrasted with the more egalitarian and collaborative approach prevalent in Western companies. Sensitivity and adaptability were needed in bridging this cultural difference. I stressed to those around me that mutual respect, and a culture of co-operation in which the best ideas could rise to the fore regardless of their source, was what was needed.

Stealthy But Strategic

The covert strategy I used to convince AMP to subcontract to Sun Fibre Optics was firmly rooted in corporate behaviour. Officially, the company was being run by Thomas John, a former senior official of Keltron, simply in order to avoid any possible conflicts of interest. In fact, in my mind, I was justified in treating it as a covert operation with a clear conscience as it was to the benefit of AMP, and I wasn't earning a penny from the outsourcing business. Based on my business philosophy that sometimes unorthodox means are required to achieve strategic ends, especially with the promise of major benefits in a larger view, this was a rational choice.

Impact On India's Economy And The Technology Sector

This move of outsourcing benefited AMP deeply and also India's economy. For AMP, it meant systems manufacturing of high quality at a lower price. In comparison with foreign competitors' finished products, these systems gave us more of an edge over them. For India, it marked the appearance of a new era of technology and systems work. The success story of Sun Fibre Optics bore testimony to the capabilities possessed by Indian engineers and manufacturers, opening a path for other such projects.

Local Talent Empowered

This move also had a big influence on our local workers. By going to India, we're giving opportunities to local talent and contributing to their development and competence. The engineers and technicians who worked on these projects gained much-needed exposure to international standards, which would serve them well later in India's technology field as an offshore provider of IT services.

Expansion And Legacy

Following the success of the first outsourcing project, Sun Fiber Optics moved on to the production of a modem, and more contracts came to AMP. That same year, in 1991, AMP set up a wholly-owned subsidiary in India to produce production tools, dies and special purpose machinery; taking the production link with China a further step forward. This expansion was a reflection of our confidence in the capabilities of Indian manufacturers and our intention to incorporate India fully into our global supply network.

The Outsourcing Phenomenon Is Ignited

The decision to outsource to India was a vision that brought about a new trend in the industry. What my initiative pointed out was that by using global talent high-quality products could be made at lower cost. What this did was to provide an 'injection' for other companies in the tech industry, encouraging them to undertake more outsourcing – with the result that India 's technology sector grew rapidly. Western corporations working with Indian factories share a long and successful history: a forerunner of things to come.

A New Era In Technology

Outsourcing to India under my initiative amounted to a mature stage of multicultural economic cooperation: it is both about cutting costs and creativity. That method sets the stage for a world that can generate enormous innovation through global collaboration. This strategic move has shown once again my belief in viewing matters from a broad perspective and that bold decisions must be taken when things are most uncertain.

Birth of GISB: From Connectors To Solutions
A Transformative Vision

By the start of the 1990s, AMP had arrived at a crucial crossroads. Although the business was known for its high-quality connectors, changes in technology occurred rapidly. It seemed to me that AMP had to move from being just a connector company into a global interconnection solutions provider. This vision was prompted by the technological advances transforming the industry and the challenge from global players who were ready to find markets for new technologies at a sprint.

The Strategy Articulated

In an interview with AMP's in-house newsletter, *Exceleration*, written by the company's Executive and Human Resource Planning Division and published in September 1992, I laid out our strategic direction. "AMP must maintain growth rates commensurate with those for an interconnection systems solutions company. We can't compare our growth now with our growth as a connector company," I said. This realignment of goals was critical to bringing the business's targets into harmony with evolving market requirements.

I pointed out the changes in technology that had taken place at AMP. "Simply stated, the United States invented semiconductor technology--the technology that set off the information explosion. Ripples from that explosion created new multi-billion U.S. corporations: Apple, Digital, IBM, Microsoft, Compaq, and so forth. AMP, as a components supplier, benefited and participated in its growth. Today, however, the global technology playing field is level. The Europeans and the Asians do just as well as Americans. And in some cases, they're faster to commercialize their technology."

A Strategic Vision:
Global Interconnect Systems Business (GISB)

From 1993 onwards, my strategic vision began to take real concrete form. I was promoted to Corporate Vice President of Strategic Businesses, and with the support of the board of AMP I and the force of my tireless efforts, I established a separate business unit: the Global Interconnect Systems Business. This new unit was intended to drive Amp's metamorphosis into a leader in interconnection technologies and solutions.

Operational Independence

In order for GISB to work with the independence necessary to innovate, I moved its offices to a different building several miles farther south of AMP's main office on Fulling Mill Road. This relocation signalled a departure from traditional corporate structures and gave GISB the space it needed to mould its identity and operational structure.

Expanding The Product Portfolio

The establishment of GISB involved more than just changing structures. It was a cultural transformation aimed at broadening our product base. Under the GISB umbrella, we incorporated various teams, including:

- **Optical Interconnection Systems Team:** focused on fiber optic products.
- **Cable Interconnection:** working in cables.
- **Printed-Wiring Board Systems:** specialising in printed circuit boards.
- **Signal Conditioning Products:** concentrated in products to improve signal quality.
- **Smart Connector Systems:** concentrated on smart components.
- **Microwave Signal:** specializing in microwave signal components.

We used strategic reorganisation to offer a full spectrum of interconnection solutions, positioning AMP as an important player in the industry. In 1995, this made AMP the strongest corporate as far as this is concerned.

Faster Growth Through Mergers And Partnerships

For a man intent on reaching his destination quickly, I found it impossible to be so patient as to build the entire division brick by brick. From the moment GISB came into being, I was set on using corporate mergers and strategic partnerships to build it. To this purpose I devoted several mergers and investments, each carefully selected to complement our strengths and help us reach new markets.

Notable Mergers and Partnerships (1993–1995)

1993

- **MicroModule Systems:** Designer of Multi-Chip Modules- Within months of the founding of this company in 1992, AMP became a strategic partner and one of its biggest suppliers. AMP also invested in Micro Module to integrate advanced technologies in keeping with our product offerings.

- **Atmel Corporation:** Struck a partnership to acquire flash devices for use in AMP IC cards.

- **Integrated Circuit Systems Inc.:** Worked together for sound cards, broadening our product line in the electronics market in doing so.

1994

- **Raylan Corporation:** Purchased this company to enter the Fiber-to-the-Desk market, extending AMP's presence in the field of fiber optics.

- **ADFlex:** Formed this partnership to jointly develop products and applications for flex-based interconnection systems. ADFlex produced flexible circuits and assemblies based on flex.

- **Connectware Inc.:** Established a subsidiary to produce asynchronous transfer mode (ATM) products--often our gateway into high-speed networking technologies.

- **Ocean Power Technologies Inc.:** Acquired a minority stake in this company, which produces hydro-piezoelectric generators that change ocean wave power to electricity. This investment showed our commitment to sustainable energy technologies.

1995

- **Alcatel Optronics:** Established a joint venture with this French company to make a series of opto-electronic products for telecommunications applications. This cooperation recognized AMP's entry into the opto-electronics industry.
  M/A-Com Inc: Bought out this Lowell, Massachusetts based company to enter the rapidly expanding wireless market. This purchase allowed us to broaden our product mix and join the growing demand for wireless communications technologies.

Investing In Innovation

As GISB started to bring in some serious money, I was able to persuade the directors of AMP to reinvest much of this income into research and development (R&D). By 1996, GISB was devoting $300 million to R&D, which was 5 percent of AMP's total income and half again more than its entire research budget. This investment testified to our faith in innovation and our understanding of how important it is to create new products to keep ahead in the marketplace.

Ensuring Market Focus

I was an executive, eager to fully productize R&D. I wanted to make sure that every dollar spent on R&D had a direct market orientation. So my goal was to see to it that AMP controlled a big slice of the interconnect business, which had been forecast anywhere from $15 billion to $20 billion within four years.

In an interview published in Business Times with the Malaysian newspaper Nni this September 1996, I further justified our substantial R & D expenditure; My aim is to ensure that we capture at least (not less than) $3 billion of this total. Making the investments now is cash-draining, but absolutely essential because this is an industry where soon there will be only a few major manufacturers and many suppliers."

An Ambition Across Borders

'I always set my sights on the highest and best in my career.' When I first started at IBM, I wasn't content just to be a small cog in the corporate wheel but aimed at becoming its leader. So, I aspired to take on a role even more important. At the time, it was clear that if something big was done or said, I would have to bear the ultimate responsibility. As with so many of its peers in the industry, becoming a division president at IBM was considered a sign of success. Despite these successes, I was unable to ascend the Glass Ceiling above Vice President here. It was a watershed moment for me. The realization that I couldn't realize my ambitions at IBM made me set off in a new direction.

In 1988, I had an offer from AMP. On the face of it, this seemed like nothing more than a backwater place in Pennsylvania, but for me it offered an opportunity to pursue and realize my ambitions. In this new environment where there are few constraints and rigid structures like those at IBM do not exist, I thought that by taking up its challenge one day, I might rise to become its leader. When Jim Marley, an experienced AMP executive who would be my mentor, confirmed that I should go to this place, it was another shot in the arm, and he played a key influential role throughout my career. This man, or 'rabbi' as I liked to call him, believed in my capabilities and was able to help me achieve the aims that deserved achievement.

AMP had a considerable list of challenges. One of the biggest problems was Bill Hudson, Vice President for Asia Pacific Operations. The company's connector business was divided into three geographical sectors: Asia Pacific, Europe and the Middle East, Africa (EMEA), and the Americas. A vice president led each of those. Hudson, as director of the Asian-Pacific division, wielded the most power. My division, GISB (later renamed Global Communications), had an independent existence. This gave me some freedom to operate. By and large, though, it was known throughout AMP that Hudson and I didn't get on. This rivalry between him and me was virtually a corporate axiom.

Where Hudson had someone looking out for him is in the person of Harold McInnes, Vice Chairman of the Board. McInnes had served in various leadership roles at AMP for more than ten years and was President from 1981 to 1986. His influence was considerable, and he was a big backer of Hudson. This made my own trajectory to management all the more difficult.

Staying Afloat In Corporate-Change Floodwaters

The corporate landscape within AMP underwent drastic changes beginning in 1990. Walter Raab, who had served as Chairman and CEO for virtually the entire life of the company (four decades), retired. Raab was only the third person to hold the title of Chairman at AMP, following its originator Whitaker and then company President Joseph D. Brenner, who took over from him. Although he retired, Raab performed the role of figurehead for another five years and so maintained some degree of influence in AMP affairs.

McInnes took over Raab as chairman and CEO, while Marley became chief operating officer, retaining his old title as president. This threw a major bone to Hudson. He was now seen as de facto 'CEO-in-waiting' by about this time, the inevitable result of it being McInnes' term to retire the general retirement age in AMP is 65. On October 1, 1992, McInnes announced his own retirement, and Hudson's elevation was underway.

Immediately after McInnes' promotion, Hudson, who had been responsible for AMP's Asia-Pacific division, was named business executive vice president in charge of all international operations. One year later, in 1991, Hudson was elected to AMP's board of directors, thus solidifying his position within the company hierarchy.

In this period of change, I had my first significant promotion at AMP. In 1991, I was elected corporate vice president for Technology and Strategic Products –a jump a not-so-insignificant one from my previous position as divisional vice president of technology. This promotion was further evidence of the potential and contributions that I had made throughout my time with AMP up until then.

Another major change took place in 1993. Marley was elected Chairman of the board, and Hudson became CEO and President. This was a turning point in AMP's organizational and corporate leadership structure. Although influential to some extent as chairman, Marley's power both on the board of directors and in the organization started gradually to wane. This directly impacted how I would fare within AMP.

Power Dynamics: The Birth Of A New Power Trio

The relationship between Marley and Hudson was complex and fraught with tension. Both men were engineers, but their backgrounds and natures were worlds apart. A tall and athletic man, Marley was a state school man by birth. He loved to go hunting and enjoyed all kinds of sports. He was a man of easy approach and strikingly pleasant personality, a person whom every employee loved. But news of an affair with a female employee injured his reputation, possibly influencing the board in their management reorganization decisions.

In contrast, Hudson was short and bookish and more distant from people. He was disciplined and conventionally narrow in thinking. In college, Marley would have been the type of person to score the winning touchdown and party all night; whereas Hudson would be in the library hitting the books as if his life depended on it. Both leaders were capable, but because they had dissimilar natures and styles they rubbed each other the wrong way constantly.

In a significant power move, Hudson brought in Robert 'Bob' Ripp as AMP's Chief Financial Officer in 1994. A fellow alum of IBM, Ripp was the first Chief Financial Officer hired from outside the company. Unlike myself, an outsider for the duration of my time at AMP, Ripp was quickly absorbed into the fold by the board and top management. He rapidly became part of the triumvirate that ran the firm: Hudson, McInnes, who stayed on as a board member.

Ripp's arrival marked a turning point for my future with AMP. Despite the fact that GISB, my division, was generating the most revenues at AMP, I only saw myself becoming further marginalized within the organizational hierarchy. With his rise, Ripp was destined to take over from Hudson as CEO – putting another stumbling block in my way.

Strategic Reorganization In 'My Last Shot'

Although my division, GISB was racked by several headstrong power struggles, it continued to perform its work exceptionally well. By the mid-1990s, it had become the highest revenue generator of any AMP division. We were able to overcome this situation because of all our hard work, and this type of success marked me out as a person of some authority and power within the business.

In May 1997, AMP reorganized its communications divisions and units into one big division, Global Communications Business. This move aimed at grabbing a considerable portion of the $39 billion communications market. I was named President of this brand-new division, responsible for managing multi-unit and segment operations.

This reorganization brought a number of senior executives under my aegis. They included N. D'Arcy Roche, Alan S. Keizer, and William J. Stape.

The new Global Communications Business division included three industrial units: Premises Systems, Communications Service Providers, and Communications Equipment Manufacturers. In addition, four product units, Cable Systems, High-Flexible Optical Cable and Accessories, Communications Connector Systems, and Optoelectronics, were also integrated into the division.

This point reflected the growing importance and performance of the communications units under my leadership. Together they had contributed over one quarter of the company's $5.47 billion sales in 1996, up from just over a fifth in 1993. The fiber-optic products area – under my direction achieved a remarkable 40% growth. In a company news release, both Hudson and I had our say on the reorganization.

For Hudson, "We perceive it as a chance to amalgamate AMP's strengths and skills in communications technology and provide better service for our customers."

I said, "Today's markets comprise customers demanding solutions, not just goods. As we ourselves are the only company in optoelectronics that spans all stages (from materials through devices) and components from chip to systems at present, we offer a comprehensive capability in these three areas by networking together at various levels."

But even though I had taken charge of a division so strong that it ranked first in earnings across the entire corporation, it was clear that my chance to become CEO was slim.

Where the leadership of the company was concerned, it was dominated by a ruling triumvirate of Hudson, McInnes, and Ripp. I no longer had any place. Even though I had built a division that was one of the biggest money-makers within AMP, the truth is that power within the company was against me.

No Compromise With My Ideas And Principles
- The Spinoff Proposal

Leaving me with no access to top management, I launched a far-reaching proposal: let GISB become independent and entirely another company.

A division of the old company had earned more than $1.5 billion in revenues during last year. I visited Hudson and put forward my case for achieving a market value in excess of $8 billion as against AMP's $3 billion.

I claimed that liberation alone of the Global Communications Business (GISB) would unlock tremendous value.

At the time, fibre optic technology was booming on Wall Street. Companies like Bell Atlantic, the successor to Verizon, had begun to set up their own fibre optic systems. If AMP had spun off optical fibres division, then it could have acquired Wall Street's high valuation. Ultimately, the spinoff company might have been larger than what remained of AMP, an old technology firm whose price-earnings ratio bottomed out due to its poor prospects in this area right now.

But Hudson saw things differently. He viewed the spinoff proposal as a threat to his authority and shut it down immediately. He was aware that with the spinoff, I could come back stronger, challenging his position.

Since Hudson had shot down the proposal, I decided to approach the board directly.

In the next board meeting, I made my case, emphasizing the high gross margins and future prospects of GISB. I chose not to use the podium and instead spoke as I walked about the conference room. All the board members, who of course, were white and male, listened carefully.

I began, 'My gross margin is 35 percent. I know that because I buy the stuff and I know its cost. I know how much I sell it for, and I know what the margin is. But I am charged with all this overhead as well. Well, when these figures are correctly stated, you will find that GISB is a very attractive business. We're growing the business, we have the margins, but when all overhead costs are added, then it's not that appealing."

Hudson said, 'Jay, don't worry. Left pocket, right pocket, it makes no difference.' I parried, 'Bill, you are saying that whether it's the right pocket or the left one for the company doesn't matter. But when you put it in the right pocket, numbers like this are very attractive. Fit it in the right pocket, this is a highly attractive business, a lot better than what's shown here, and I'm saying so openly.' They did not accept my arguments. My proposal was defeated by the board, which was dominated by Hudson and McInnes.

My direct denial to the company president's face was akin to cutting my own throat in the presence of the board. The end had arrived; in effect I was resigning.

That autumn I left AMP. This was the end point of my journey with the company.

Valuable Insights: From My Experience To Your Success

Lessons Learned and Advice for Aspiring Entrepreneurs/Leaders

Staying True to Your Ideas and Beliefs

In that challenging environment, I realized that staying true to your principles, ideas, and philosophy is paramount. It's easy to get swept up in corporate politics, but maintaining integrity ensures that you stay anchored in your core values. Core values such as these will determine your leadership and legacy.

Why Being True to Your Ideas Matters

- **Authenticity Creates Trust:** When you stick to your beliefs and principles, you build trust with your team and colleagues. Genuine leaders breed loyalty and devotion. In addition, people are more likely to follow somebody who they believe keeps their word and has 'walked their talk'.

- **A Clear Sense of Purpose and Leadership:** Sticking to your own ideas gives you a clear vision and direction. It provides for decisions in tune with long-term goals rather than being swayed by short term profits or external pressures. This clarity helps bring order out of chaos and keeps you focused on what truly matters.

- **Resilience in the Face of Difficulty:** Staying with your principles gives you the inner strength to cope with challenges and setbacks. If your core values are clear and present, you can use them as a foundation you can rely on when confronted with adversity. This represents an internal toughness that is key for overcoming barriers and emerging still stronger from problems.

- **Driving Innovation and Change:** All new ideas are born of dissatisfaction with what exists and the desire to create something fresh. With your knowledge and belief backing you up, it is possible to stand at the head of innovation and drive change. Those leaders who dare to trust their own instincts, skill and ability to direct and lead on a different course are the ones that differentiate their companies.

Remain Respectful but Fearless

It is equally important to stand up for your ideas fearlessly yet maintaining respect. Respectful but fearless leadership means standing up for what you believe in. Even if it means challenging authority or established norms.

- **Courage to Speak Up:** There have been many instances throughout my career where I had to oppose popular wisdom. Fearless disagreement and constructive argument are conditions for an organization to progress well. When presenting your ideas fearlessly, get others to follow your train of thought while also listening. This is how an atmosphere of mutual respect is created and enduring improvement.

- **Handling company politics:** It calls for a good balance between assertiveness and diplomacy. By being fearless, you can successfully negotiate the power dynamics while making sure that your own voice is heard and ideas taken seriously. This assertiveness helps break down barriers and bring about meaningful change.

- **Leading by Example:** A fearless leader sets an example for his or her team. When they see you standing up for your principles, it empowers them to do likewise. This atmosphere of integrity and courage can lead to a more innovative and motivated workforce.

Prepared to Move On

There also comes a time when, in spite of one's best efforts, you find yourself hampered by the existing power structures. At that point, it is essential to be prepared to move on.

- **Recognizing When to Move On:** We must recognize when the environment no longer nurtures our own growth, or realization of what we have set out to accomplish. Remaining in a place that stifles potential can lead to frustration and stagnation. Knowing when and how to move on makes it possible for you to seek opportunities more in line with your goals and values.

- **Exploring New Horizons:** Being ready to move on means keeping an open mind about new opportunities and challenges. It means putting your trust in your capabilities and being ready to walk into the unknown to achieve your aims. This kind of pioneering spirit toward the unknown can only help make life more fulfilling.

- **Leaving a Positive Legacy:** As you move on, do so gracefully and leave a positive legacy. The relationships you form and the influence you exert are lasting strengths. Make sure that your departure is polite and helpful, building bridges rather than burning them and leaving doors open for future collaboration.

My Resolve Tested: Staying True To My Beliefs

Throughout my time at AMP, I was faced with many trials that tested my spirit and tenets. While the restructuring of the communications division was an example of my leadership qualities and ability to innovate, it also showed the importance of maintaining consistency in one's beliefs so that one does not shrink back from tough choices.

My division was a great success, but it became clear that my path to the top was being obstructed by one hurdle after another. The entire power hierarchy within AMP was obstructing me, especially the three leaders, Hudson, McInnes, and Ripp. Knowing that my scope to effect changes from inside was limited, I reluctantly decided to suggest that the GISB division be spun off.

The proposal was shot down in the end, but it was a watershed fore me. It reinforced my belief in the importance of pushing hard for your ideas and standing by your principles. It confirmed the adage that one must be ready to move on when necessary, though that in itself is no easy path. Hard though this decision was, it was a reflection of my dedication and my willingness to take bold measures.

A Rocky Start: The Hostile Takeover Attempt

Even after saying that I was retiring from AMP, I soon discovered my time with the company was far from over.

On the day following my retirement, AlliedSignal Inc, a huge aerospace and transport conglomerate located in Morristown, New Jersey, made an aggressive bid for AMP.

This sudden turn of events threw me back into the heart of AMP's turbulence, though from a different vantage point. AMP was already navigating through troubled waters, sales were plummeting, the Asian markets fluctuated and a strong U.S. dollar forced the company to put 22,000 U.S. employees out on salary suspension and to even offer 2,200 employee early retirement. Our stock had lost 50%, so from the perspective of market watchers and calculations experts, AMP became an increasingly appealing acquisition for AlliedSignal. However, its offer of $9.8 billion was received as a daring and opportunistic raid on a weakened company. The AMP board and senior executives regarded it as a hostile takeover. They thought the offer was too low, and that AlliedSignal didn't fit into the long-term vision of AMP. To deal with the threat, AMP placed Bob Ripp, executive VP of global business at that time, in the chair and chief executive's post. He succeeded Bill Hudson, who remained as Vice Chairman. At the same time my mentor, Jim Marley, was within a month of retirement and there would be quite a vacuum left in management.

The Unexpected Call

A few days after leaving AMP, I was surprised to receive a call from Bossidy himself. He directly asked for my help in the takeover, suggesting that I could run the company after AlliedSignal gained control of it. Although this offer was certainly attractive, I had known for some time that it was time to move on. My loyalty to AMP and its management which had stretched back through eleven years of service, told me I could not act against the company. 'I'm not going back', I told Bossidy. 'I'm moving on.'

A Sense Of Loyalty

Loyalty from every employee is vital for successful careers. In my own case, this was particularly true; even when there were attractive offers elsewhere and prospects looked good, my commitment to AMP never wavered! This loyalty was not blind adherence-to the company but rather a heartfelt belief in its future and a sense of responsibility towards the people I had worked with for so many years. The decision to refuse Bossidy's proposal was not taken lightly. It reflected the personal relationships and trust which I had built up within AMP. Those ties, nurtured over many years through unity and shared trials, were far too important to discard for quick gains.

The White Knight Arrives

AMP was rescued by Tyco International in the following months. Known in business circles as a 'white knight', Tyco stepped in to save AMP from AlliedSignal's hostile bid. Tyco, an expanding industrial giant whose principal interests are electronics, security systems, medical equipment and industrial valves, paid $12.22 billion – some $2.42 billion more than AlliedSignal.

The agreement, ratified on April 5, 1999, gave AMP shareholders about two-thirds (0.7507) of a Tyco share for every share of AMP.

The Aftermath Of An Acquisition

After I retired from AMP, I moved to a Philadelphia suburb. Here at last my undivided attention could be directed to running the company I had just bought. But my connection with AMP was not over. I was living in Blue Bell, Pennsylvania and only a hundred miles away was Harrisburg, the scene of all these developments. So I kept a sharp ear for what might happen next.

The Tyco Acquisition Meant Big Changes For AMP Afterwards

As happens in many acquisitions, Tyco immediately began to make an impact on AMP. By the end of April, they announced that 8,000 of AMP's 48,800 employees worldwide would be laid off--including 2,100 jobs in Harrisburg. Bob Ripp was supposed to head the new company and join the board of Tyco. However he resigned abruptly, his leaving accompanied by rumors of pressure from Dennis Kozlowski, the CEO of Tyco. Jurgen Gromer, a man who had worked for AMP for 16 years, took his place.

One of Tyco's earliest decisions at AMP was to prune surplus companies and turn it into a single line, connectors. This included the sale of Raylan, a business that had engaged in the manufacture and sale of fiber optic media converters and networking devices. I couldn't bear to see the venture that I had started go down the drain, so I bought it back through Nestronix, itself a division of my company SFO.

Seizing Opportunities

Instead of seeing a setback, when AMP decided to sell off the Raylan business I saw my chance. This was an opportunity to ensure that my efforts, my inventions and my vision for a Raylan product line did not go to waste. Acquiring Raylan via Nestronix was not only saving a part of AMP but was also 'seizing an opportunity in an industry I have always been deeply convinced of'. My move was to continue building on the foundation laid at AMP and achieve even greater things under my own direct control. It was a strategic move to further develop the expert capabilities I had acquired and also continue independently innovating in fiber optic technology.

Corporate Karma

Ripp himself, before his resignation, actually had the idea of shutting over 50 plants and offices. Those employees were simply laid off, and whatever business they were doing went to auction. It was a painful but necessary step to streamline operations and focus AMP's strengths. One plant that went this way was the Raylan product line, which I had a hand in creating. The products needed by Raylan, primarily fiber optic media converters made by SFO, were essential to my vision. When AMP placed Raylan on the market, it pained me. Using Nestronix I took the company over, for my creativity and Raylan's future.

Reflections And Lessons

Reflecting on this tumultuous period, there are many lessons for aspiring entrepreneurs and industry leaders.

First of all, there is no substitute for the importance of loyalty and integrity in business. Despite the temptations of a lucrative offer from Bossidy, I decided to remain faithful AMP – one decision rooted more deeply in my values and loyalty to the company which I had served for over ten years.

Loyalty isn't just about staying with a company; it's about honoring the relationships, trust, and commitment you have built up over time.

Secondly, adaptability and resilience are crucial in navigating corporate turbulence. The attempted takeover and subsequent acquisition into Tyco were full of ambiguities and unrest. Sometimes companies have to change their tune fast just to survive. AMP's leadership, including myself, responded strategically, securing a better deal and striving to protect our employees and shareholders.

Personal Growth And Innovation

This chapter in my life emphasized to me the importance of continued personal growth and innovation. I left AMP to begin a new entrepreneurial existence along with the acquisition of Raylan and its amalgamation into Nestronix.

This move not only preserved my creation but also allowed me to innovate further, leveraging my expertise in fiber optic technology. This ability to see opportunities where others see challenges is a crucial trait for any entrepreneur. This move has been both a measure of preservation for my creation but also gave me the opportunity to continue my quest for innovation. This facility for seeing possibilities, when others see problems is an essential character of a strong entrepreneur. First, by taking over the Raylan business I was able to turn loss into acquisition.

A Humble Selective Voice

Throughout my career, I have continued to maintain both a humble and confident attitude. Confidence without humility can bring hubris, as seen in the case of Kozlowski.

On the other hand, humility without confidence may mean lost opportunities. Balancing these two states has for me been crucial to navigating complex problems and availing myself of opportunities for growth.

Looking Ahead

I hope that by learning from these experiences, entrepreneurs and future leaders of industry from around the world will find these insights useful to shorten their learning curve toward even greater success. The world of business is unpredictable, full of challenges and opportunities in equal measure. Nevertheless, if one can be true to their values, be adaptable, and retain an attitude of humility mixed with confidence, then it becomes possible to navigate these complexities successfully.

For the future leaders among you, my suggestion is to embrace change, keep learning from all experience and never sacrifice your integrity, for any reason. The lessons learned from that failed hostile bid and eventual buyout had been invaluable to me in my career and in my business ventures at all levels. They sustained my course with unswerving resilience, entrepreneurial spirit, and integrity.

Remember, every setback provides an opportunity for growth; every challenge is an opportunity to innovate. Stick to your values, be adaptable and lead with humility and confidence. Your travels, like mine, will be sprinkled with both failures and successes, each one making you a stronger, and more capable leader.

Unexpected Twists

Tyco relentlessly pursued the restructuring of operations and improvement of efficiency. This called for large numbers of layoffs and the closing down of many plants. It was harsh but necessary, and a somber reflection on the future for multitudinous ex-colleagues.

The departure of Bob Ripp stands out particularly. He had been a major figure in securing Tyco as AMP's white knight, and his sudden resignation raised eyebrows. It was whispered that Dennis Kozlowski, Tyco' s flashy CEO, had given Ripp the boot. Whether true or not, Ripp's exit was a surprise turn from fate. On second thought, corporate loyalty may be a passing phenomenon.

Fallout From Tyco's Scandal

Tyco came across its own troubles when it succeeded in the tender for AMP. Kozlowski's involvement in a colossal scandal shook the business world. Accusations of embezzlement and misuse of company funds stained Tyco's background. Kozlowski was at last thrown into prison for defrauding Tyco stockholders, and the evidence against him included unapproved bonuses and extravagant personal expenses. The scandal was not only a setback for Tyco; it threw a dark shadow over AMP's future as well.

AMP plummeted in value as the scandal broke, and this was followed by other changes. In the years after Tyco's acquisition, AMP underwent a number of reorganizations and finally divided into three different companies. This splintering brought an abrupt end to a company that had once been a pioneer in the connector industry.

The What If?

As I slowly made my way into the world of business, I couldn't help asking myself *'what if'*. What if I had accepted Bossidy's hint to help him take over AMP on behalf of AlliedSignal? Could AlliedSignal have managed AMP more effectively than Tyco? Could AMP have escaped the troubles and the scandal that followed

These reflections were not just idle thoughts: they offered valuable pointers on decision-making and foresight.

The decisions we make, based on our values and instincts, determine our paths in ways that are not always predictable. In my case, sticking with AMP and looking for new things to do felt like the right decision even though it meant having to cope with uncertainty and dislocation.

The Importance Of Ethical Leadership ·

Kozlowski's fall was a stern reminder of the necessity for ethical leadership. His behavior not only brought dishonor to himself, but also did serious injury to Tyco and AMP. To those who covet leadership jobs, this is a warning: you may think unethical behavior has short-term benefits, but the ripple effects can go for years and hurt an entire company along with its employees.

Integrity, ethical behavior, and effective leadership go hand in hand. At least, if you adhere to these principles, you can win the trust of others, motivate your group, and deal with the complexities in the corporate world with semblance.

It's been my own experience that to lead with integrity not only protects your private image, it also creates a good working environment and improves output.

Loving Change And Innovation

What I've taken from my years of experience is this: You should not only accept change but love it. Companies are always changing; staying ahead requires you to be adaptable and able to innovate. In trying to acquire the Raylan business and integrate it into Nestronix, I upheld this belief. By grabbing opportunities and using my abilities to the utmost, I opened up entirely new paths of development and success.

To hold your own in the uncertain world of business, a company needs to be able to innovate and adapt. By doing so, you can turn challenges and uncertainties into opportunities. You have resilience *and* creativity.

Navigate Complexities – Hit Your Goals

Each of these episodes, whether it was the hostile takeover bid, the purchase by Tyco or my entrepreneurship experiences, offered valuable lessons and insights. However, after mulling over all these experiences and putting the lessons into practice, I was able to achieve my objectives and navigate successfully through the complexities of corporate life.

How can we inspire future leaders? As I think back on all my experiences and the lessons they afforded me along the way, there is a profound sense of gratitude that occupies space within my heart these days. From my time with AMP, to the opportunities that I have enjoyed in my own businesses, each chapter has contributed toward turning me into a leader.

To the Business Leaders and Entrepreneurs of Tomorrow, I leave you this tip: Stick to your credos, rarely stay still, and lead with integrity and humility. Your journey will brim with trials and successes, but with perseverance, creativity, and conviction, you can go for the gold.

You need only remember that setbacks can be turned around into opportunities for growth and that challenges offer fertile ground on which to innovate. Be confident in your leadership, every experience is a learning exercise and encourage those around you who are still coming up to do their best. Like mine, your own journey will testify to the power of tireless persistence balanced with integrity and enlightened leadership.

Personal Reflections: And Hot Tips

Looking back, my journey with AMP and the birth of GISB were defining stories in my career. They carried lessons about leadership, innovation, and strategic thinking, which have stuck with me ever since. I was lucky enough to work with visionaries like Narinder Singh Kapany and work hard to serve the exigence of markets worldwide.

These experiences sharpened my skills and have shaped the way I do business. At AMP, my journey has not only been about heartfelt improvement but also uninterrupted progress. It taught me about leadership, innovation, and the importance of diversity. By viewing change as an empowering phenomenon, I was able not only to continue moving forward when faced with adversity but also to stay focused on my goal.

To aspiring young entrepreneurs and future industry leaders, I offer this advice: Embrace change with love and take risks. Innovations often come from stepping out of the comfort zone where you have grown comfortable and explore new areas. Surround yourself with talented advisers who share your vision and can help you achieve your goals.

And above all, stay firm in your beliefs. Success means more than meeting goals or winning accolades. Invest in the future so that future generations can profit from your work and legacy.

Three Attributes Worth Cultivating

1. **Ambition should blend seamlessly with adaptability.** In a corporate environment, the power games and various feuds are liable to undo anything you have so carefully planned for yourself. If you want your ambitions realized, you must keep your options open.

2. **Mentorship and alliances are key.** My relationship with Jim Marley brought me much-needed support and advice. It is equally important, however, for one to realize when any alliances shift and navigate these shifts skillfully. In corporate life, relationships are very changeable, and recognizing this can help keep you ahead.

3. **Resilience is essential.** Despite countless setbacks and challenges, the success of my department and the impact I had at AMP stand as a monument to effort and devotion. Even when you feel the way forward is completely closed out, creativity and fresh ideas can always turn obstacles into opportunities. We must continue moving forward, no matter how high the odds against us.

My time at AMP was full of ambition, struggle, and achievement. I well understood how to maintain one's own direction within the intricate web of corporate politics. For all those who are aiming to lead, remember that every difficulty is an opportunity for growth, and every setback is a stepping-stone to success.

Keep up your strength, stay flexible, and never lose sight of your goal. Redirect your mind to - *'The Art of the Possible'*.

Section 3

My Entrepreneurial Odyssey
Embracing Opportunities
Growth With Resilience
The Art Of The Possible

An Introduction
To My Entrepreneurial Odyssey

Beginning an entrepreneurial journey is like sailing out into unexplored oceans, held on course by the compass of two critical traits - ambition and determination. My story, chronicled in the following pages, stands as a tribute to the indomitable spirit of human tenacity, adaptability, and foresight. From modest beginnings to leadership of a business empire. My journey has been marked by singular moments, pivotal decisions, and faith in the art of creation - *'The Art of The Possible'*.

Early Influences: Seeds Of Entrepreneurship

I grew up breathing the very air of entrepreneurship.

My grandfather and uncle were pioneers in India's international trade fields and shipped lemongrass to Europe and America. Further, my parents were also made of the stuff of fortitude and innovation. My father went from policeman to successful farmer, and my mother managed a coconut oil factory out of the house where we lived. These early experiences taught me that entrepreneurship was more than just making money; it was about creating value and improving lives as well.

As I grew up in the bustling merchant cities of Aluva and Kochi, the role models who surrounded me were the ones who turned problems into opportunities. My family's businesses in agriculture, exporting spices, construction and a bank presented a rich texture of experience which nourished my understanding about ways to produce wealth. These early teachings have since become a major guiding beacon for my entrepreneurial philosophy: wealth building is based on hard work, adaptability and continually seeking better results.

The First Venture: Turning A Dream Into Reality

In 1962, I launched my first venture. I was still an apprentice at Hindustan Machine Tools Company (HMT), working there with the sole aim of acquiring experience and knowledge. It was a casting company. Together with my immediate boss, Mr Menon, we managed to construct a furnace in the corner of my one-acre plot This humble beginning tested my perseverance and resourcefulness, teaching me that anything worth having is worth waiting for and the importance of life-long learning in business.

More than just a business, this venture allowed me to put into practice what I had always believed: entrepreneurship at its best. Better than a university class on entrepreneurship itself, it taught me that rolling up your sleeves and getting your hands dirty is entrepreneurship, that success and failure are facts of life, and one can learn lessons from both. Every little improvement fed my confidence. To enhance the development of any company, real rather than theoretical knowledge is needed. Experience tells me this.

Bridging Cultures: The Grandfather Clock Business

During my days at IBM, I began a novel business venture – making teakwood grandfather clocks in cooperation with George Micklus. This business aimed to bring the precision of German watchmaking and the elaborate woodcarving of India together.

We took our raw teakwood from Kerala and our components from Germany, inspired by my father's antique grandfather clock. But despite our best efforts, the advent of quartz watches in the 1970s brought an unpredicted change in market preference. This business failure still meant learning a lesson, and this enterprise, while not commercially successful, reinforced for me the need to take a flexible and sensitive approach in such situations, and always to be alert to market changes.

This business was dear to my heart as it represented the blend of traditional respect and modern innovation. George had highlighted for me the importance of cultural synergy in business. The goal was to create a product representing both precision and craftsmanship, but the change of market dynamics was disadvantageous. This experience reinforced the need for flexibility and market awareness. It also enabled me to carry over the lesson that preserving cultural heritage in business is something which should go hand in hand with every venture.

Diversification And Setbacks: Business Number Two

In the early 1980's, I began Nagoor Trading Corporation to market spices from my father's farm. Simultaneously, I invested in a construction business in Libya which was unfortunately destroyed by geopolitical turmoil. These experiences have shown me the uncertainties inherent in business and the necessity to diversify and mitigate risk. They also strengthened my resolve to keep on trying to never be vanquished by setbacks.

The establishment of Nagoor Trading Corporation was a big step to add value from our agricultural products. I felt a deep obligation to elevate my native agricultural area. This venture taught me the importance of knowing international markets and building strong supply chains. As a result of these experiences, when the construction venture in Libya failed due to political instability, it was a heavy reminder of the uncertainties in business enterprises. Nevertheless, they gave me a foundation upon which future ventures could diversify and mitigate risks.

Investing In Innovation:
Processors Systems (India) Private Limited

My first major investment in my personal capacity was Processor Systems (India) Private Limited (PSI), one of India's first computer companies, established by my friend Veetikad Krishnabhavan Ravindran. Through the development of healthcare software, I demonstrated that a practical approach worked. It was also a way of fulfilling my promise to Ravindran.

As I pursued my entrepreneurial career, I also continued to work for IBM, and it was during this time that I both observed the transformative power of technology for the first time and felt its potential to create new markets. It was at that point that I back tracked and truly made Ravindran's health software dream a reality.

My work at IBM provided me with financial security, and my investments enabled me to pursue my passion for technology. The combination of these two roles allowed me to understand and follow time management, strategic thinking and the importance of perseverance. Above all, it has shown me that a stable foundation is essential when aiming towards ambitious goals.

My experience in PSI was a very informative time for me as I witnessed the power of new markets and business ways wit h my own eyes, and personally seen their transforming effect on technology. It was this balance that spelt out to me the importance of having a stable base and ambitious goals: In the end you must be able to balance risk, and always to do something for the long term.

Lessons of Adaptability, Resilience, And Networking

Ventures and initiatives taught me key lessons:

- **Adaptability:** It is vitally important in a market that is continually changing to have the ability how to pivot and embrace change.

- **Resilience:** In any journey, there will be setbacks you must learn from, and it is necessary to persist through challenges.

- **Networking:** If you develop strong relationships and use networks, they will certainly offer more opportunities.

A Fresh Start In Quakertown:
Further Transition To Entrepreneurship

Venturing into entrepreneurship in Quakertown, Pennsylvania, I left a secure corporate career at 58. I wanted to innovate and lead in my own way, free from bureaucratic interference, it was this impulse to call the shots that drove the change. Years of experience in setting strategy and designing efficient operations, which I had gathered during my time at AMP were very beneficial for the business I set up afterwards. This phase marked the beginning of a string of entrepreneurial endeavors, from network monitoring systems to acquisitions and partnerships that would rebrand industry standards. Stepping out of the comfort of working in a corporation was an eye-opener for me. I had the impulse to control my destiny and challenge conventional wisdom on one side, but from another, a deep desire to do things better with greater impact. I set out to create a heritage which reflected my vision and values.

This phase marked the beginning of a series of entrepreneurial ventures that would redefine industry standards altogether.

The Art of the Possible: Innovation And Continuous Growth

Innovation and growth characterize my journey. When pioneering AM Communications as the future of network monitoring and then breaking into media with Neestream, the basic concept remains: *embrace change and take advantage of synergies, persisting in spite of all odds.*

This is the philosophy behind the success of both the NeST Group and JKH Holding. This culture of continuous innovation and growth has been the driving force behind my success. It has enabled me to navigate the challenges of various industries and emerge as an adaptable entrepreneur – one who is versatile and strong with a solid reputation for excellence and innovation.

A Legacy Of Excellence: Message For Future Leaders

Even now, every day I continue to work with the same passion and dedication. My message to aspiring entrepreneurs is simple: dream big, work hard, and keep smiling. Rethink the unthinkable.

By challenging the norms, taking calculated risks, and instilling an innovative culture in your business, *'The Future is Yours to Create'*: the arduous journey with its occasional bumps can be lightened and made joyous by the right thinking, going for initiatives you believe in, and perseverance.

From my experiences, I've come to realize that entrepreneurship is not just a job: it's an attitude and way of life. It takes passion, resilience, and belief and that ultimate quality - a deep sense for oneself. The lessons learned on my journey make good advice for every aspiring entrepreneur: adapt to change, keep at it in the face of setbacks, and forge strong networks. Guided by these principles, you will find success and make a lasting imprint on your world for the future.

My Entrepreneurial Odyssey: Part I

From Small Beginnings To Established Business Leader

My family was a major influence on me from a young age, and the entrepreneurial spirit instilled in it by nature seems to have become mine as well. In India, my grandfather Mackar Pillay and maternal uncle M.M. Abdul Hameed Pillay were among the biggest exporters of lemon grass to Europe and America. In international trade success itself laid the foundation for my lifelong dream of becoming an entrepreneur.

Entrepreneurship Roots And Early Influences

To my family, entrepreneurship was more than just a livelihood choice; it represented life. Nagoor Rawther, my father, made a great shift from a police officer to a successful planter.

Nagoor Rawther (father); MM Khadijoo (mother).

Javad and his mother.

And M.M. Khadijoo, my mother, ran a coconut oil factory from her home which was not far from ours. Endurance, adaptability, and invention were the values they successfully conveyed to me, and which have so deeply influenced my thinking today. My brother, N. Jehangir, always says that as a child I must have inherited my entrepreneurial genes and practical savvy both from them, since they played such an important role in beginning my journey.

From a young age, I was surrounded by business activities. Watching my father conduct negotiations and manage plantations and seeing my mother run a factory in the house, I learned management, finance, and how hard work pays off.

I was imbued with the conviction that entrepreneurship is of the utmost importance not only in money-making capacities but also for producing value and improving people's lives. That conviction has long stood as a cornerstone of my business philosophy.

Our extended family was engaged in many lines of business, from agriculture and spices export to construction and banking. Growing up in Aluva and the port of Kochi, where much commerce took place was one member of countless examples. These early experiences were rich soil for my understanding of commercial value creation even though I chose to make my career in engineering. The lively markets and shrewd negotiations I witnessed instilled in me the importance of flexibility and recognizing opportunities as they arise.

Vision Turned Into Reality: My First Venture In Casting

My first venture, a casting company, was started from my home in 1962, when I was an apprentice at HMT (Hindustan Machine Tools). My partner is Mr. Menon, who is also my supervisor and the foundry manager. Although I only made 250 rupees a month, I watched Mr. Menon at his work very closely and thought to myself that I would capitalize on what he's doing.

We built with bricks a furnace and in a corner of my one-acre plot set up a brick oven for melting copper. This venture concentrated on investment casting, the first time I put into practice what I had been learning about practical guidelines for entrepreneurs. It was a small step very early in my journey, and it taught me the importance of first-hand experience and know-how.

This initial venture was more than an effort to build a business. It was a test of my steadfastness and inventiveness.

Mixed feelings clouded my mind: I was both thrilled and anxious about what might happen in the future.

There were nights when I could not sleep, fretting over the possible pitfalls of this venture. However, each successful cast and every minor improvement gave me encouragement and confidence. This taught me that starting from a low level, having patience, and forever learning are essentials for entrepreneurialism.

It also hammered home for me that practical experience on the ground is invaluable. Knowledge gained through mere books is no substitute at all for the wisdom acquired from actual implementation and solving problems.

Cultures Bridged: The Grandfather Clock Business

During my time at IBM, I started a business producing grandfather clocks made of teak wood with George Micklus who was my best boss ever. This enterprise endeavored to combine German watchmaking precision with elegant Indian woodworking. Clocks crafted by us were works of art from teak wood taken out of Kerala (in the south western corner of India) and parts brought over from Germany.

The idea came from my father's prized heirloom clock, a polished wood marvel which gave out its own unique sound: 'ding-dong'. Although we planned meticulously and possessed skills, the business met many setbacks. The clock industry underwent tremendous change during the 1970s, with the big hit at that time being quartz technology. Changing consumer habits and the impact of new technology had come to disrupt our traditional skills. We didn't expect it.

This venture was close to my heart because it combined respect for traditional craftsmanship with a love of creative innovation. Working with George Micklus taught me how important cultural integration is in business. We wanted to create a product which stood for precision and scrumptiousness. While the market seemed difficult, this experience highlighted once again the need to be able to adjust the play.

It also stressed preserving our cultural legacy in business, something that guides all my endeavors even now.

I began to realize that sometimes, despite all the hard work you put in and the effort to do things right, external factors such as technology and what people want can have a decisive effect on whether your business thrives or not.

Diversified Ventures: Nagoor Trading Corporation And Construction In Libya

In the early 1980s, Nagoor Trading Corporation began in Aluva to market spices from my father's estate, primarily cardamom. Together with others produced here and there. With my brother-in-law, Abdul Khader, we tried to obtain better prices for our produce. At about the same time, I invested money in Khader's construction business in Libya. However, President Reagan's bombing of Libya in 1986 was a huge setback to this business. This venture never bounced back. Another defeat on my entrepreneurial path.

Starting a subsidiary for Nagoor Trading Corporation was a significant step toward adding value to our agricultural products. I felt a deep sense of responsibility to improve the lives of local farmers. This product introduction enabled to increase production and find better markets for our spices. Thus, the venture taught me the importance of understanding global markets and building solid supply chains. However, the Libyan construction project was a tough reminder that business is just full of uncertainties. These experiences, however, stiffened my morale to diversify and spread future risks across many ventures. I learned that diversification is not just breaking into new markets but also understanding and negotiating the intricate web of geopolitical and economic factors that can influence business.

Processor Systems (India) Private Limited (PSI)

My first big investment was in Processor Systems (India) Private Limited, a company founded by my late friend Veetikad Krishnabhavan Ravindran in 1973. Ravindran, who had a Ph.D. from Stanford, returned to Bangalore in the 1970s, before it became an IT hub. Along with a few friends, I supported his venture.

Since starting this venture, Ravindran was supported by myself and a few friends. The enterprise was cofounded by Ravindran and his wife, Junko, a Japanese. Then came the opposition to multinational companies in India, most particularly IBM and Coca-Cola. In 1983, the government of Prime Minister Morarji Desai ejected both of these multinationals from India. Initially, PSI received its capital funding from acquaintances of Ravindran. While still a worker at IBM in New York, I was an early investor. I involved my doctor friend, Dr. Enu Karavathu, in investing in PSI. We brought engineers from PSI to the United States to write a program that would facilitate quality healthcare.

The Balance Between Employment
And Entrepreneurship: Early Software Development

Even while working at IBM, a job that paid the bills, I was already an entrepreneur. PSI sent a software engineer to live in our basement to write code for a healthcare software. The operating system was MS-DOS on big floppy disks. My daughters, Naureen and Hafiza, fondly remember calling him "Mr. Guy" due to his complicated South Indian name. His presence compromised their play space, much to their annoyance, but it was a small price for pursuing entrepreneurial dreams.

With a full-time job at a corporation and an entrepreneurial career to manage, it was challenging and exhilarating to be successful in both domains.

My work at IBM gave me stability. To live and develop products as well as make the breakthroughs I was chasing, I saw my investments as complementing my corporate income. This dual role taught me time management, strategic thinking, and the value of persistence.

My experiences at PSI were particularly enlightening, as I witnessed first hand the transformative power of technology and its potential to create new markets and opportunities. The balance also underlines the importance of having a solid foundation while striving for great things. Risks must be managed, and the venture must be kept sustainable.

Key Lessons Learned: Adaptability, Resilience, And Networking

Through these ventures, successful and unsuccessful, I learned valuable lessons that I want to share with young entrepreneurs and future business leaders:

- **Be Adaptable and Keep Pace with Change:** The market and technology are constantly changing. Adaptability and openness to change are the keys to long-term success. Keep abreast of how the industry is changing and be ready to pivot when that is needed.

- *Personal Insight:* Throughout my experiences, adapting to new technology was crucial. Even very well-planned ventures can fail if they do not keep pace with change. Whatever the field you work in, it is crucial to anticipate changes and implement new strategies versus resting on one's laurels for any length of time.

- **Resilience:** Setbacks are part of the road of an entrepreneur. Equally important is one's resilience and ability to learn from one's failures. Every time there is a difficulty it also means that each challenge can be a chance for growth and improvement. One should never let a failure derail you; instead, it should be looked at as an opportunity to improve yourself.

- *Personal Insight:* The failure of my start-up companies conveyed far more to me than any of my experiences with successful ones.
  They demonstrated the importance of a gritty mindset and fresh beginnings with renewed insight. Every defeat contains a lesson, and every setback can help better prepare us for future challenges by imparting more wisdom and strength.

- **Leverage Networks:** Making friends and building networks can provide crucial support as well as many opportunities. Surround yourself with mentors, peers and collaborators - all people who will show you the way subtly as you find your path on different levels.

- *Personal Insight:* My relatives, friends and colleagues have been invaluable in my journey. They have provided encouragement, offered their own advice and collaborated with me through the complexities of entrepreneurship. Networking not only brings resources, but it creates a platform where people can receive mutual aid and grow together.

For Future Leaders: Enjoy Your Entrepreneurial Journey

Speaking to any aspiring businessman or young future leaders, my advice is: Adopt the entrepreneurial spirit, learn as you go, and stick with it. Your journey will be different, but adaptability, resilience, and leveraging people connections must be some of the adages to guide you toward success. Whether your results have been good or bad, every venture is a rung on the ladder to your eventual goal. Stay curious, stay aggressive. Never stop innovating. The whole world of business is filled with opportunity; the more passionately determined you are to seize it with both hands – the better.

Entrepreneurship is not just one's career but also one's way of life; it requires passion, perseverance, and a steadfast belief in your ideas and vision. My journey's lessons apply to all would-be entrepreneurs: Learn to adapt; remain stoic in the face of setbacks; and develop linked networks.

My Entrepreneurial Odyssey: Part 2

A New Life In Quakertown

The next part of my entrepreneurial journey began in a little town called Quakertown, a rustic hamlet approximately fifty miles north of Philadelphia. This town was settled initially by Quakers and the spirit of 'work hard, play harder' that Quakertown embodies deeply resonated with me as I started down my entrepreneurial road.

Transitioning from corporate America to entrepreneurship wasn't something I decided overnight, but it was an inevitable evolution fuelled by my belief in '*The Art of The Possible*'. After a decade-long career at AMP, where I had built up a strong and fruitful career, it felt like something was missing. This feeling of dissatisfaction led me to think deeply about what the future held and how to make sure it would be brilliant.

Leaving the comfort and security of a salaried job at the age of 58 – a time when many Indians contemplate retirement – was a significant decision. Nevertheless, driven by my craving for innovation and desire to create something myself, making this transformation was inevitable. My colleague Bret Matz, who had worked alongside me for many years in my career, put it succinctly: "*He wanted to be his own boss.*"

This wish was fuelled by both irritation with corporate red tape and an intense yearning to build something innovative and take charge on my own terms. It wasn't enough to keep within the lines; I wanted to break new ground. I wanted to create something that would reflect my dreams and values.

In the earlier stages of my career, particularly at AMP, I developed a number of essential skills. As a senior leader, I learned the significance of strategic planning, operational efficiency, and innovation. When I stepped into entrepreneurship, that experience proved crucial. The ability to think strategically allowed me to foresee possible hurdles and opportunities, which was important in steering my way through the labyrinth of a new venture. Emphasizing operational efficiency meant that our resources could be maximized, and we could provide top-quality products and services, even if we were in a start-up situation. My dedication to innovation set the stage for my entrepreneurial path. It brought continual progress and increasing success.

Pioneers Of The Future:
Network Monitoring AM Communications

The experience at AM Communications opened up new doors. Founded in 1974 by Maqbool 'Mac' Qurashi, network and status monitoring systems for cable TV and broadband communications networks became its specialty. The firm's first technical invention, OmniSTAT, came in the 1990s. This advanced monitoring system featured network monitoring as well as performance and FCC Proof-of-Performance testing, which is important for assessing signal levels or network conditions and reporting problems in real-time. Our journey to becoming a market leader threw up a number of obstacles of its own. The 1990s brought systemic changes and financial uncertainty for AM Communications. Despite the technological advances, the company was swimming in red. This was when Hoffman, a businessman from Pennsylvania, bought the majority holding and financially supported us. 'They weren't making any money and would call Alvin for money', recalls Matz. This kind of arrangement, however, was not sustainable in the long term.

Years went by and Hoffman was at last prepared to hand me the leadership I needed. In November 1998, I assumed the position of Chairman.

Hoffman held 60% of the stock, which I took as a mortgage on my aggressive acquisition of AM Communications. This daring move took both Hoffman and me out on a limb. Yet it was a bold step, and it marked the advent of my active involvement in lifting AM Communications back to life.

Applying Skills Learned In Large Corporate Management Projects To Senior Leadership

My experience at AMP had given me the ability to manage large organizations and handle complex projects. Such experiences were invaluable when I took over at AM Communications. Among my first tasks was to evaluate the company's advantages and shortcomings, one of the abilities I had developed while heading various divisions for AMP. I was able to deal with AM Corporation's early trials because of my experience in managing high-stakes projects, from financial engineering to product innovation.

The Financial Storm: Riding The Global Crisis And Its Aftermath

In 1997, a financial crisis, which originated in Thailand, began to spread globally, and by the end of that year, had affected worldwide economies, from Russia to Brazil. Wall Street's major stocks had begun to tumble drastically by 1998 and AM was not spared this turbulence. Chapter 11 bankruptcy filing for AM Corp. was made after the market crash of that year.

I remember during this period, 'I was worth $100 million because the stock was three dollars. $60 million, more than half my fortune, was wiped out in the crash. But I made a $5 million investment and took AM out of Chapter 11.'

Resilience In The Face Of Adversity

During that financially tough time, I learned many valuable lessons about the importance of keeping strong-minded and thinking strategically. The market crash did, however, offer an opportunity in which we could rebuild from the ground up, and even reorganize our corporation. This experience bolstered my faith in flexibility and always being ready to meet unexpected challenges.

For AM Communications, the task of steering the company through Chapter Eleven was a professional challenge as well as an overwhelming personal trial. It meant not only financial deftness but the courage to thrive under pressure when your future depended upon how well you could hold out. I had to persuade my people to keep up their spirits, even as I was busy negotiating with creditors and investors. It was during these difficult times that my true self—a leader - sharp, intelligent and self-disciplined—was put to the test and forged.

Crisis Management Skills In Action

At AMP, I met many challenges that demanded quick intelligence and decisive action. Securing the company through financial instability and bankruptcy meant not just strategic planning but also effective management of all stakeholders.

These skills, honed during my leadership years at AMP, proved invaluable in guiding AM Communications safely through this period of uncertainty. I realized the need for transparency and for maintaining open lines of communication with stakeholders, built trust, and fostered a team approach to problem-solving.

Rebuilding With Purpose: The Revival Of AM Communications

Immediately after leaving AMP, I brought Bret Matz in to manage AM Communications. We made Quakertown our corporate headquarters and brought in a number of software professionals from India. On December 26, 2003, My conglomerate, NeST Group, bought AM Communications' Broadband Products Divisionazines. We stabilized business and founded AM Networks, Inc., with a vision even broader for the broadband industry.

Cultivating A New Vision

The first decade of the new century brought further turmoil. The 2008 financial crisis obliged us to submit for bankruptcy once more, and the court split the company into several parts. I bought the original AM remote monitoring business rebranding it as AM Networks. Not just about simply surviving, this process was also about nurturing a new kind of vision, which was in step with the changing requirements of broadband technology. Reviving AM Communications called for a broad range of measures. It was necessary to recover the confidence of our customers, steady its finances, and work out a strong strategic direction. Importing Indian software professionals was one means of employing fresh thinking and global talents to build the company. With these resourceful and enthusiastic workers, we were able to develop new products which met the needs of the changing marketplace.

In our transformation, my motto was *'The Art of The Possible'*, leading us to explore new areas and stretch our imagination.

Taking Leadership Of Innovation And Action

I had always stressed the importance of innovation and strategic vision in my previous jobs. At AMP, I led the way to many advances in technology and efficiency. This mentality played no little part in energising AM communications. By creating an atmosphere of creativity, we were able to develop some highly original solutions and make major breakthroughs. This method not only lifted us out of financial troubles but also gave us a leap over other broadband industry leaders.

Partnership For Success: The Alpha Collaboration

A strategic decision was taken in 2008 to cooperate with Alpha the market leader in power supplies, which paid off. A large contract, which we secured with Comcast captured Alpha's attention. Partnering with Alpha, we developed transponders worth over $150 million, which meant AM became a single-customer company. However, this partnership came with many obstacles.

Our salespeople were at first apprehensive of this new direction, however by focusing on relationship building we found our way through.

Building strong partnerships was key to our success. Our cooperation with Alpha proved that joining hands with industry leaders can open up new arenas and drive growth. This partnership led to large contracts securing a strong income flow. It established trust in each other and we could all work with the clarity of mutual benefit.

The choice to adopt a single-customer model involved risks.

It called for a leap of faith and a shift in our fundamental business direction. This move also enabled us to streamline our operations and focus on providing top-quality products to our customers, which in turn reinforced our reputation in the industry. My nonconformist mindset and willingness to challenge convention were crucial in the success of this partnership.

Networking And Communication Skills

Over the years, I realized the importance of networking and developing strategic partnerships. In AMP, several high-stakes deals were negotiated successfully which sharpened my skills even more in this area. These experiences proved most useful when developing an alliance with Alpha. Successful negotiation, with a clear mutual benefit in mind, made this collaborative venture possible. My ability to build and sustain strong relations with important stakeholders was crucial in securing the long-term success of this partnership.

Efficiency And Focus: Operations Finely Tuned

Our operations were streamlined, and by focusing on our own core competencies we improved profitability.

In effect, AM Networks became a supply chain company: SFO Technologies, a NeST Group subsidiary, took over manufacturing work in India at a local factory. This allowed us to concentrate on innovation and customer service. It meant that when the industry began heading towards software, new challenges arose, and we stood firm, providing precious software products, especially to Latin America.

SFO Technologies – Pivotal Role

SFO technologies quickly became a crucial part of our operations, handling the manufacturing processes in India. Materials were sourced from there, prices negotiated, and all activities managed. It was a streamlined process handled by the then Vice President of Operations and Global Supply Chain of AM Technologies, Abraham Chandy. This streamlining meant that the final products were shipped straight to Alpha from the factory without going via AM. Things became more efficient and less costly.

It not only streamlined our supply chain, but also helped us to get the best out of the manufacturing excellence of our Indian factory operations. Collaborating across oceans is a fine example of how efficiency or even basic operation costs can be reduced. By doing our own part well while getting others to do theirs through contract manufacturing we freed funds for innovation and service. This approach reflects my belief in *'The Art of The Possible.'* It demonstrates how unconventional methods can yield extraordinary results.

Implementation Of Operational Excellence

Senior leadership taught me the importance of operational excellence.

At AMP I found so many process improvements. That improved our efficiency and productivity.

At AM Networks I focused on streamlining operations and optimizing our supply chain, using these principles.

While working in concert with the strengths of SFO Technologies, we were able to save vast amounts on costs and refine our operations.

This method not only increased our profits, it also meant that we could offer our customers better products and services.

Industry Shifts - Opportunity Through Adaptation

The industry was now prioritizing software over hardware.

In the software era, many US enterprises created and maintained their own software systems. In this sector we faced stiff competition.

But in coping with these pressures, we still continued to offer valuable software solutions. Latin America was one of our strongholds for product demand.

Being Competitive In The Software Market

It was difficult to compete in the software market when so many companies had their own engineers who could build software in-house.

Our software product, while still part of our business, shrank in emphasis. We were under attack from companies in Europe, particularly in Belgium, and struggled to maintain our position in this gruelling market.

Shifting from hardware to software was such a major change in both business model and strategy that we had to learn new skills, technologies, and processes. It was not an easy transition but necessary given the insatiable demands of customers and trends in the industry.

We remained focused on our innovation to serve the market well – we were moving with the times and my commitment to challenge conventions pushed us to continually break new ground.

Driving Innovation In Technology

Working for AMP, I was intensively involved with driving technological innovations. This stood me in good stead when AM Networks shifted its emphasis from hardware to software. Recognizing the overall technological environment--and identifying trends that were beginning to develop kept us ahead of the pack. By making R&D investments and energizing our team of experts worldwide we produced innovative software products. My technology background helped us to stay with and often ahead of the changing industry trends which were happening at a crazy pace.

Innovating For The Future: Igniting Growth

My experience in AM Communications was the start of a rampant period of acquisitions and creation.

In the past two decades, I have launched or acquired more than a dozen companies in fiber optics, software, system integration, IT infrastructure, healthcare IT, and digital media. Each venture has been one more step on the road to achieving a greater vision.

A Conglomerate In The Making: The NeST Group

In the previous decade, the Group was formed to amalgamate all the corporations that had been founded by Jehangir and myself.

NeST, led by Jehangir in Kerala, became a symbol of our growth and creativity. By combining the various business units under one roof, we ensured that our ventures in diverse areas would be aligned over common goals.

The NeST Group's foundation was an odyssey of innovation, collaboration and strategic development. Every merger and collaboration was cautiously examined with an eye toward complementing our current business practices and creating synergies. This comprehensive method allowed us to capitalize on our collective strengths and give our customers all-encompassing solutions. My guiding principle for this conglomerate is *'The Art of The Possible'*, which keeps us looking for ways to break new ground and what can be achieved.

Growth And Integration Of NeST Group

I had held many senior management positions and successfully managed large projects integrating diverse teams. These experiences were instrumental to building the NeST Group. Strategic development needs careful planning and execution, as each takeover must offer added value and further our overall vision. By cultivating a culture of collaboration and innovation, we forged a nimble organization capable of adjusting to market changes and seizing fresh opportunities.

Winning Through Difficulty: Lessons Of Resilience

There were obstacles along the way. The challenges of getting through financial crises and ramping down the company to adapt to market changes, taught us that resilience is not a choice but a vital strength. The market crash of 2008 was particularly difficult, but it also reinforced the importance of making strategic decisions and being flexible.

The Importance Of Strategic Partnerships

One of the key lessons we learned on our journey was the value of forming strong, strategic alliances. Our collaboration with Alpha was a turning point, showing how joining forces with industry leaders can open up new possibilities and spur growth. This partnership allowed us to land major contracts and maintain a steady stream of income even in tough times.

The various financial crises and market volatility we had to face taught me about the importance of being strategically flexible. In other words, being able to change with the times, whether through restructuring, forming fresh alliances or innovation, was pivotal for our survival and prosperity. These lessons in tenacity were invaluable and have influenced my business style. Making the best use of my rational problem-solving style and coupling it with unflagging determination, we overcame these challenges one by one.

Adaptive Leadership

Throughout my career, I faced many challenges that called for adaptive leadership. The capacity to be flexible, even in the face of drastic change, is what made the difference in overcoming setbacks. At AMP, I had been involved in a number of projects that required rapid adjustments to market shifts and technological changes. These experiences helped me to create a mind-set that was instrumental in taking the NeST Group through its various difficulties. Combined with adaptive leadership and a focus on the long-term rather than immediate gains, it ensured we could turn adversity into opportunities for progress.

The Power Of Innovation

Innovation has been the core of our business from the start. From providing advanced monitoring systems to embracing new technologies, it is innovation that has kept us ahead all along. By shifting our emphasis from just hardware to including software solutions also, we showed that our policy of innovation continued even in a volatile and dynamic industry.

Hello Change, Nice To Meet You: A Continuing Journey

Embracing change became a continuous journey.

Whether it was from a corporate career to entrepreneurship or adapting when markets shifted, the ability to welcome change and alter our path according to need was vital for our success. Every change brought new opportunities and challenges. Our pioneering spirit driving creative growth innovation remained constant and energized.

Innovation is not just about new products or technologies. It refers to a frame of mind. It's about always looking for better ways to do things, always being open to new ideas, and staying ahead of trends in any industry. This innovative spirit has been with our business from the start; now it forms one of the fundamental values at NeST Group.

In the company, I always remained open to breaking from the norm and taking a non-conformist, more progressive approach. This courageous path continues to serve us and has hugely contributed to our achievements.

Nurturing An Innovative Environment

At AMP, I had created an environment where innovation and creative thinking were promoted. Such innovation was essential for driving continuous improvement and growth.

In the NeST Group too, I lived by these standards: Innovation was valued and before long became a tradition and norm of thought. We gave our teams the authority to innovate. This allowed them always to produce cutting-edge solutions that met with the evolving needs of our clients continuously. As for the innovation culture, it was an essential element in our success as a business; it put us ahead of all competitors.

A Global Presence In The Making

Another milestone was to make our operations global. Together with sales offices situated at Redmond Headquarters in North America, UK, Madrid, Dubai, India and Japan we had a very strong global presence. As a result we established an excellent market reach but also tapped into fresh opportunities and diversified operations.

Integration Of Operations That Creates Synergy

Creating synergy across our global operations was vital to our success. By harmonizing our manufacturing, sales and new approaches for developing products, we ensured that the highest standards of quality and efficiency were met in both our products and services. The resulting synergy was a key factor in preserving our market position.

My philosophy of global expansion is to turn a network of interlinked business entities into a matrix with multiple responsibilities. By leveraging our international network, we could offer clients from all over the world complete solutions and unrivalled service. This global strategy also gave us a broad perspective and helped us to understand different markets and cultures better. I believed in 'The Art of The Possible', and my unconventional methods of thinking enabled us to break new ground and expand the horizon we faced.

Global Leadership And Integration

Running a global company requires a full understanding of various markets 'lay of the land' and different cultures.

At AMP, I was involved in international projects and so got insights into global business dynamics, which were later used to help expand the NeST Group step by step. We became smart in how to integrate our global operations effectively so that we could maintain equal quality and service worldwide. Being able to cope with cultural differences and develop close international contacts, won our company international prestige.

A Vision For The Future

Looking to the future, our vision is built upon innovation, growth and global cooperation. We must be constantly expanding on our strengths, exploring new markets and welcoming the arrival of new technologies. This will be the next stage in our development.

My Message For The Next Generation

The next generation of entrepreneurs and future business leaders can draw many lessons from my experiences:

- **Embrace Change:** Don't be afraid to leave your comfort zone. When I left a secure job at age 58 to open something new up, these successful 10 years taught me the value of change.

- **Make Strategic Acquisitions:** Look for strategic opportunities even in bad times. When AM Communications came up for sale during a financial crisis, nobody wanted to buy it. But it was a good move.

- **Be Flexible:** Don't be afraid to change direction. In 2008, we had to readjust our strategies and align ourselves with industry leaders in order to survive the market collapse.

- **Build Strong Partnerships:** Our partnership with Alpha transformed our business. Building strong, mutual–interest partners can take you into entirely new fields.

- **Continuous Innovation:** Keep ahead of the times in industry trends and always be innovating. It is what took us from hardware to software and from there to down – the supply chain efficiencies.

Your business will have its highs and lows. Stay strong, learn from defeat and don't forget the original vision and experience on the road.

The accounts and teachings from my life experience are proof that determination, methodology and continuous innovation will produce results. With these principles as a guide, you too can reach the top. Never forget, *'The Art of The Possible'* is a matter believing in possibility and challenging standards to bring truly remarkable outcomes.

My Entrepreneurial Odyssey: Part 3

Kerala To The Top Of World Entrepreneurship: Proud Journey With My Brother – A Business Vision

I often reflect on the many twists and turns, challenges and triumphs involved in shaping my life. It's not only the story of my own personal success, but also has rich significance for those who are just starting out as entrepreneurs or those who are going to lead business enterprises in the future. I hope my experience will be able to inspire and guide whoever still dares to dream and work determinedly to realize their dreams.

Meet Challenges Head-On: Resilience In Adversity

In 1989, at the age of 33, my younger brother Jehangir drove his life in a direction that would change it dramatically and one day produce one of India's leading contract-manufacturing operations. Before that turning point, Jehangir had been deeply involved in the pharmaceutical distribution business in Kerala, a major employer. However, destiny had very different plans for. Our father fell extremely ill; Jehangir gave up a number of years caring for him. The business took a nosedive leaving Jehangir at a crossroads after our father's death.

Emerging from that grim period his spirit was rekindled. In those tough years Jehangir reflected and understood that with perseverance, great achievements can happen again. Exploring new opportunities was driven by an insatiable desire for success, though he knew little beyond the fact that contract manufacturing in United States had potential. The suffering he underwent during that period became a new boost that kindled stronger determination than ever before.

In his philosophy, Jehangir adopted my belief in *'The Art of The Possible.'* Even in the darkest time, there were opportunities waiting to be discovered. This thinking gave him the tools to turn problems into stepping stones for success. When everyone else saw big problems, he looked at where successful development was possible. He started to see the biggest difficulties as powerful opportunities rather than problems.

Seizing The Moment: Insights From The U.S. And New Challenges

Jehangir's first stop in the United States was Harrisburg, Pennsylvania, where I was with AMP International. The timing of this visit was perfect. AMP was in the midst of explosive growth and looking at manufacturing in Asia.

By 1988, AMP had already established plants in South Korea, Taiwan, and Singapore. It wasn't until I joined the company that they really started to seriously consider India as a new manufacturing destination. Under its President, Jim Marley, AMP began to realize the vast skilled potential of Indian engineers. The company's need for PCBA (Printed Circuit Board Assembly) production coincided with this realization. AMP decided to place the manufacturing in India, a major change in its worldwide manufacturing strategy. During his visit to AMP's facilities, Jehangir observed and learned about the company's markets and their needs. AMP was a global leader and for Jehangir to move forward it was essential to understand the way they operated. This period was an eye-opener and it gave him a new understanding of global business. More importantly it showed him that if timing is right, then take the opportunity that comes along.

He was becoming a pioneering businessman and comfortable to look beyond the norms. Jehangir processed all of this understanding and conceived of India as a manufacturing base. It was with this outlook that he was able to look not just at what existed, but beyond and ahead – before others.

The Birthplace Of SFO: A Leap Of Faith And A Legacy

Jehangir established Sun Fibre Optics Pvt Ltd (SFO) in August 1990, just a few months after returning to India. That location is also known as the Cochin Export Processing Zone, today. At the inauguration, our mother Khadijoo lifted the shutters. They opened the empty shed with festivity and hope, opening up their own path. Their first customer was none other than AMP, who were looking to expand their product range beyond electrical connectors. The initial large-scale project was to reverse-engineer an IBM eight-port Token Ring Network. To undertake this project they turned to the design house of Processor Systems India Pvt Limited (PSI) in Bangalore.

SFO's creation was a step into the unknown. There was worry in those early days and struggle as well as a touch of anticipation and aspiration. That empty shed was not only a space; it was also the canvas for their dreams. Jehangir's faith that SFO could grow into something big kept him going, and the help of our family was also very important to him. Establishing SFO meant not just doing business but making history.

Unconventional by nature, Jehangir played an important part in this. He daringly challenged established systems and held that there was more than one way to skin a cat, ways of thinking he often says were influenced by me. Many people doubted the viability of starting such an enterprise in Kerala.

For Jehangir, however, things were quite different. He saw another opening here and told me: 'Only by forging ahead with confidence, tenacity and a touch of wildness can we really achieve great things.'

Overcoming Difficulties: A Challenge In Confidence And Credibility In Business

Over the years, SFO's development has morphed the company into India's largest production center for printed circuit boards. But the road was not smooth at all. When AMP decided to subcontract production to Jehangir's company, discontentment spread to some corners of their organization and a conflict-of-interest investigation was begun.

A group was sent to Cochin to investigate. In spite of worries on the inside, we had the clear backing from AMP President Jim Marley. He saw the importance of the strategy in having local contacts in India. He knew the added-value Jehangir could supply. This faith from Jim helped to quieten their internal disputes, and it meant we could go on cooperating with AMP.

Dealing with these problems taught Jehangir invaluable lessons about credibility and trust.

He understood that maintaining integrity and building good relations are essential for long-term success. His experiences only confirmed his belief in building bridges and that business should be conducted in an ethical way. Getting through these difficulties was not only about resolving conflicts, but proving your value and earning the trust of other people.

My spirit of possibility was a beacon for Jehangir. He believed that with persistence and ideas, they could overcome any obstacle. He concentrated on just proving SFO's capabilities and winning confidence. Their own determination and new approaches to the problem thus enabled them to make their way successfully through these difficult times.

Scaling Heights: Transforming SFO Into A World-Class Production Power

Our partnership with AMP was mutually beneficial. SFO supplied AMP with high-quality connector parts at a fraction of their former cost, thus lowering AMP's production costs. SFO, under Jehangir's leadership, had morphed into a well-known Indian production company that catered to customers from around the world. They brought Toshiba, General Electric and numerous small and medium enterprises to become part of their client list.

To reach the heights of excellence requires unwavering effort and commitment. We invest in the latest technology and develop teams of talented people. Each step towards their goals is a new milestone, reflecting their commitment and hard work. Transforming SFO into a world-class production center was the product of shared effort and shared vision. Its empire was built through mutual cooperation.

A maverick by nature, I had learned to step away from the norm and break ground. This served Jehangir and taught him to look at possibilities where others only saw constraints. That mindset determined the upward trajectory and immense triumph of SFO. This change in mindset, from the impossible to possible, infused them with a new philosophy of seeking for higher and striving more.

Forward Thinking: Branching Out And Expanding

Being an Electronics manufacturing services (EMS) company, SFO's journey did not end here. They transformed themselves into original design manufacturers (ODMs) and then an ODM-plus solution provider with their own IP assets. This strategic change showed the company's interest in innovation and its capacity to provide complete technology packages.

They dabbled into the likes of cutting-edge technologies such as Internet-of-Things (IoT), analytics, cloud computing, artificial intelligence (AI) and more. This diversification had them in tune with the direction of their industry and marked SFO as an agile operator within technology.

Innovation has been central to SFO's mission from its beginning. They were early adopters of new technology and always on the lookout for ways to improve their product. There was always a need for diversifying and this moving into the new frontiers helped to stay at least one step ahead of time in terms of what their customers wanted. They continue to innovate, always interested in delivering value and maintaining relevance with their solutions as the world changes around them.

Innovation is the fight against complacency and consistently finding new ways to bring value. Jehangir says he embraced my faith in him and imbibed the message that keeping a constructive mind of possibility works and bring achievement. This approach ensured that SFO continued to be at the forefront of innovation in our industry which fostered growth and adaptation.

SFO Today And The Future Of Excellence Through Visionary Leadership

SFO Technologies is today the biggest Indian-owned electronic contract manufacturing company. They have facilities located at Cochin, Thiruvanthapuram, Bangalore, Mysore and Pune They have scaled new highs to establish a cult that changed the economic lore of Kerala.

Kerala has a history of an agrarian economy and spice trade. The state's powerful labor union movement was seen as a possible brake on industrial expansion. However, with the operations department in the Cochin Special Economic Zone, they overcame these hurdles and propelled SFO to become CSEZ's biggest exporter.

Very soon, Kerala surpassed the rest of India in the literacy index, and with time Keralites were recognized everywhere for being highly literate. This major paradigm shift showed the capacity of Kerala of delivering technological excellence beyond the state's traditional economic strengths.

One of Jehangir's greatest pleasures has been leading SFO towards vision and purpose. It is a living example of how anything can be achieved with determination and a strategic approach. This is not a business that has been run successfully, it also involved the careers of economic investment in their own region. For all their innovation, they still draw inspiration from SFO's tradition of excellence.

Jehangir was guided by my most important principle to convert the impossible person into possible. With an inspiring vision and steely determination, he was sure they can accomplish great things. This healthy perspective helped achieve success and the legacy-building that followed. It has also reminded them of the requisite humility and grounded-ness that should accompany their success, no matter how great.

Mentorship and Leadership: The Role Of Family And Vision

I am proud of my younger brother, Jehangir, and his capability. He claims that I played a very important role in his journey. Yes, I did guide him, but he took the opportunities I opened up for him with both hands. Mentorship and connections are both invaluable in achieving success. With over 12,000 staff and strike-free operations for more than three decades. SFO alone leads to the creation of $300 million in revenue per year.

Mentorship and leadership truly go hand in hand. I mentored Jehangir in his leadership journey. This help and guidance lead him through the ebbs of business life. We owe our family so much for it is one of the greatest contributors to us achieving success. It was a launching pad from which we can take off and live the life of our dreams. The same family values have been guiding us all along, assuring that we keep moving towards our goals.

I had planted that seed of dreaming big and pushing the boundaries. Jehangir embraced this vision with full force and the result is evident.

Women Empowerment: Reducing The Widening Gap In Workplace Bringing Growth And Equality

Jehangir currently serves as chairman of NeST Group which has actively promoted women empowerment and gender equality. Consequently, women constitute 35-40 percent of their workforce and are working across roles in plants and development centers around the world. More than 60 OEM customers trust us for their service, which is now available in almost every country (56 countries) and with the leading telecom players as our customer base.

Part of NeST's growth strategy has always been to empower women. They are of the opinion that only through diversity and inclusion can they all grow together. They have every reason to be immensely proud of the accomplishments which their female employees achieve, and an indication in itself as to why diversity is such a powerful asset. In this way, their growth and equity performance more than fuels the business, it contributes to societal advancement as well.

As an innovator and maverick I have been questioning those norms from the very beginning. One of these changes is allowing women to be empowered in the workplace. That is what making the impossible possible truly comes down to; it is about removing roadblocks and generating opportunities for everyone. This strategy, consequently, has driven their growth and also serves as a benchmark to others.

Looking Ahead: Positioning For Future Growth

SFO Technologies is set to grow at 12 percent year-on-year, and it has lined up about $100 million in major expansions in the next three years.

A leading provider of product design, working capital management, and market development for high-tech products it is expanding its scope to include such services as R & D, hardware engineering, software engineering, manufacturing sheet metal fabrication, plastic injection molding, cable wire harness, relay transformer, fiberoptics, PCBA assembly and more.

NeST's future goals are geared to the forward thinking and out-of-the-box mentality that pursue innovation, define standards of quality in their own right. They continue to look for ways to innovate and invest in technologies that will change the future. They create their strategies based on expansion and innovation.

This will keep the success going and add long-lasting value for their stakeholders.

The concept of the possible continues to be what inspires them into their future planning, following Jehangir. He looked forward to the unlimited possibilities for growth and creativity. They continue being respected as the industry leaders, which can only be achieved by focusing on expansion and remaining technologically competitive.

Takeaways: Advice To Future Entrepreneurs

The story of Jehangir transforming into an international leader – A true example for hope and dream. Here are some of the key lessons we can learn from his story, for budding entrepreneurs and future business leaders;

Accept Challenges and Reshape

Expect the unexpected; life happens with a multitude of challenges - accept them as a chance to build and evolve. The key to survival is flexibility and adaptation. When Jehangir saw the pharmaceutical business going down and our father being unwell, he took it as an opportunity and pivoted into looking at more opportunities.

Build and Leverage Connections

This step is significantly important as it helps you build relationships and be connected with the best people and entities to operate from new markets or industry fields. The power of networking and relationships opens up doors giving you incredible support. The connections I had at AMP played a huge part in helping them establish themselves early on. It was through these relationships that they were able to prove themselves and land their first large customer.

Continuous Innovation

Emphasis on continuous innovation & diversification. It is essential that we remain ahead of the curve with industry trends. Your business strategy needs to make innovation the ultimate deliverable. SFO's commitment to innovating and adapting in a rapidly-evolving industry has allowed them to ingrain themselves as the cornerstone of their business domain.

Empower Your Team

Your best resource is a strong and capable team. Create a collaborative environment within which each team member feels they are valued and able to contribute with their own discipline. The NeST Group's venture into IT enabled services was bolstered by an accommodative and empowering culture that has helped their female employees accomplish more!

Stay Resilient and Persistent

The path towards success is inconsistent with many obstacles. Hang in there, get back up when you stumble and keep going. The key to a life well lived is persistence and determination. SFO and NeST came into the journey with a lot of bumps in their road, but they were able to push through and find success.

A Memo for the Next Generation

Jehangir's story is not just one of his personal achievements, but also the making a dream into reality and for contributing to Kerala's economy. May his journey get your entrepreneurial zeal to flow and motivate you head on for achieving. Even the unlikeliest of places, in AMP's case, Kerala, can transform into focal points for innovation and growth when paired with vision and determination.

My Entrepreneurial Odyssey: Part 4

Turning Vision Into Reality: NeST Group And Opterna Lessons

Together with the establishment and growth of NeST Group, as well as Opterna, I have dealt with various business obstacles; I hope my experiences are a source for inspiration and insight during your journey.

Foundation Stone: Genesis Of NeST Group

The birth of NeST Group was based on a single fundamental principle, to establish an idea from conceptual stage till commercial production and emerge as "One Stop Solution" for all technology needs. The NeST Group - Network Systems & Technologies (P) Ltd. For me, this entire journey has always been about *'The Art of The Possible'*, that with vision & persistence; nothing is impossible.

Creating The Blueprint: Co-founding For Growth

At the time I co-founded NeST Group, my strategy was to create businesses based on product/ geographic focus. This approach helped us to perfectly address an array of industry requirements. NeST became the vehicle for us to bring together several companies, reorganize operations and create maximum value in various business domains.

- **Learnings and Emotions:** Initially, when I advanced in my business ventures - they were the days of uncertainty leveraged with enthusiasm. As such, I was very invested in learning the nuances of every industry we entered. It required the right strategic planning and an additional willingness to dive into market research as well as customer needs. I often felt like I was a discoverer, in search of alternate continents and preparing the way for future victories. I was well informed by my favorite creed – the world of possibilities, which helped me not to be limited but forced and motivated me to see beyond limitations. I moved forward to materialize the theory turning it into tangible business with innovation and hard work.

- **Impact and Results:** We achieved a healthy mix of customers because we were able to easily develop solutions for nearly any industry, meaning our reputation was incredible. This strategic approach to the business world enabled us to overcome intricacies of different markets and we flourished as a multi-divisional, multidisciplinary conglomerate.

Centralized Excellence – SFO's Pivotal Role

Southern Fiber Optics (SFO) was our manufacturing arm. This was essential in maintaining efficient and low-cost production. My younger brother Jehangir and I recognized that putting our manufacturing resources in SFO would be the best juxtaposition for us to maintain the design community of all these brands together. This not only boosted operational efficiency but also permitted our firms to be staffed with a lean workforce. Most had one or two people doing the sourcing, marketing and sales across each company.

- **Lesson Learned:** As we started large batching assembled goods at SFO, our lesson was clear - centralize manufacturing in SFO for optimized impact and outcomes. By doing this, it not only made us even more productive but also contributed to our own quality and innovation aspirations. Through resource optimization, we developed a reputation for value and quality that helped us to improve our position in the market.

A Clientele Of Giants: Operational Efficacy

From the start, our motto has been obvious to all: *'Translating ideas into products'* and *'a home for your technology needs.'* Over the years this constellation of companies under NeST has been privileged with providing our services to global giants like GE, HP, Hitachi, Philips, Siemens. Sony, Toshiba and TycoElectronics. This is a validation of our approach in designing and deploying an organizational model that pens out into innovation, effectiveness and agility within the dynamically shifting business landscape.

- **Lessons and Tips:** Working with large clients of this scale has really put into perspective the importance of building trust and delivering what you promised. Each project we worked on was an opportunity to demonstrate our capabilities and reinforce our reputation. My advice to aspiring entrepreneurs is, always first focus on quality and reliability. In business, the most valuable thing is your reputation. To push the envelope and work to perfection in everything you do is a key trait of high achieving business trailblazers.

Harness Synergy: The Power Of Collaboration

One of the main reasons for NeST Group's accomplishment was how closely My brother Jehangir and I worked together. I worked on innovative ideas and direction, as Jehangir managed the operations functioning to ensure Kerala was an ideal performance ecosystem. We built trust and mutual success in our relationship, which helped us to drive the business.

A Relationship Beyond Business: The Partnership With Jehangir

Despite the 16-year age gap between Jehangir and me, I was often his mentor, helping to show support and guide him through the intricacies of the business world. Jehangir so poetically puts it — 'He's like a father figure for me. He is a mentor. He is second to my parents, otherwise he would be the first. He helped make me who I am.' It was a key element of our success, this close relationship.

- **Personal Insights:** My relationship with Jehangir goes beyond just a professional concern, it is our family that has driven us to do this and push the limits! Watching him grow into a capable leader has been one of the most rewarding parts of my life. If you are a member of the younger generation entering your family business, put as much enjoyment into building these relationships with others in and around your family. They will pay off.

- **Impact of this Work:** Our collaboration was so tight and both sides were in synch with one another which significantly contributed to very quick and well-informed decisions being made. The second mechanism behind our success has been the synergy between strategic vision and operational execution. We expanded the limit constantly on what was possible from both of us.

Worldwide Ambitions, Local Expertise

Jehangir was always the man inside - negotiating local politics, regulations, and overall systems. He had a background in operations and sales & marketing which I was lacking but aligned with my strategic vision. We laid a strong foundation together on which the NeST Group could prosper.

- **Results:** Jehangir, using his local knowledge and experience cut through regulatory hurdles to solve operational difficulties.

He was the person who managed things on ground which meant our strategic plans were implemented impeccably. They had also been a big driver in our success: the confluence of strategic vision and operational excellence.

Joining Family Ties With Business Triumphs

Jehangir works with his daughter and son, who are both engineers. City-based Nazneen is in charge of the software division while Hyderabad's Althaf heads the hardware team. The family integration into the business is an echoing reflection of our relationships and direction that results in success.

Lessons Learned And Tips

Every family has its struggles in the business, but there is no greater degree of trust or commitment than a fully integrated family unit. Working with family members who share your principles and aspirations can be beneficial for budding entrepreneurs. It is vital to keep the three C's in mind - *communication, consistency* and *capitalize* on all your passion.

But always ensure that these principles operate within the basic boundaries of professionalism.

Global Presences And Strategic Mergers: Spreading Wings

Two Additional Manufacturing facilities were set up in UAE and India, providing a finger on the pulse of the Middle East manufacturing needs along with North America, where the NeST Group expanded its foot-print globally by establishing offices in the UK, Dubai & Japan. Most of our companies were bootstrapped, acquired for a song, or founded from the wreckage of other startups. One illustration of this or near tactical acquisitions could be found in our 2007 acquisition of Ashling Microsystems Ltd based in Limerick, Ireland.

Strategic Match: The Ashling Acquisition

Ashling Microsystems was focused on state-of-the-art embedded software and hardware development tools. This acquisition was basically a part of an overall strategy to transition our development tools business into a comprehensive embedded systems development services entity. This was in line with our aggression to expand the embedded software services business, leveraging both our engineering depth and regional presence.

When the deal was completed, I noted that "Ashling is a natural extension for us here at NeST. Ashling's real-time embedded software development tools business has significant growth potential, and we will use our engineering strength and international presence to grow this business. In a nutshell, this move showed our talent for finding undervalued assets and turning them into profitable businesses.

Reflections and Insights: An acquisition is not merely a financial transaction; it also has great potential for successful growth if well fitted in the strategy appropriately. The risks paid off with the acquisition of Ashling Microsystems. My advice out there for potential first-time buyers would be to do your homework and take the time to see how it will fit into what you are already doing, or what other business opportunities this can enhance.

Impact and outcomes: With this strategic acquisition, we were able to grow our capabilities and offerings by leaps. With the Ashling acquisition we were able to get product enriched and expanded our customer base footprint.

This new chapter was a testament to our belief in *'The Art of The Possible'* and working endlessly towards that vision.

Hidden Gems Week: How Opterna Was Born

For me, the acquisition and growth of Opterna marked a turning point in my career. This is an example of how my entrepreneurial sense created success out of the unknown.

Finding Opportunities: The Purchase Of Raylan Corporation

In 1994, I was leading AMP's Global Interconnect System Business, and we bought a company out of Irving Texas called Raylan Corporation. Raylan was a specialist in electro-optic transceiver technology and fiber optic networking installation within buildings. Most buildings were connected by copper cables, which are slower than fiber optics.

When Tyco International bought AMP in 1998, Raylan started to encounter drastic changes. I purchased Raylan's product line and assets from AMP after seeing an opportunity. This was the decision which gave birth to Opterna.

- **Golden Reflections:** The power of perception and adaptation is fundamental in an entrepreneurial journey! The Raylan Corporation acquisition was purely a "bet" on the future of fiber optics technology. But for others who want to get in the game, answer what your gut tells you and then validate that with more research and planning.

- **Results and Outcomes:** Entering the fiber optics market with confidence as we acquired Raylan Corporation. This move highlighted our skills in recognizing and cashing in on new technologies. A tremendous real-life example of *'The Art Of The Possible'*, taking a tough situation to an absolute business win.

The Founding Of Opterna

Particularly affected by the AMP restructuring was Bret Matz, the engineering director for products within AMP's fiber optics division. I hired Matz to run the operations of our new fiber optics company. We faced some steep challenges, but Matz and I still believed in a new vision for fiber optics technology going forward.

Our new venture, originally called Sun Conversion Technologies (SCT), was to be a high-value provider for fiber-networking applications. The company changed its name to Opterna based on feedback it received in 2002.

- **Valuable Learning:** Starting a new business is one of the most exciting and also scariest endeavours to take on. It needs boldness and conviction to get everybody else around you on board with your train of thought. One might think that the name of a company is trivial and that it does not matter, but this step can be one of the most important in terms of branding aspects and market positioning. I would advise owners of companies to be carefully choose the name, it's a major point of success.

Building Opterna: The Making Of A Company

Starting up with nothing but the name, we had only ideas and have worked tirelessly for months to build something real. The move allowed us to rebrand and pivot as we got feedback from the market, which meant that our desire for quality became more visible. This experience reconfirmed to me that as an entrepreneur, the world of 'The Art of The Possible' lives right there in front of your eyes and even after having started such a small setup from scratch could make us one of the most respected players on Global map.

Adversity Overcome: Challenges Faced With Resilience

By 2001, Opterna was on the brink of a major breakthrough – a deal with the Pentagon on the horizon. But the tragic events of September 11, 2001, changed all that and we had to rethink our market strategy. Opterna, however showed its mettle and only grew further

- **Impact and Outcomes:** 9/11 was a terrible reverse, but it also taught me how to be more resilient. We had to change direction with our plan and figure out where we could grow instead. This moment provided me with my faith that situations are transient and can be reversed if it is what you truly desire.

- **Face Challenges:** In every business journey, you are guaranteed to face challenges. How you handle them and persevere is the important part. What differentiates successful entrepreneurs from those who come up short is their resilience to be knocked down and get back out there again. Adopt 'The Art of The Possible' mindset that any challenge is an opportunity for growth and learning.

Strategic Partnerships And Growth: The Verizon Breakthrough

Opterna's big break came through a large infrastructure contract with U.S. telecom giant Verizon. This partnership included providing fiber-optic solutions for Verizon's FiOS service and delivering top-quality internet, video, and phone services to millions of homes in several U.S. cities. By performing this well-executed collaboration, it secured Opterna a spot in the fiber optics game.

Reflections and Insights: Strategic partnerships are game changers for any business. Collaborating with Verizon allowed us to enter into new markets and partnerships.

My advice to entrepreneurs: go out and find partnerships that complement your strategy and ideology as a business.

- **Impact and Outcomes:** The Verizon partnership marked a pivotal moment in Opterna's history. We have all the qualifications to provide fiber optic solutions and it put us into a good validating position. The success was a testament to our key mantra: 'The Art of the Possible', as we leaned on those strategic relationships to grow faster than anything I had ever experienced before.

Diversification And Apps

In addition to telecoms, Opterna ventured in many areas like mobile applications. We launched an entire division devoted to the creation of mobile apps for emerging markets. This diversification also showed how we could adapt and innovate new products with changing market needs.

- **Impact and Outcomes:** Diversification helped reduce risk as well as provide us with a new source of revenue It also placed us as a forward-looking company that was ready to take on the new era of technology. Staying ahead of industry trends and diversifying your offerings is a big help to entrepreneurs in increasing the growth horizon for their businesses.

- **Reflections and Insights:** A willingness to explore new potential opportunities combined with a calculated risk mindset is what embracing diversification is all about. We got into mobile apps because we saw it coming and wanted to innovate. The approach illustrated all about exploring the open field of possibilities, and it allowed us to endlessly challenge the limits of what we could do.

Strategic Exit: Opterna Sale

I sold Opterna in 2019 to Belden Inc., a large company active in developing networking, security, and connectivity products an d solutions. By the time it was sold, Opterna employed over 375 people in eight countries. This momentous strategic exit defined my colorful entrepreneurial expedition.

Reflections and Advice: Exiting is as important as entering into a business. The sale of Opterna was a strategic move made to unlock significant value and refocus our efforts on the next chapter in our journey. For aspiring entrepreneurs, timing your exit is a critical factor in extracting the highest returns and ensuring your capacity for re-investment in new potential.

- **Impact and Outcome:** The sale of Opterna was a product of several years' worth or hard work, creativity, asset development. It yielded a large ROI and allowed me to venture into new opportunity sectors. This exit was a validation of our focus on 'The Art of The Possible': the mantra that we followed in changing this startup into something everyone thought was worth owning.

Key Insights Gained From Success

As I look back on my journey, a number of lessons come to mind.

1. Vision, Strategy and Operational Efficiency

Success takes a strong strategic vision and efficiency in operations. A combination of centralized manufacturing and a lean organizational structure helped us maximize resources while minimizing costs.

Advice: Entrepreneurs should keep a clear vision on what they want to achieve and optimise their process. Concentrate on what you are naturally strong at and always strive to deliver more efficiently. Cultivate a spirit of seeing possibilities in all situations - being able to see the future and working for nothing less than the best outcomes.

2. The Power of Collaboration

Working together and developing good relationships is key. One of the key reasons for our success was my close partnership with Jehangir. Surround yourself with people that believe what you believe and fill the gaps where your weaknesses show through.

Advice: Surround yourself with like-minded people who have the same drive and vision. Solving business problems requires breaking silos and collaborating to find sustainable solutions. Cut the '*im*' in *impossible*, which will inspire and reassure your team allowing you to connect with your people and generate collaboration.

3. Resilience in the Face of Adversity

Obstacles and setbacks are simply par for the course. Remain tenacious and flexible. That Opterna was able to recover after 9/11 is a tribute to our perseverance.

Advice: Be resilient and open in the face of changes. Remember, setbacks are not failures - they are temporary challenges that require patience and resilience. Reconfigure challenges as learning and growth opportunities.

4. Strategic Acquisitions and Diversification

Recognizing underpriced assets and turning them into successful businesses takes vision, strategy, and tactically excellent execution. Moving into new and growing areas of the market allows for diversification, as well.

Advice: Keep an eye on the opportunities others are not looking at. Stay relevant and follow trends by varying your offering. Explore and attack new frontiers in a stealthy entrepreneurial manner, keeping your mind and eye on opportunities.

5. Build and Foster Relationships

Successful managers will tell you that the strongest component of their business is having deep relationships with clients, partners and also, employees. Some of the biggest names in the industry were our clientele, and it was thanks to our tight-knit, co-operative team that we grew so quickly.

Advice: Take care of the people that you do business with, clients, partners, and associates alike. Confidence, reliability, and trust are vital components to business success. Keep nurturing deep, trust-centered relationships.

6. Creative Advancement

In a rapidly changing world, innovation and adaptability are more important than ever. Always be looking for new avenues for your capabilities and nurture your abilities to match new opportunities. And when the need arises - change course.

Advice: Accept change and always look for new ways to do things Keep up with industry trends and be ready to modify your strategies according to the evolving demands of the market. Practice '*The Art of The Possible*' - Go for maximum, keep pushing the boundaries on what's possible.

Final Notes for Aspiring Entrepreneurs
And Future Leaders: Crafting Your Path to Success

My advice to aspiring entrepreneurs, and future leaders is simple: stay true to your vision and believe in it even when no one else does. Keep fighting through those tough times knowing that the end goal will be reached by a mind focused on the possible. Build a strong supportive network around.

Building a successful business can be tough and daunting, the road may seem long with its challenges and victories but if you try to look further, adopting the learnings from my experience and how we approached business and work, you are sure to get there. Be strategic in your vision, collaborate well, know yourself, your talents and strengths and be adaptable – great destinations are certain.

Please keep in mind that success does not always mean money; often innovation, creating value and positively affecting others is a better definition of success. Keep pushing your values and commit to lifelong learning as you start on this adventure.

The future *is* yours to shape.

My Entrepreneurial Odyssey: Part 5

From Vision To Reality - How NeST Technologies Was Built And How A Random Encounter Led To A Vision: Finding That Perfect Future Partner

During the late 1990s, as the President of Global InterConnect Systems Business at AMP International I found myself in an important meeting with New Jersey Institute of Technology (NJIT) and arrived to Teterboro Airport. This is where I found Richard Schatzberg, former head of corporate development and marketing for NJIT while also an adjunct professor. On the drive to NJIT we talked readily, and Richard was obviously extraordinarily bright and inquisitive. I bought into his excitement and felt he could be part of something important.

It occurred to me much later, that the meeting was not just another chit chat but a turning point for NeST Technologies. The thoughtful questions Richard asked and the fact that he clearly put thought in to understanding my vision strongly suggested that I was dealing with someone who was not only talented at what he did, but also looking to achieve big.

I wrote down Richard's cellphone number after that first encounter. During the summer, I called him with an exciting offer. I said to him, " - I'm starting a US-based company called NeST Technologies, and would like you as a part of it. On that same phone call, I invited him to visit Harrisburg the next Saturday morning 8:30 am.

When it comes to how I built NeST Technologies, where others saw roadblocks, I saw opportunity, and where common sense was lacking a compass rose of experience. I loved that Richard was curious and open to trying new things, which is exactly what I wanted him to do.

Jumping In The Deep End:
The Journey Of NeST Technologies

Intrigued but uncertain, Richard mentioned it to his wife before driving into Harrisburg.

On arrival, he met three other strangers in the basement of our home. I spoke to this group, sharing my vision about NeST Technologies and invited them to be the founding executives. I was clear about the conditions: the starting salary would be low and only two of them would remain after a year. All four took the risk. Richard quit NJIT to become the Chief Commercial Officer of NeST Technologies, and we were off.

NeST Technologies was born out of necessity and a desire to compete. When I bought AM Communications, we needed programmers and instead of outsourcing or building an in-house team, I decided to create a separate entity. Our early headquarters were in the spare office space of AM Communications in Quakertown, and indeed our first client was AM Communications itself.

It was an exciting time to be doing something new. Of course there were times of doubt and unease, yet it was mostly quelled by our combined spirit and conviction. The team was small, but the vision was tremendous. Our work was our mission, and we were convinced that it could be succeeded through determined effort.

I am an innovator and a non-conformist when it comes to out of the box thinking. I was hell bent on breaking conventions by doing something extraordinary. I thought that if we were focused and determined, with a tendency to challenge the status quo we would be able to pull off some incredible success. With our attitude of making opportunities possible, we were unafraid to take risks and wade into deep waters filled with unknowns.

Early Challenges:
A Time Of Uncertainty And Innovation

In those days, the USA was grappling with the potential threat of Y2K, and they needed huge Indian software talent, which created a major influx in people solving these upcoming challenges. To better integrate them into the American work culture I enlisted a former Pakistan Air Force veteran, Durrar Aidrus. Together, we trained our team through the cultural intricacies of American ways, staying in a guesthouse in Quakertown.

Our resilience and adaptiveness were tested early on. The Y2K crisis was a tough situation, but it also gave us an opportunity to showcase our potential. We spent countless hours, late at night working to prepare our client's systems for the new millennium. This period of hard work also served to strengthen our team and helped cement a reputation for being dependable and competent.

Although NeST Technologies faced its own share of teething problems, the company rapidly established a firm foothold in an ultra-competitive industry landscape. We were geared up to deliver high-quality software engineering services and expanded our global presence with US-based operations, expanding across Europe, Middle East (UAE and Saudi Arabia), India as well as several countries in Asia. Our client roster grew to feature the big global names such as First American, Corning, GE and Hitachi along with Motorola, Nokia, Philips Seibels Tata and Texas Instruments.

This is a testament to our execution and commitment to excellence, as we continued the positive momentum and achieved strong client retention rates above 90 percent.

My personal *'The Art of The Possible'* philosophy shone through in how we dealt with these challenges. Every hurdle looked like a chance to create something new and exciting. We were able to do this because of a desire not just to twist and tweak the same old system, but rather to re-think it entirely.

The Power Of Synergy: Harnessing Collaborative Potential

NeST Technology's success has shown with extreme clarity how my philosophy of business ventures is effective, and it works by building on synergies in our businesses and using resources efficiently across different companies. Because of this strategic implementation we were able to realize and output the maximum value for our clients.

Today, after a span of twenty-six years, Richard continues as the Chief Commercial Officer at NeST technologies. The other person present at that initial meeting was Dr. Robert Smith (B.S. from GA Tech and a Ph.D in Engineering). A Ph.D. in optics, he was our Chief Technology Officer. Robert worked with the company for over 20 years: he was a Former National Science Foundation Fellow, and before retiring due to Covid-19 pandemic. He also served as an ex Senior Member of Technical Staff at Sandia National Laboratories. Robert was our core, alongside Bret Matz and Richard, working at the many companies I headed.

The synergy within our ventures was much more than a mere strategy; it became our essence.

An atmosphere where collaboration and sharing of resources were not only promoted but a pre-requisite. As a result, we were able to innovate continuously, pooling our collective knowledge and expertise to solve complex problems and create cutting-edge solutions.

As an unconventional visionary, I really knew the value of synergy. We created an ecosystem of innovation and mutual success by blending different talents together. We harnessed individual expertise into a collaborative force.

Strategic Separation For Expansion: The Rise Of JKH Holding

My brother Jehangir and I decided that for efficiency and growth, we should separate our businesses. Jehangir became the chairman of the NeST Group, overseeing its diverse ventures, including the flagship company SFO Technologies. All my business entities were consolidated under the newly founded JKH Holding.

SFO serves as a key manufacturing hub for various entities within JKH Holding, such as AM Technologies and Nestronix.

The same time, JKH Group companies made a mark across several technology and service areas like IoT (internet of things), fiber optics products & solutions, software development services, electronic manufacturing services, healthcare IT, RF and microwave technologies and also media. Combined, the companies provided services to more than 400 customers - including several Fortune 100 organizations- and a workforce of over 4,000 employees around the world.

The reason for choosing to create JKH Holding was our ambition of optimizing the business and sharpening its strategic focus. By combining our businesses under one umbrella made it a better aligned, more streamlined entity.

Further, this restructuring positioned us to better focus our resources and strengths for a more sustainable future.

That shift was embodied in my philosophy as *'The Art of the Possible'*. I saw the opportunity to build a more integrated & responsive organization: one that could operate effectively in today's fast changing business world. As an innovator, I took on the opportunities from change head on change and to create a future that aligned with my vision of limitless possibilities.

Breaking New Ground: Hightailing It Out Of The Box

The companies held by JKH Holding included NeST Technologies, Ashling, Nestronix Inc., and Qual-Pro Corporation. Headquartered in the United States, Nestronix is a North American supplier of engineering and manufacturing services into many industries. In 2020, I acquired Qual-Pro Corporation based out of Gardena California. Formed in 1972, Qual-Pro added critical manufacturing facilities providing a strong US and Thailand presence to our growing global footprint.

In addition, Ecell Healthcare offered various medical information technology solutions across the board with turnkey options including a modular hospital management system.

The expansion into new markets and sectors was based on a strategy to mitigate our business risk. We diversified across industries and product lines, which allowed us to build multiple revenue streams and lower the risk of being driven by any one market segment. This also provided us the ability to leverage new opportunities and trends.

As a rebel who has always played by my own rules, I embraced the expansion for what it was: a bold and pioneering adventure. *'The Art of The Possible'* was a thread that ran through all if it, helping us to take strategic decisions across sectors and innovate to create meaningful value.

Entering Media Land: The Next Chapter

After decades in tech, I decided to break new ground and enter the media industry. It was a personal passion. We acquired a Cochin-based software firm that developed world-class streaming platforms for international clients in 2016. With this investment, I could leverage the growing digital content consumption market.

Building on this we launched Neestream in 2020, which is a streaming platform for the Malayalam (Kerala) audience across the globe.

In 2022, I extended my media stint by establishing a local news portal in Kerala - responding to the surge demand of credible and relatable content in this subject area.

It was a bold move to go into the media industry, and it was indeed out of conviction and passion. We identified the increasing need for digital content and saw that we could use technology (and our experience with it) to build a platform to serve the audience in an expanding market.

My unconventional journey into media came from my attitude of not conforming and embracing *'The Art of The Possible'*. I went against the grain and sought an unusual and novel route.

The will to challenge norms and lean about new opportunities was what got us there.

Reflecting On Learnings And Insights:
Advice For Aspirational Leaders

I continue to stay my course at 83 focusing on my love for bringing value and making a difference. Five days a week, I continue to work out of the office, with the same passion and dedication that has characterized my entire professional journey.

Below I am sharing critical lessons from my entrepreneurial journey to serve aspiring entrepreneurs and the next generation of business leaders.

- **Curiosity and Intuition:** Always be curious, and trust your gut instinct. Innovation comes from curiosity, and seeing the uninhibited flow of opportunities arising on the horizon. And, intuition is what you rely on to guide the excellence of your decisions when clarity seems obscured and the times seem tough.

- **Take Calculated Risks:** Success requires you to get out of your comfort zone by taking a risk. Consider outcomes and act accordingly, but never fear difficulty. The greatest accomplishments are borne out of the courage to go forth.

- **Associate With the Best:** Put together a team of high-quality, dedicated people. A good team will enhance your efforts and sure up top achievement. By investing in and keeping your professional network strong, the payoff is huge.

- **Value Synergy:** Find synergy between your ventures. Efficient use of resources through collaboration will enhance results. More than just 'working together' it focuses on working from your strengths to get brilliant outcomes.

- **Adapt and Readjust:** The business landscape is volatile and perpetually changing. Remain relevant by being adaptable and open to innovation. Constantly remain in touch with new opportunities. Change is the name of game; be ready to pivot as needed to stay ahead.

- **Strive for Excellence:** Invest energy and resources in the highest-quality products and services. This will translate into repeat clients and make your business grow. Do your very best, and make quality a standard.

- **Be resilient:** Challenges and setbacks are guaranteed.
  Remain determined, focused and persevere to navigate through difficult times and emerge stronger. Resilience is about bouncing back and learning from failures to grow and improve.

- **A Learning Machine:** Always be in search of new knowledge and learning points. Educating yourself is key to making wise choices and remaining proactive. Life is always about learning - if you stop then the wins will stop.

I am still excited to embrace the new adventures. My message to you is - dream big, have a clear vision, work with dedication and determination, and keep your goals at the forefront of your mind. The future is yours to shape.

Transforming Vision To Thriving Reality: NeST Technologies

The NeST Technologies story is a classic example of visionary leadership, perseverance and strategic thinking! This success didn't just happen overnight. It was the result of meticulous planning, dedication to what we were doing and that commitment towards excellence. He created a healthy business that thrives to this day, and we did so by maximizing synergy, using few resources yet focusing from each part of the group on delivering value to our markets.

Looking back on my journey, I am reminded how important it is to take risks and be constructive about uncertainty. For the people who I had invited to join at the start of NeST Technologies, including Richard Schatzberg, my vision was clear and resonated with everyone as were the challenges ahead. Their courage to take the leap of faith and believe in the vision was instrumental in shaping the company's direction.

This transformation was fired by my belief in *The Art of The Possible'*. Where others saw obstacles, I envisioned potential and was dead-set on bringing that vision to life. It is this mindset that drove our success, and laid the foundation for a healthy growth.

Why Building A Strong Foundation Is Essential For Success: Laying The Groundwork

A key lesson I acquired is the criticality of laying a solid foundation on which you can establish and secure your business growth. It was a time when dedication and hard work were the hallmarks of NeST Technologies. We have always concentrated on quality customer services and long-term relationships with our clients. A focus on excellence early in our tenure set us up for this success, and gained us a reputation that continues to fuel top clients paying top rates.

As we grew, so did the number of our international customers while ensuring that quality and client satisfaction always came first. This tactic was not only advantageous in terms of on boarding new clients but secured an excellent post-purchase retention rate. We were able to create a customer base that knew we would be there for them when they needed us because they trusted we would provide this level of quality all the time.

'The Art of The Possible' directed our efforts to build a strong foundation. We believed that by driving determination and a commitment to excellence, any challenge could be overcome and achieve lasting success.

Success Through Synergy And Strategic Thinking: The Perfect Sambar

Synergy mindset is one of the major principles driving my business psychology. To cook the perfect *sambar* (a South Indian lentil and vegetable curry) the perfect balance of all 20-25 ingredients is what makes it delicious. Non-synergistic cooks will add extra flavoring, spices, or vegetables and the taste is ruined. Some people put the wrong proportion of lentils to vegetables and the texture is ruined.

Similarly, in business, this synergistic balance between the right resources to serve the right clients is the secret to success. Strive for the perfect *sambar* my friends.

Then match it with the perfect *dosa* (rice galettes), which in business means collaborating with the right and best people. You have a perfect dish and a perfect business.

At NeST Technologies and then JKH Holdings, by capitalizing on the strengths and resources of various ventures, we were able to create a powerful network to drive innovation and growth. This collaborative approach allowed us to maximize efficiency, generate new products and solutions for the market, and achieve incredible results.

Our success was determined by strategic thinking. A good strategy can help you remain focused, while helping to make informed decisions - be it in identifying market opportunities or managing challenges. Entrepreneurs-to-be need to adopt a strategic mindset and be on the hunt for how synergies can be created plus value added.

As a non-conformist and visionary, I always regarded synergy and strategic thinking as crucial to unlocking 'The Art of The Possible.' By optimizing our capabilities and uniting our collective strengths, we were able to achieve exceptional results.

Flexibility and Innovation:
Staying Ahead Of The Curve

The ability to adapt and innovate is essential in the current fast business environment. During my entire career, I have always been open to change and believe that something can be accomplished in a new or better way. We excelled in pioneering into different sectors whilst integrating new technology for innovation.

An example of this diversification was our media industry venture.

It was sparked by a strategic vision to tap into the growing market for digital content. To capitalize on this demand we acquired a software company specializing in streaming platforms. This move diversified our portfolio and opened up new avenues for growth.

People called me a maverick and innovator, and I felt I was; committed to adaptability and innovation as *'The Art Of The Possible.'*

We were able to adapt and develop by adopting new ideas, concepts, and opportunities.

Building a Legacy Of Excellence: Creating Lasting Impact

NeST Technologies and the JKH companies are testimonies of how vision, toil and strategic thinking have re-defined destiny! We deliver this excellence worldwide through our clients. Our global presence and impressive clients list show our commitment to continuous search for excellence and innovation.

- **For aspiring entrepreneurs:** Think big, work hard and never take your sight from your goals. Keep excellent relationships with all stakeholders, whether employees, partnerships, suppliers, or others. Welcome challenges and always aim for perfection. Although it is a difficult journey, the returns in achievement and self-satisfaction well outweigh anything else.

  My guide in building a legacy of excellence has been viewing the possible in every situation. Resultantly, we have made an enduring difference in a way that never ceases to energize and propel our ongoing success.

Future Directions: Moving Forward

At the time of writing, I am in my early 80s and still have some way to go. It has been a remarkable journey with NeST Technologies and beyond, full of rocky roads leading to lessons learnt the hard way as well. I look forward to how my story will encourage you to go on your own confident journey.

Your success is a culmination of more than just what you achieve - it should be how you rose to where, and the journey itself.

Master *'The Art of The Possible'* and be great.

Section 4

Captivating Interviews With Javad Hassan
And Colleagues: Invaluable Insights
And Masterful Learnings

Section 4: Captivating Interview With Javad Hassan, Accompanied By Durrar Aidrus

Invaluable Insights And Masterful Learnings

To complement this autobiography, here is a series of interviews with Javad Hassan and individuals closely associated with him throughout his professional, corporate, and entrepreneurial career. The interviews have been transcribed and edited to be used as powerful case studies.

The Significance Of These Interviews

- **Beyond Modesty:** Autobiographies can often reflect the modesty of the individual. These interviews bring out the full extent of Javad's impact through the eyes of others and the interviewer's extraction of his essence.

- **Inspiration for Your Journey:** these interviews from Javad's experiences and those of his close associates will help you accelerate your own entrepreneurial and leadership development.

Invaluable Cruxes

- **Insightful Stories/Case Studies:** To gain a deeper understanding of Javad Hassan's philosophy and approach through first-hand accounts.

- **Practical Lessons:** Use these interviews as a guide to enhance your own leadership and strategic thinking skills.

- **Broader Perspective:** These interviews provide an external view of Javad's brilliance, offering a more comprehensive picture than an autobiography alone.

Part 1: Three Interviews With Javad Hassan

Interview With Javad 1: The Avant-Garde Innovator And Perpetual Business Mastermind

- A Global vision implemented.

- Always ahead of the curve.

- Serial entrepreneur – creating businesses from trends.

- Javad Hassan's 5 Ps formula for success.

- Beyond Business: A Legacy of Integrity and Human Connection.

Interview With Javad 2: Challenging The Status Quo At IBM

- A significant moment at IBM when Javad boldly proposed doing a project for 20% of their planned approach.

- Showcases his clarity of thought, dedication, passion, and courage.

- A true visionary's thinking v complicated executive approaches.

Interview With Javad 3: The Ground-breaking Pioneer Of Outsourcing

- Discusses how Javad became a trailblazer in the technology outsourcing industry, earning the title 'king of outsourcing.'

- Provides insight into the early days of what is now a massive industry.

Part 2: Interviews With Associates/Employees

Features seven interviews with colleagues who have worked closely with Javad for many years. These interviews offer:

- **Lessons Learned:** Valuable takeaways from their experiences.

- **Vital Traits of Leadership:** Insights into Javad's exceptional qualities as a leader, boss, visionary, and entrepreneur.

Part 1: Interviews With Javad Hassan

The Avant-Garde Innovator
And Perpetual Business Mastermind:
The Change-Maker Who Saw Beyond Borders

My entrepreneurial odyssey has been shaped by a relentless pursuit of innovation and a commitment to excellence. Although I've achieved considerable success, I consider myself a simple man who has been fortunate to see the world through a unique lens. This is my story of vision, persistence, and the unwavering belief that with patience and passion, anything is possible.

From a young age, I was fascinated by how things worked. Growing up in a modest household in South India, I was always curious and eager to learn. My education provided a strong foundation, but it was my innate curiosity that drove me to explore new horizons. Moving to the United States opened up a world of opportunities, and I was determined to make the most of them.

- **Key Lesson:** Awaken your curiosity and always seek to learn.
  Your background or starting point doesn't define your potential;
  your drive and passion do.

The Early Days At AMP:
Sparking The Outsourcing Revolution

My entrepreneurial journey began in earnest during my tenure at AMP. It was a company deeply rooted in the traditions of small-scale operations, with factories scattered across Pennsylvania.

However, I saw the limitations of such a localized approach. It was clear to me that the future lay in thinking bigger and broader.

"We have to go find, you know, go outsourcing," I often told my colleagues. This simple idea was revolutionary at the time. I pioneered the concept of outsourcing, long before it became a global business norm. My vision was to leverage global talent and resources, thus setting the stage for a new era in manufacturing and technology. It wasn't about being a trailblazer; it was about doing what made sense for the company's growth and sustainability.

Implementing this vision required convincing the leadership at AMP to take a leap of faith. It wasn't easy, but I believed in the potential of global collaboration. We began by setting up small operations in India, demonstrating that high-quality work could be done efficiently and cost-effectively. This move was not without its challenges, but it laid the groundwork for what would become a global industry standard.

- **Key Lesson:** Don't be afraid to challenge the status quo. Innovative ideas often face resistance, but persistence and a clear vision can turn skepticism into success.

- **Advice for Aspiring Entrepreneurs:** Always look for ways to improve and innovate. Be prepared to take calculated risks and advocate for your ideas with conviction.

Founding SFO And NeST: Building A Global Network

This vision took a significant leap forward with the establishment of SFO Technologies in Kerala, India. To me, it wasn't just about expanding operations; it was about demonstrating that global outsourcing was a viable strategy. Kerala, with its abundant skilled labor, became the perfect location. With strategic leadership from individuals like Thomas John and my brother Jehangir, SFO quickly became a cornerstone of AMP's diversified manufacturing strategy.

At the same time, I founded NeST (Network Equipment Systems and Technology), a software company that complemented SFO's hardware focus. NeST grew rapidly, serving major clients like GE Healthcare and expanding globally with Nihon NeST in Japan. The burgeoning software talent in India was a key factor in this growth.

Creating these companies was never about seeking accolades. It was about addressing needs and solving problems. I was fortunate to work with brilliant minds who shared my vision and dedication. We built a network that spanned continents, each step reinforcing the belief that great ideas know no boundaries.

- **Key Lesson:** Collaboration and leveraging diverse talents are key to building successful enterprises. A strong team with shared goals can achieve remarkable feats.

- **Advice for Aspiring Entrepreneurs:** Surround yourself with capable and like-minded individuals. Invest in building a team that complements your strengths and shares your vision.

An Instinctive Innovator: Always Ahead Of The Curve

My success wasn't limited to outsourcing. During my time at IBM, I worked on semiconductor manufacturing machines, laying the groundwork for future industry leaders like Applied Materials Technology and Lam Research. My innovative mindset was evident early on, as I developed technologies that would later become industry standards.

"I never thought I was working for anybody," I often reflect. "I did what I wanted to do wherever I was, whether at IBM or AMP."

My approach was always simple: identify the problem, find a solution, and move forward. I didn't see myself as a pioneer; I saw myself as someone who wanted to make things better. This mindset allowed me to contribute significantly to the technological advancements of my time.

- **Key Lesson:** Focus on solving problems and creating value. Your work should always aim to improve existing processes and technologies.

- **Advice for Aspiring Entrepreneurs:** Stay ahead of the curve by continuously learning and adapting. Innovation often comes from understanding current limitations and envisioning better solutions.

Embracing New Challenges: The Serial Entrepreneur

My restless creativity led me to start numerous ventures, each with a distinct focus. From PSI in Bangalore, instrumental in early outsourcing, to Nestronics, a contract manufacturing company in the US, my ventures showcased my knack for identifying opportunities and turning them into successful enterprises.

"I lose interest after a while," I admit. "I get things started well, and after a while, I want something different." This wasn't because I was fickle, but because I believed in constantly challenging myself and those around me.

Each new venture was an opportunity to learn and grow. My goal was never to build a vast empire but to create solutions that addressed real needs and to enjoy the journey along the way.

- **Key Lesson:** Welcome change and be willing to start over. Each new challenge is an opportunity to grow and innovate.

- **Advice for Aspiring Entrepreneurs:** Don't be afraid to pivot and explore new ideas. The entrepreneurial journey is about continuous learning and adapting to new circumstances.

The Philosophy Of Success: The 5 Ps

In a commencement speech at NJIT, where I was honored with an honorary doctorate in engineering, I shared my philosophy encapsulated in the '5 Ps':

- Passion

- Patience

- Persistence

- Perseverance

- Practice

This framework has guided my approach to life and business, emphasizing sustained effort and unwavering dedication.

"You have to have patience and a passion for something," I advised the graduates. "Then you have to have persistence and perseverance."

These principles are simple, but they are powerful. They reflect the values I hold dear and the approach that has helped me navigate the complexities of life and business. I believe that success is not a sprint but a marathon, requiring consistent effort and a deep-seated commitment to one's goals.

- **Key Lesson:** Success is built on a foundation of core principles. Passion fuels your journey, while patience, persistence, perseverance, and practice ensure you stay the course.

- **Advice for Aspiring Entrepreneurs:** Develop your own guiding principles and stick to them. They will help you navigate challenges and stay focused on your long-term goals.

Beyond Business:
A Legacy Of Integrity And Human Connection

I have always had a disdain for authority and bureaucracy, but I deeply value people. My interactions, whether with employees or business partners, are characterized by genuine respect and consideration for individuals over profit.

"People matter to you most," a close associate once told me. "Products have been great fun things to do, but people to you have been really important."

For me, business has always been about building relationships and fostering a sense of community. Success is not just measured by profits but by the impact we have on those around us. My fondest memories are of the people I've worked with and the relationships we've built together.

- **Key Lesson:** Value relationships over transactions. Genuine connections lead to lasting success and fulfillment.

- **Advice for Aspiring Entrepreneurs:** Focus on building strong, meaningful relationships. Treat your team and partners with respect and integrity, and they will support you through your entrepreneurial journey.

A Restless Mind: Forever Seeking The Next Challenge

My relentless pursuit of new ideas and ventures is both my strength and my defining characteristic. From buying luxury cars to acquiring properties, my actions reflect a restless, creative mind always seeking the next challenge.

"It's a restless mind or a creative one," I muse. "I think I have this restless leg syndrome also."

This restlessness has driven me to continually push the boundaries and explore new frontiers. It is not about accumulating wealth or accolades but about the joy of discovery and the thrill of innovation. I believe that life is too short to settle into a routine, and there's always something new to learn and explore.

- **Key Lesson:** Embrace your restlessness as a source of creativity and innovation. Use it to drive continuous improvement and exploration.
- **Advice for Aspiring Entrepreneurs:** Let your curiosity and drive for new experiences fuel your entrepreneurial spirit. Always be on the lookout for the next opportunity to grow and innovate.

My journey has been a compelling narrative of innovation, persistence, and the pursuit of excellence. My contributions to the fields of outsourcing, technology, and entrepreneurship have been monumental, shaping industries and inspiring future generations. This story is not just about business success but about a visionary leader who dared to dream beyond borders and conventional wisdom.

In the end, I am just a simple man who believed in the power of ideas and the importance of hard work. My story is one of gratitude for the opportunities I have had and the incredible people I have worked with along the way. Together, we have built something remarkable, and for that, I am deeply thankful.

Key Lessons And Advice For Aspiring Entrepreneurs

1. **Embrace Curiosity and Continuous Learning:** Your background doesn't define your potential; your drive and passion do.

2. **Challenge the Status Quo:** Innovative ideas often face resistance, but persistence and a clear vision can turn skepticism into success.

3. **Build Strong Teams:** Surround yourself with capable individuals who share your vision and complement your strengths.

4. **Focus on Solving Problems:** Your work should always aim to improve existing processes and technologies.

5. **Embrace Change:** Each new challenge is an opportunity to grow and innovate.

6. **Develop Core Principles:** These will help you navigate challenges and stay focused on your long-term goals.

7. **Value Relationships:** Genuine connections lead to lasting success and fulfillment.

8. **Harness Restlessness:** Use it to drive continuous improvement and exploration.

I hope my journey and these lessons inspire you to pursue your own path with passion, patience, persistence, perseverance, and practice.

A Story Of Free Thinking, Simplicity, And Resilience

Javad Hassan's story is one of simplifying business, resilience, and unwavering integrity. As a pioneering figure at IBM, Javad navigated a predominantly white corporate world, challenging the status quo with his practical, cost-effective approaches to technology and business. His ability to foresee the potential of small-scale operations like Micron Technology and his fearless advocacy for efficiency over grandeur set him apart from his contemporaries. This story needs to be told to inspire future leaders and innovators to embrace simplicity, challenge conventional wisdom, and pursue what is right, regardless of the obstacles. Javad's journey is a testament to the power of integrity and vision in driving true progress.

The Story: The Largest Producer Of The Lowest-Performance Memory Chips In The Universe.

Interviewer: When you went to IBM at Fishkill, and they were all white American executives, right? How did you get along with them, both the educated executives and the uneducated workers?

Javad Hassan: It was just my instinct for survival. Darwinian. I had to survive, right? Whatever the environment is, you make it work. No meaning in bitching and moaning about it.

Interviewer: You don't seem to be much concerned. Was it your openness, curiosity to learn, or being nice to them that made it okay?

Javad Hassan: Maybe that. I have to survive. It was all about survival.

Javad Hassan's journey at IBM Fishkill is a testament to his adaptability and resilience. Despite facing an environment where he was often the only person of color, he navigated the complex social and professional dynamics with a pragmatic approach. His focus was always on survival and excellence, which helped him earn the respect of his peers and superiors.

In the predominantly white, hierarchical structure of IBM at the time, Javad's presence was an anomaly. Yet, he managed to build relationships across different levels of the organization. His ability to connect with both the executives and the workers in the plant stemmed from his genuine interest in people and his innate ability to relate to their experiences. This unique quality allowed him to bridge gaps and foster a collaborative environment, even in challenging circumstances.

Challenging The Status Quo At IBM

Interviewer: Tell us about the IBM corporate office management committee meeting and the story of Micron Technology.

Javad Hassan: I was telling them that building a big facility in Burlington, Vermont, wasn't the right way. Micron in Idaho was making 64KB chips in a small building with much less investment, around $50K. Spending $250 million in Burlington made no sense.

Interviewer: Why did you feel that the $250 million investment was unnecessary?

Javad Hassan: The Atkinson brothers were building Micron Technology in Idaho with much less money. They were making 64KB memory chips in a potato field financed by a potato magnate from Idaho. Meanwhile, IBM wanted to invest heavily in a project that didn't make sense.

At IBM, Javad didn't shy away from voicing his opinions, even if it meant confronting the top brass. His practical insights often clashed with the grandiose plans of the executives, but his focus was always on efficiency and value. During a critical meeting, Javad stood up against a proposal to invest $250 million in a new facility in Burlington, Vermont. He argued that smaller, more efficient operations like Micron's in Idaho were achieving similar technological advancements with significantly less investment.

Javad's criticism wasn't just about the financial aspect; it was about the philosophy behind the investment. He believed that innovation and practicality should drive technological advancements, not grandiose projects driven by fear of competition. His stance highlighted a fundamental difference in thinking – while the IBM executives were reacting to the perceived threat of Japanese technological dominance, Javad was advocating for a more grounded and innovative approach.

A Visionary's Insight

Interviewer: You mentioned that the Atkinson brothers were building Micron Technology in Idaho with much less money. Can you elaborate on that?

Javad Hassan: The Atkinson brothers were making 64KB memory chips in a small building, financed by a potato magnate from Idaho. They were achieving remarkable progress with limited resources, which contrasted sharply with IBM's massive investment in Burlington. It didn't make sense to me.

Javad's ability to foresee the potential of smaller, more efficient operations like Micron's highlighted his visionary approach. He recognized the value of innovation over sheer scale and grandeur. This foresight was not just about saving money; it was about fostering an environment where technological advancement could thrive without unnecessary financial burdens.

His visit to Idaho, where he discovered the Atkinson brothers' work, was a turning point. He saw firsthand how innovation could flourish in unlikely places with the right mindset and resources. This experience reinforced his belief that IBM needed to rethink its approach and focus on practical, cost-effective solutions rather than expensive, large-scale projects.

Standing Up For What's Right

Interviewer: When you stood up in that meeting, were you confrontational? How did you describe your stance?

Javad Hassan: I was sitting in the gallery, outside the main circle of executives. I spoke up because I believed we had become the largest producer of the lowest performance memory chips in the universe. Spending millions on outdated technology didn't make sense.

Interviewer: Did Bob Evans or anyone react to your statements? What was the aftermath?

Javad Hassan: IBM is a serene society; nobody reacted openly. Bob Evans didn't say anything. I was seen as a traitor to the president of IBM at that meeting. Later, I got a job in Tucson, Arizona, thanks to Dr. Bertram, another iconic figure who thought highly of me.

Javad's courage to speak out, despite being an underling in the hierarchy, showcases his commitment to integrity and technological advancement. He wasn't afraid to challenge the prevailing norms to advocate for more sensible and forward-thinking strategies. His stance during the meeting was not about seeking confrontation but about highlighting a critical flaw in the company's approach.

Despite the lack of immediate recognition or support, Javad's boldness did not go unnoticed. Dr. Bertram, a respected figure within IBM, saw potential in Javad's practical approach and offered him a leadership position in Tucson, Arizona. This opportunity allowed Javad to continue his work in a more supportive environment, where his ideas could be implemented more effectively.

The Path To Leadership

Interviewer: What made you speak up without fear of the consequences?

Javad Hassan: Maybe I was dumb. I didn't think about becoming something else. I just said what I had to say. I was a simple guy, not over-thinking.

Interviewer: So, when you are rising in Fishkill and Armonk, did you have in your mind the next position, the next position, and let me work for that?

Javad Hassan: No, I just went along with the flow. People around me saw my talent, I guess.

Javad's simplicity and fearlessness stemmed from his focus on doing what he believed was right. His lack of concern for personal gain or fear of repercussions allowed him to navigate his career with a unique sense of freedom and integrity. He didn't plan his career meticulously; instead, he followed his instincts and made decisions based on what he believed was best for the company and the technology.

This approach resonated with many of his colleagues and superiors, who recognized his talent and potential. Despite facing numerous challenges and obstacles, Javad's dedication to his principles and his willingness to speak out eventually led to numerous opportunities for growth and leadership within IBM.

The Legacy Of A Trailblazer

Javad Hassan's journey from a lone voice in the gallery to a leader in the tech industry is a story of resilience, innovation, and unwavering integrity.

His ability to challenge the status quo, advocate for practical solutions, and maintain his principles in the face of adversity left a lasting impact on the industry and those who worked with him.

Interviewer: Did Bob Evans or anyone acknowledge your contributions later on?

Javad Hassan: No, Bob Evans didn't say anything directly. But I did get the opportunity to lead the Tucson, Arizona lab, thanks to Dr. Bertram, who believed in me.

Javad's legacy is defined by his fearless pursuit of excellence and his unwavering commitment to doing what he believed was right. His journey is a testament to the power of integrity, resilience, and the courage to challenge the status quo. Through his innovative approach and practical mindset, Javad Hassan has left an indelible mark on the tech industry, inspiring future generations of leaders and innovators.

Visionary Leadership Beyond The Boardroom

Javad Hassan's story is a powerful reminder of how true visionaries often diverge from the conventional paths taken by suited executives in boardrooms. While corporate leaders may focus on grandiose plans and massive investments, a visionary like Javad sees the potential in practical, effective solutions that drive real progress.

Javad's approach was rooted in a deep understanding of

technology and an unwavering commitment to innovation. He wasn't swayed by the allure of grand projects or the fear of competition. Instead, he championed cost-effective, efficient strategies that harnessed the full potential of available resources. His ability to foresee the value in smaller, innovative operations like Micron Technology, and his courage to voice his insights, set him apart from his peers.

In a world where corporate decisions are often driven by fear of competition and a desire for grandeur, Javad's story highlights the importance of practicality, simplicity, and integrity. His fearless pursuit of what he believed was right, without concern for personal gain or fear of repercussions, is a testament to his visionary leadership.

Javad Hassan's legacy serves as an inspiration for future leaders and innovators. It underscores the value of challenging the value of challenging the status quo, thinking beyond the conventional, and advocating for practical solutions that drive true technological advancement. His journey reminds us that visionary leadership isn't about making big plans in boardrooms; it's about having the courage to see things differently and the integrity to act on those insights.

Key Lessons For Aspiring Entrepreneurs And Future Leaders

1. Adaptability and Resilience

- **Story Reference:** Javad Hassan thrived in IBM's predominantly white corporate environment by focusing on survival and excellence. He built relationships across all levels by showing genuine interest and relating to others' experiences.

- **Lesson:** Embrace adaptability and resilience in challenging environments. Build meaningful connections and focus on personal and professional growth regardless of obstacles.

2. Challenge the Status Quo

- **Story Reference:** Javad questioned IBM's decision to invest $250 million in a large facility when smaller operations like Micron were achieving similar results with much less investment.

- **Lesson:** Don't be afraid to challenge prevailing norms and voice your practical insights. Innovation often comes from questioning and improving existing approaches.

3. Value Practicality Over Grandiosity

- **Story Reference:** Javad highlighted the efficiency and innovation of Micron Technology, which operated with limited resources but achieved significant progress.

- **Lesson:** Focus on practical, cost-effective solutions that drive real progress. Large investments aren't always necessary for technological advancement.

4. Stand Up for What's Right

- **Story Reference:** Despite being an underling, Javad spoke out against inefficient investments, showing his commitment to integrity and technological advancement.

- **Lesson:** Have the courage to stand up for your principles and advocate for sensible, forward-thinking strategies, even if it means challenging higher-ups.

5. Embrace Simplicity and Fearlessness

- **Story Reference:** Javad's simplicity and lack of concern for personal gain or fear of repercussions allowed him to navigate his career with integrity and freedom.

- **Lesson:** Maintain simplicity in your approach and be fearless in your decisions. Focus on what you believe is right without overthinking the potential consequences.

6. Foster Innovation in Unlikely Places

- **Story Reference:** Javad's visit to Idaho and his discovery of the Atkinson brothers' work in a small, resourceful setup reinforced his belief in practical innovation.

- **Lesson:** Recognize that innovation can thrive in unexpected places. Support environments that foster creativity and resourcefulness.

7. Resilience Leads to Opportunities

- **Story Reference:** Despite initial resistance, Javad's practical approach and boldness were eventually recognized, leading to a leadership role in Tucson.

- **Lesson:** Stay resilient and committed to your principles. Opportunities will arise from your consistent efforts and integrity.

8. Visionary Leadership Requires Integrity

- **Story Reference:** Javad's journey is marked by his fearless pursuit of excellence and unwavering commitment to doing what he believed was right.

- **Lesson:** Lead with integrity and a clear vision. Your commitment to excellence and practical innovation will inspire others and drive true progress.

9. Think Beyond Conventional Paths

- **Story Reference:** Javad's ability to foresee the potential in smaller operations like Micron set him apart from conventional corporate leaders.

- **Lesson:** Embrace unconventional thinking. Practical, effective solutions often lie outside traditional paths and require a visionary approach.

10. Legacy Through Practical Innovation

- **Story Reference:** Javad's innovative approach and practical mindset left a lasting impact on the tech industry, inspiring future generations.

- **Lesson:** Aim to leave a legacy through practical innovation and integrity. Your contributions can inspire and shape future leaders and entrepreneurs.

The Ground-Breaking Pioneer Of Outsourcing

A New Direction In Pennsylvania: The Birth Of Outsourcing

Javad Hassan's career at AMP marked a significant shift in how manufacturing was approached. AMP was originally established by Whittaker, a German entrepreneur, who set up small factories across Pennsylvania. However, Javad saw the need for a different strategy.

"When I came to AMP, I said that this is no longer the way to go. Because that was okay right in those days when he started in the hinterlands of Pennsylvania, which is huge, and so I said, we have to go find, you know, go outsourcing." Javad recalls. This foresight led to the pioneering of outsourcing, a concept that would revolutionize the industry.

Javad's insight was that small, local manufacturing units scattered across Pennsylvania were no longer viable in a rapidly globalizing world. He recognized the need for more efficient and cost-effective manufacturing solutions, leading him to conceptualize and implement outsourcing, even before it became a buzzword in the business world.

- **Guidance Lesson #1: Embrace Change and Innovation**
  Javad's ability to see beyond traditional methods and embrace change was crucial. Aspiring entrepreneurs should be open to innovative ideas and not be afraid to deviate from established norms. Change can lead to significant breakthroughs and competitive advantages.

Building Bridges: From Pennsylvania To Kerala

Javad's innovative approach wasn't just about outsourcing; it was also about leveraging global talent. He started a factory in Kerala, India, challenging the norm and proving that high-quality manufacturing could be done outside the traditional industrial hubs.

"Kerala has plenty of labor. So I bought a Bangalore guy called Govardhan and Satish Babu later they all left then Mr. Jehangir (Javad's younger brother), taken over from there." Javad's move was brave, considering Kerala wasn't known for its industrial base at the time. Yet, his decision was driven by a desire to diversify and innovate.

This factory in Kerala was more than just a business venture; it was a statement. Javad believed in the untapped potential of regions that were often overlooked. By setting up in Kerala, he was not only creating jobs but also fostering a culture of industrial development in a place not traditionally associated with it.

- **Guidance Lesson #2: Recognize and Leverage Global Talent**
  Entrepreneurs should look beyond geographical boundaries to tap into global talent. Recognizing the potential in different regions can open up new opportunities and create a diverse and innovative workforce.

The Political Balancing Act

Setting up a business in India came with its own set of challenges, especially the political landscape. Javad navigated these waters skillfully, understanding the importance of local connections and political goodwill.

"SFO was inaugurated by the Minister for Industries at the time. I made him inaugurate it. My mother was inaugurating. But he was there I gave him the honor."

This move not only garnered political support but also showcased Javad's ability to blend personal and professional elements seamlessly. Javad's diplomatic approach ensured that his ventures were well-received. By involving local politicians and dignitaries in his projects, he ensured a smoother operational path and created a sense of local ownership and pride in the factories he established.

- **Guidance Lesson #3: Navigate Political and Cultural Landscapes**
  Understanding and navigating the political and cultural landscapes of the regions where you operate is crucial. Building strong relationships with local stakeholders can lead to better support and smoother business operations.

From Vision To Reality: Expanding Horizons

Javad's ventures didn't stop at one factory. He expanded SFO to other cities like Bangalore, Mysore, and Pune, eventually playing a crucial role in India's space missions.

"They did the major electronic work for ISRO or Indian Space Research Organization in Trivandrum. They put more than 20 components in the Chandrayan which landed on the Moon." This achievement underlines the impact of Javad's foresight and leadership.

The involvement of SFO in ISRO's Chandrayaan mission was a crowning achievement. It highlighted the capability of Indian manufacturing and engineering on a global stage. Javad's vision had come full circle, with his factories contributing to one of India's proudest technological achievements.

- **Guidance Lesson #4: Think Long-Term and Aim High**
  Javad's long-term vision and high aspirations allowed him to contribute to significant projects like India's Chandrayaan mission. Aspiring leaders should think beyond immediate gains to achieve lasting impact.

The Advent Of NeST: A Global Network

NeST, which stands for Network Equipment, Systems, and Technology, was another brainchild of Javad, conceived while he was still with AMP. NeST embodied a comprehensive approach, covering everything from hardware to software, making it a global entity.

"I convinced AMP that we should outsource. We cannot keep on doing it in the Pennsylvania labor. We have to outsource and I said we will do India. And I pointed out as we start this when demonstrators can be done." Javad's knack for identifying market needs and acting on them was pivotal in NeST's success.

NeST was not just a company but a concept that encompassed the entire spectrum of technology and systems. Under Javad's leadership, NeST grew into a formidable entity, proving that outsourcing was not just a cost-saving measure but a strategic advantage.

- **Guidance Lesson #5: Identify Market Needs and Act Decisively**
  Entrepreneurs should always be on the lookout for market needs and be ready to act decisively. Identifying gaps and providing solutions can set the foundation for successful ventures.

Fun And Innovation: The Core Of Javad's Philosophy

Despite his many achievements, Javad never lost sight of the joy of innovation. He often moved on to new projects once they were up and running, a trait that defined his career.

"I am a guy who loses interest after a while. I get things started well, and after a while, I want something different." This restless energy drove Javad to constantly seek new challenges, keeping his work dynamic and exciting.

Javad's approach to business was unconventional. While many entrepreneurs seek stability and growth within a single venture, Javad found joy in the initial phases of creation and innovation. His restlessness was a testament to his creative spirit, always pushing the boundaries and exploring new horizons.

- **Guidance Lesson #6: Embrace Your Creative Restlessness**
  Don't be afraid of moving on to new challenges once you've set things in motion. Embrace your creative restlessness and use it to fuel continuous innovation and exploration.

The Japanese Connection: Nihon NeST

One of Javad's notable expansions was Nihon NeST in Japan. His experience there was both challenging and rewarding, reflecting his ability to adapt and thrive in different cultural environments.

"They are different. They're pretty honest. They're honest. If they tell you that you will get the business you will deliver no wishy-washy." Javad's appreciation for the Japanese work ethic and culture was evident, and it helped him build strong business relationships.

Japan, with its unique business culture and stringent standards, was a challenging market to penetrate. However, Javad's ability to understand and respect cultural differences allowed Nihon NeST to thrive. His ventures in Japan solidified his reputation as a global business leader.

- **Guidance Lesson #7: Respect Cultural Differences**
  When expanding internationally, respect and understand cultural differences. Building strong relationships based on mutual respect can lead to long-lasting business success.

The Restless Creator

Javad's tendency to move from one project to the next, whether it was in business or personal interests, like his fleeting enthusiasm for luxury cars, painted a picture of a man driven by a relentless pursuit of new experiences and challenges.

"I just wanted to have fun. That's it. Fun creating solutions." This philosophy extended to every aspect of his life, making him a unique figure in the business world.

Javad's personal interests mirrored his professional life. His brief enthusiasms for luxury cars and other ventures were not about materialism but about the thrill of new experiences. His restless nature was a driving force, constantly seeking out the next challenge.

- **Guidance Lesson #8: Find Joy in Creation**
  Find joy in the process of creating and exploring new ventures.
  Let your enthusiasm for innovation drive your actions, rather than just the pursuit of success.

A Legacy Of Innovation And Fun

Javad Hassan's journey is a testament to the power of visionary thinking and the importance of enjoying the process of creation. His contributions to outsourcing, manufacturing, and global business strategies have left a lasting impact, driven by a restless yet creative mind. "I'm not interested in building a big thing. I just wanted to get things started and have fun with it."

This legacy of innovation and joy continues to inspire those who follow in his footsteps.

Javad's legacy is not just in the companies he built but in the way he approached life and business.

His story is a source of inspiration for entrepreneurs and innovators, reminding them that success comes from passion, creativity, and a relentless pursuit of new challenges.

- **Guidance Lesson #9: Create a Legacy Through Passion**
  Create a legacy that reflects your passion and creativity. Your journey should inspire others to pursue their dreams with the same enthusiasm and dedication.

Part 2: Interviews With Associates/Employees

An Interview With Jim Helm

Jim worked under Javad at AMP and then went on to work for him in many parts of the entrepreneurial journey —India, and NeST Technologies.

Javad: The Visionary Without An Ego
Introduction: A Remarkable Journey

"Jay is the best boss I ever had". Jim Helm

In a candid conversation, Jim Helm reveals the inspiring journey of working with Javad, a visionary leader with a unique blend of humility and ambition. Their collaboration at AMP Incorporated and beyond showcases the power of trust, innovation, and the drive to create something meaningful.

Meeting Javad: A New Beginning

From IBM Innovator To AMP Visionary

Jim Helm was a manufacturing manager at AMP Incorporated when Javad joined the company, brought in by the chairman, Jim Marley. Coming from IBM's research department, Javad was tasked with elevating AMP from merely making connectors to becoming a systems-level business. His arrival, however, was met with skepticism and resistance from the existing staff who viewed him as an outsider.

Breaking The Ice: Overcoming Skepticism

Despite the cold reception, Javad began to change the company's direction. While many were resistant, Jim was one of the few who saw potential in Javad's vision. He admired Javad's deep thinking and innovative approach and chose to support him from the outset.

Building The Future: Key Projects And Innovations Revolutionizing Fiber Optics

Jim was instrumental in starting the manufacturing of fiber optic products at AMP, introducing numerous styles of connectors, and establishing global supply chains. When the company aimed to expand into active components, Javad played a crucial role in inspiring this transition. This initiative wasn't just about expanding the product line; it was about transforming the company's core identity. Javad's vision drove AMP to integrate active noise within connectors and develop wavelength division multiplexers (WDMs) with lasers, pushing the boundaries of their technological capabilities.

A Promise Kept: The India Project

During a large meeting, Javad expressed his desire to build a factory in India. Jim, ever the man of action, volunteered for the task. Despite initial challenges and skepticism from colleagues, Jim successfully established the factory, spending months in India to ensure everything was in place. This move not only fulfilled Javad's vision but also honored a personal promise Javad had made to his mother to create opportunities for young women in India.

Jim's Hands-On Approach In India

In India, Jim faced logistical challenges, from securing the right materials to training local staff. His dedication was evident as he spent considerable time away from home, integrating into the local community and ensuring the factory met all operational standards. This hands-on approach was instrumental in overcoming cultural and logistical barriers, making the project a success. He recounts how he taught the local team to think innovatively, shifting their mindset from a purely mechanical and hierarchical approach to one that embraced creativity and proactive problem-solving.

Efficiency On The Factory Floor

Jim recalls a pivotal meeting where he asked the local team why the factory floor was not completed. They explained they were waiting for specific brown tiles that were unavailable. Jim asked if any other color was available, and when told there were blue tiles in stock, he ordered the switch. This decision saved weeks of delay, demonstrating Jim's practical approach to problem-solving and his commitment to efficiency.

Crafting Connect Well: Merging Seven Companies

Javad acquired seven networking companies and tasked Jim with integrating them into a single subsidiary called Connect Well. Despite the complexity of merging various engineering disciplines and manufacturing processes, Jim's dedication and Javad's unwavering trust in him led to successful integration and operational excellence.

Navigating Corporate Mergers

Merging seven companies required a strategic approach to align different corporate cultures, streamline processes, and unify goals. Jim's role as Vice President of Operations was pivotal in navigating these challenges. His ability to foster collaboration among diverse teams and implement efficient systems ensured the success of Connect Well, further solidifying Javad's vision for a cohesive, innovative enterprise.

Javad's Unique Leadership Style
Leading Without Ego: Javad's Humility

One of the most striking aspects of Javad's leadership was his lack of ego. Unlike many leaders who seek to bolster their own importance, Javad was solely focused on achieving his vision. He trusted Jim's ability to execute his ideas, creating a powerful dynamic where vision met action.

Javad's humility allowed him to build strong, trust-based relationships with his team. He valued results over rhetoric and was always open to feedback, fostering an environment where innovation could thrive. This lack of ego also meant that Javad was willing to take risks and make bold decisions, knowing he had the support of capable individuals like Jim.

Informed Decisions: Trusting The Right People

Javad's decision-making was heavily reliant on the quality of information he received. Jim ensured that Javad had accurate data, enabling informed decisions. This trust-based relationship was crucial, as illustrated by Jim's intervention in preventing unnecessary expenses for polishing equipment in India, saving significant costs.

Vision Meets Action: Mutual Respect

Throughout their professional relationship, Javad and Jim developed a mutual respect. Javad valued Jim's ability to get things done, while Jim admired Javad's visionary thinking. This combination of skills and trust led to numerous successful projects and a lasting professional bond.

Jim's proactive approach and Javad's strategic vision created a synergy that drove the success of multiple initiatives. Their mutual respect and complementary skills were key to overcoming challenges and achieving their goals.

Dedication Beyond Retirement:
Executing Javad's Vision: Building The Virginia Factory

In 2015, Javad asked Jim to build a factory in Virginia. Despite his retirement, Jim agreed to help. Javad, once again, outlined his vision, and Jim executed the plan flawlessly. He spent four years, from 2015 to 2019, establishing the factory, ensuring it was fully operational and met all required standards.

Javad's approach remained consistent: he provided the vision and trusted Jim to handle the execution. Jim's dedication and expertise were instrumental in bringing Javad's ideas to life, reinforcing their strong professional relationship.

Tough But Necessary Decisions: Closing The Factory

After the successful establishment and operation of the factory, Javad made a strategic decision to close it. Despite the emotional and professional challenges of this decision, Jim understood and respected Javad's reasoning. This move demonstrated Javad's ability to make tough decisions for the greater good of the business, always keeping the broader vision in mind.

Saving $148,000: A Strategic Intervention

One notable story that underscores Jim's critical role was his intervention to save $148,000 in unnecessary expenses. The team in India had requested this amount for additional polishing equipment, claiming they lacked capacity. Jim analyzed the situation, demonstrated that the existing equipment was sufficient if used efficiently, and convinced Javad to reject the request. This move not only saved significant costs but also highlighted the importance of accurate information and strategic decision-making.

Ensuring Profitability: Challenges In Dallas

As Vice President of Operations for Connect Well, Jim faced significant challenges. Javad once instructed him to go to Dallas and not return until the operations were profitable. Jim spent three and a half months in Dallas, working tirelessly to streamline operations and cut unnecessary costs. During this period, he discovered financial discrepancies where costs for other projects were being unfairly allocated to his division. Jim's meticulous attention to detail and relentless pursuit of transparency led to the removal of the financial manager responsible and the appointment of someone more trustworthy. This story illustrates Jim's dedication to ensuring operational efficiency and financial integrity.

Conclusion: A Legacy of Innovation And Trust

Jim Helm's stories about Javad paint a picture of a leader who defied conventional expectations. Javad's lack of ego, visionary mindset, and reliance on trusted individuals like Jim created a legacy of innovation and success. Their partnership is a testament to what can be achieved when visionaries and doers come together with mutual respect and a shared goal.

Their collaborative efforts transformed AMP and later ventures into industry leaders, setting new standards for innovation and operational excellence. This legacy continues to inspire future generations of leaders and innovators.

Javad's Vision: A Final Thought

The stories and experiences shared by Jim Helm illustrate Javad's exceptional qualities as a leader and visionary. His ability to inspire, coupled with his humility and strategic acumen, made him a unique force in the industry. The legacy of their partnership serves as a powerful reminder of what can be achieved through mutual respect, trust, and a relentless pursuit of excellence, and a relentless pursuit of excellence.

Reflections: Learning From Javad's Leadership

Javad's leadership style offers valuable lessons for aspiring leaders:

- **Humility in Leadership:** True visionaries focus on their goals, not their egos.

- **Trust and Delegation:** Trusting capable individuals to execute a vision is crucial for success.

- **Informed Decision-Making:** Relying on accurate information and feedback ensures sound decisions.

Jim's reflections and stories not only highlight Javad's exceptional qualities but also serve as an inspiration for future leaders aiming to create impactful change. Their partnership exemplifies the power of visionary thinking combined with practical execution, paving the way for groundbreaking achievements in any field.

An Interview With Guy Rabat

Guy began working with Javad at AMP and then went on to work for him in many parts of the entrepreneurial journey – Including SFO (India), Opterna and NeST Technologies.

The Visionary Leader: Javad 'Jay' Hassan
A Journey Begins

Guy Rabat recalls his first encounter with Jay Hassan in the mid-1970s at IBM. Jay was already a few levels into management, while Guy was just starting his technical career. Their professional relationship blossomed over the next 50 years, transitioning from colleagues to friends and collaborators in various entrepreneurial ventures. Jay's journey from IBM to becoming a successful entrepreneur was marked by his relentless pursuit of innovation and his unique ability to connect with people.

The Power Of Connection

One of Jay's standout characteristics is his unparalleled ability to network. Guy describes him as a "people person" with an extraordinary memory for names and faces, even those he may not have always agreed with. Jay's charm and approachability made people feel comfortable around him, regardless of their background. This quality helped him build an extensive network of loyal contacts, which played a significant role in his success.

Jay never forgot anyone and was always ready to reconnect, even with people he had disagreements with. This extroverted nature, combined with his genuine interest in others, allowed him to cultivate relationships that were beneficial both personally and professionally. Guy emphasized that people liked to connect with Jay because of his charm and the genuine care he exhibited in his interactions.

Vision And Intuition

Jay's vision and intuition are other defining traits. Coming from humble beginnings in India, Jay developed a keen sense of foresight, especially in the realm of technology. Guy highlights Jay's early contributions to the tech industry in India, noting his involvement in areas like AI, VLSI, and fiber optics long before they became mainstream. Jay's ability to foresee technological trends and his deep love for India and its potential were instrumental in his professional achievements.

Jay's vision was not just mystical but based on keen observations and facts. He had an uncanny ability to predict technological advancements and understand their implications. His love for India and his desire to see it advance technologically were evident in his contributions to the tech sector there.

Jay's foresight in technology and his commitment to India's development were crucial aspects of his career.

Balancing Innovation With Practicality

Jay's entrepreneurial spirit is evident in his approach to business. He constantly balanced innovation with practicality. Guy recounts Jay's involvement in pioneering expert systems at IBM and later in fiber optics at AMP. Jay's ability to understand complex technologies and simplify them for broader application was crucial in these ventures.

He wasn't just a visionary but also a practical businessman who could see projects through from conception to implementation.

At IBM, Jay worked on the development of expert systems, which were early forms of artificial intelligence designed to mimic human decision-making. This innovation, though ahead of its time, showcased Jay's ability to envision the future of technology. Later, at AMP, Jay's focus on fiber optics marked another significant contribution. He guided AMP into new directions, demonstrating his ability to drive technological innovation within a business context.

One notable project at IBM was the development of a knowledge system for semiconductor design. Jay and Guy worked together to turn vast amounts of data into practical applications for self-testing chips and devices. Despite the potential, IBM's focus on hardware over software meant this innovation remained internal. Jay's ability to navigate these corporate challenges while pushing the envelope of technology exemplifies his balanced approach to innovation.

Loyalty And Trust

Loyalty and trust are core to Jay's interactions with others. Guy emphasizes Jay's commitment to his team and his ability to inspire loyalty in return. Despite making some mistakes in his career, particularly in selecting executives, Jay's resilience and the loyalty of those around him helped him recover and thrive. His willingness to take risks, coupled with his capacity to bounce back from setbacks, underscores his entrepreneurial spirit.

Jay valued loyalty highly and built strong bonds with his team members. He believed in giving people opportunities and trusting them to do their jobs well. Even when mistakes were made, Jay's ability to rebuild and move forward was remarkable.

His approach to leadership, which combined trust with a willingness to take calculated risks, was key to his long-term success.

Guy recalls a pivotal moment when Jay was considering leaving IBM for AMP. Jay was uncertain, but Guy encouraged him, emphasizing the importance of securing a solid contract. This advice proved invaluable when Jay faced challenges at AMP, reinforcing the deep trust and mutual respect between them. Jay's commitment to his team and his ability to inspire loyalty were crucial in his entrepreneurial ventures.

The Role Of Luck

Guy acknowledges that luck has played a part in Jay's success. Jay has made errors, some could have been damaging, but he was always resilient and clear visioned and managed to recover. This resilience, combined with the loyalty of his team and his own capabilities, enabled him to navigate challenges effectively.

Jay's career is dotted with instances where his resilience was tested. Despite facing significant setbacks, he always found a way to recover. To Jay's inherent ability to learn from his mistakes and adapt quickly. This combination of luck and resilience has been a significant factor in Jay's enduring success.

For instance, Jay had a tendency to trust people who sometimes turned out to be unreliable. However, his ability to recover quickly and his network of loyal, competent executives helped mitigate these risks.

A True Entrepreneur

Jay's journey from IBM to AMP and eventually to leading his own ventures, such as Opterna and the NeST group, showcases his entrepreneurial drive. Guy describes how Jay's vision for 'fiber to the home' transformed Opterna into a major player in the fiber optics industry. Jay's long-term perspective and willingness to invest time and resources into building profitable, sustainable companies set him apart as a genuine entrepreneur.

Jay's entrepreneurial spirit was evident in his willingness to leave the security of established companies like IBM and AMP to start his own ventures. His vision for 'fiber to the home', which aimed to replace traditional copper cables with high-speed fiber optics, was revolutionary. Under his leadership, Opterna grew from a small distribution company into a major player in the industry, eventually being sold for a high valuation.

Jay's journey with Opterna began in Dubai, where he successfully navigated a complex joint venture with a UK firm. This venture laid the foundation for Opterna's growth. Jay's strategic vision and determination turned Opterna into a key player in the fiber optics market, securing major contracts with global companies like Verizon and Orange.

Influence And Legacy

Throughout his career, Jay has influenced countless individuals and organizations. Guy mentions how Jay's advice and support were pivotal in his own career, reflecting Jay's broader impact. Jay's legacy is not just in his professional achievements but in the lasting impressions he leaves on those he interacts with.

Jay's influence extends beyond his professional accomplishments. He has mentored many individuals, including Guy, and has been a reference point for them throughout their careers. Jay's willingness to offer advice, support, and mentorship has left a lasting impact on those who have had the privilege of working with him.

Guy recalls Jay's role in encouraging him to transition from technical work to management. Jay's belief in Guy's potential and his guidance were instrumental in Guy's career growth. Jay's influence is evident in the careers of many he has mentored, reflecting his commitment to developing talent and fostering growth.

An Unconventional Path To Success – Defying Norms

Jay's story is one of defying norms and pursuing innovation for its own sake rather than for monetary gain. Guy notes that making money was never Jay's primary goal; it was a byproduct of his passion for innovation and his ability to execute his vision. Despite his significant wealth, Jay lives modestly, underscoring his focus on substance over superficial success.

Jay's approach to success is unconventional. He has always been driven by a desire to innovate and make a difference rather than by the pursuit of wealth. This passion for innovation has led to significant financial success, but it has never been his primary motivator. Jay's modest lifestyle reflects his focus on what truly matters to him: creating value and advancing technology.

Even after achieving significant financial success, Jay remains focused on innovation and growth. He continues to explore new opportunities and mentor others, driven by a passion for making a meaningful impact rather than accumulating wealth. Jay's unconventional approach to success serves as a powerful example of what can be achieved when one prioritizes vision and innovation.

A Unique Personality

In summing up Jay Hassan, Guy describes him as a multifaceted individual who leaves a lasting impression on everyone he meets. Jay's intelligence, vision, and personable nature make him a rare personality in the business world.

His ability to balance professional success with genuine human connections is what truly sets him apart.

Jay is a unique personality in the business world. His intelligence and vision are complemented by a genuine interest in people and their well-being. He is not just a successful businessman but also a person who values relationships and human connection. This combination of professional success and personal warmth makes Jay a truly remarkable individual.

Guy highlights Jay's ability to connect with people from all walks of life, making them feel valued and understood. This quality has been instrumental in building strong, lasting relationships both professionally and personally.

Jay's unique blend of intelligence, vision, and genuine care for others sets him apart as a truly exceptional leader.

Conclusion

Jay Hassan's life is a testament to the power of vision, innovation, and human connection. His journey from a young engineer at IBM to a successful entrepreneur is marked by his unique ability to see the future, connect with people, and turn ideas into reality.

Jay's story serves as an inspiration, highlighting the impact one individual can have on technology, business, and the lives of those around them. Jay's legacy is one of innovation, resilience, and human connection. His journey from IBM to leading his own ventures showcases his ability to envision the future and make it a reality.

Jay Hassan is not just a successful entrepreneur but a unique personality who has left an indelible mark on the people and industries he has touched.

Key Learning Points For Aspiring Entrepreneurs And Future Leaders

- **Build and Nurture Networks:** Jay Hassan's success was greatly aided by his ability to connect with and maintain relationships with a wide range of people, highlighting the importance of networking.

- **Balance Vision with Practicality:** Combining forward-thinking innovation with practical implementation allowed Jay to turn visionary ideas into successful business ventures.

- **Value Loyalty and Trust:** Jay's emphasis on loyalty and trust within his team fostered strong relationships and created a supportive environment, essential for long-term success.

- **Resilience and Adaptability:** Despite setbacks and errors, Jay's resilience and ability to quickly adapt and recover were crucial in navigating challenges and sustaining growth.

An Interview With Durrar Aidrus

Durrar has been Javad Hassan's 'right hand man' for over twenty-five years.

The Revolutionary Entrepreneur:
The Remarkable Journey Of Javad Hassan
A Legacy Of Innovation

Javad Hassan's entrepreneurial journey is a testament to his unwavering dedication and relentless pursuit of innovation. Through the words of his close associate, Durrar Aidrus, we gain insight into the myriad of ventures Javad spearheaded, each reflecting his unique blend of shrewd business acumen, technical expertise, and an indomitable spirit. Durrar's admiration for Javad is evident in every anecdote, revealing a leader who inspires through action and foresight.

AM Technologies:
Pioneering Field Service Automation

In Quakertown, Javad took on the challenge of AM Technologies, a company focused on monitoring and field service automation. The company, founded by the brothers Ashraf and Maqbool, initially struggled under mismanagement. Despite early setbacks, including a brief and tumultuous collaboration with Mr. Maqbool, Javad's vision remained steadfast. Durrar recalls how Maqbool's extravagant and unnecessary expenses, such as purchasing 100 pickup trucks, almost derailed the company.

However, Javad's decisive leadership turned the situation around, showcasing his ability to navigate and rectify challenging business environments.

AM Technologies specialized in field service automation, deploying trucks to monitor and repair cable networks. Javad saw potential in centralizing and streamlining these operations. Under his guidance, the company developed a more efficient system for field monitoring, setting the stage for future ventures in technology and service automation.

ECL Technology: Revolutionizing Communication

Javad's foresight was evident in his venture into communication technology with ECell Technology. Partnering with experts from India, he developed a groundbreaking technology called "Cells in Frames," aimed at revolutionizing communication through sophisticated coding and packet switching. This project highlighted Javad's commitment to pioneering new technologies and his ability to secure significant investments, such as the notable support from investor David.

Durrar fondly recalls the ambitious nature of the project and Javad's relentless pursuit of excellence. "He saw potential where others saw obstacles," Durrar says. "He wasn't just thinking about the present; he was always a step ahead, envisioning the future of communication technology."

Nestronix: The Lean, Mean Profit Machine

Javad's approach to business was not limited to large-scale operations. Nestronix, run by a competent manager, became a model of efficiency with minimal overheads and substantial profitability. This venture, along with the profitable acquisition of a company in France managed by Michel Privat, underscored Javad's knack for identifying and nurturing lean, profitable businesses.

"JH knew how to make the most out of every opportunity," Durrar notes. "He could see value where others couldn't, and his ability to turn around struggling businesses was remarkable."

Nihon NeST: Conquering The Japanese Market

Venturing into Japan, Javad established Nihon NeST, a software solutions provider catering to giants like Toshiba and Hitachi. Starting from scratch, he meticulously built the company, navigating language barriers and cultural differences to achieve remarkable financial success. Durrar remembers the challenges they faced, especially with the language barrier and the intricacies of Japanese business culture. Despite these hurdles, Javad's determination and strategic thinking led Nihon NeST to thrive.

Eventually, Nihon NeST was packaged and sold to Quest, marking another successful exit for Javad. "It wasn't just about making money," Durrar explains. "For JH, it was about building something impactful, something that could stand the test of time."

Opterna: Leading The Fiber Optics Revolution

One of Javad's most significant ventures was Opterna, a company he built from the ground up to address the burgeoning demand for fiber optics technology. Securing a major contract with Verizon, Opterna developed innovative products like FTTH (Fiber to the Home) systems.

Javad's hands-on approach and collaboration with talented individuals like Atikam ensured the company's success.

Durrar vividly recalls a particular incident involving a fiber optic box delivery to Verizon that encountered issues. "There was a malfunction, and JH, along with Atikam, brainstormed tirelessly to identify the problem. It turned out to be a small grommet issue. JH's hands-on involvement was crucial in resolving it quickly," Durrar shares.

Opterna's success attracted the attention of Belden, a public company, leading to its acquisition. "JH's ability to see the potential in fiber optics and execute it flawlessly is a testament to his visionary leadership," says Durrar.

NeST Technologies: A Household Name In Kerala

NeST Technologies became synonymous with innovation and success in Kerala, employing thousands and making significant contributions to the local economy. Despite its eventual sale to Quest, the legacy of NeST Technologies and its impact on the community remain a testament to Javad's vision and leadership.

Durrar fondly recalls the company's prominence in Kerala. "NeST was a big deal. You'd see banners at the airport, and everyone knew about it. It employed about 4,000 people, and it was a source of pride for many in Kerala."

SFO: Pioneering Outsourcing Solutions

In 1998, Javad's foresight led to the creation of Sun Fibre Optics (SFO), a company that revolutionized outsourcing in the semiconductor industry. By convincing major companies like AMP to embrace outsourcing, Javad demonstrated his ability to identify and capitalize on emerging trends, establishing SFO as a key player in the market.

Durrar highlights Javad's role as a pioneer in outsourcing. "He saw the potential of outsourcing long before it became a trend. His ability to foresee market trends and convince major companies to adopt these practices was remarkable."

Neestream: Transforming Media And Entertainment

Javad's entrepreneurial spirit extended beyond technology into media and entertainment with Neestream. Focused on providing unfiltered news and high-quality Malayalam movies, Neestream quickly gained popularity, showcasing Javad's versatility and his commitment to addressing diverse market needs.

"Neestream was another example of his ability to adapt and innovate," Durrar says. "He saw the need for honest news and quality entertainment, and he filled that gap with Neestream."

A Mind Always Thinking Forward

Javad Hassan's career is marked by his relentless pursuit of new opportunities and his ability to adapt and thrive in various industries. His ventures, whether in technology, communications, or media, reflect a visionary mindset and an unwavering dedication to innovation. Through hard work, strategic thinking, and an innate ability to inspire those around him, Javad has built an impressive legacy that continues to influence and inspire.

"He is always thinking ahead," Durrar notes. "His mind is constantly buzzing with new ideas. He's always looking for the next big opportunity."

Hands-On Leadership And Unmatched Dedication

Javad's hands-on approach to business, combined with his sharp financial acumen, set him apart as a leader. He was deeply involved in the operations of his companies, ensuring that every detail was meticulously managed. His ability to recall intricate financial details and his insistence on thorough accountability made him a respected and sometimes feared figure in the business world.

Durrar shares an anecdote that highlights Javad's meticulous nature. "If you told him a number, he'd remember it. And if you came back with a different number later, he'd call you out on it. His attention to detail was unparalleled."

The Joy Of Work: A Life Fueled By Passion

For Javad, work is not just a means to an end; it is his passion. He derives immense joy from his entrepreneurial endeavors, often stating that work is his form of enjoyment. This relentless drive and love for what he does are key factors in his numerous successes and his ability to overcome any setbacks with grace and determination.

"He always says that work is his enjoyment," Durrar recalls. "He never gets tired of it. His passion for what he does is evident in everything he undertakes."

Constantly Innovating: The Drive To Diversify

Javad's mind is always buzzing with new ideas.

His ventures into AI and other cutting-edge technologies demonstrate his constant desire to stay ahead of the curve. This drive to innovate and diversify ensures that he is never complacent, always looking for the next big opportunity to seize.

"JH is always thinking about what's next," Durrar says. "He never settles. He's always looking for the next big thing, whether it's AI or something else."

A Visionary Leader Ahead Of His Time

Javad Hassan is truly a visionary leader, always ahead of his time. His ability to foresee market trends, coupled with his strategic thinking, allows him to build a diverse and successful portfolio of companies. His legacy is one of constant growth, adaptation, and an unwavering commitment to excellence.

Through the eyes of Durrar Aidrus, we see a portrait of a man whose energy, dedication, and innovative spirit have left an indelible mark on the world of entrepreneurship. Javad Hassan's journey is a powerful reminder of what can be achieved through hard work, strategic thinking, and a relentless pursuit of one's passions. "You've got to give credit to this man," Durrar concludes. "The energy, the dedication, it's incredible. There aren't many like him around."

Javad Hassan's story is not just about the success of his businesses but also about the qualities that make him a remarkable leader. His passion, dedication, and innovative mindset continue to inspire those around him, leaving a lasting legacy in the world of entrepreneurship.

An Interview With Richard Schatzberg

Richard started working for Javad in late 1990s and is now his Chief Commercial Officer at NeST Technologies

A Visionary Lands In New Jersey

It was the late 1990s. Javad Hassan flew into New Jersey on a corporate jet, the young executive named Richard Schatzberg was there to greet him. At just 24 years old, Richard was the head of marketing and corporate development at the New Jersey Institute of Technology (NJIT), where Javad was set to receive an honorary PhD. Richard recalls their first meeting vividly: "His vision was clear from the start—he wanted to bring world-class American education to Kerala. He believed that education was the key to economic growth, especially in a state with a 100% literacy rate."

Javad's passion for education was evident in his detailed plans and enthusiasm. During the drive from Teterboro Airport, he passionately discussed his vision with Richard. "He was so strategic," Richard remembers. "He saw education as the foundation for economic development in Kerala. His idea was not just to build an institution, but to ignite a movement that would uplift the entire region."

The Unlikely Businessman

Richard, at that time, was balancing his university role with a small IT consulting practice. Javad's assessment of him during their car ride was unexpected but insightful.

"What are you doing at a university? You're a businessman," Javad declared. This comment struck a chord with Richard, who had always seen himself as more than just an academic.

Six months later, Javad called Richard with a life-changing invitation: *"Be at my house on Saturday at 8:30 in the morning."*

The Breakfast That Changed Everything

At Javad's house in Harrisburg, Pennsylvania, Richard met the other three men who would form the core team of Javad's new venture, NeST Technology. Javad's approach was direct and uncompromising. He informed them that they all had to quit their current jobs to join this risky endeavor. "He said, 'I just want you to know, a year from now, only two of you will still be here,'" Richard recalls. This statement wasn't just a prediction; it was a challenge that set the tone for a competitive, high-stakes journey.

Building A Business From Scratch

The four men faced intense competition, but Richard and Robert Smith, one of the team members, found a way to collaborate. "Robert was a hardcore PhD techy guy, and I was the business guy. We realized our skills complemented each other."

This partnership helped them thrive, even as the other two members eventually left the company.

The Birth Of A Global Enterprise

Javad's vision for NeST Technology was grand. He put Richard and the team through rigorous training, which Richard fondly refers to as 'Hassan 101'.

This was an intensive education in business fundamentals, from financial modeling to strategic planning. "The greatest gift of my life was that education," Richard says. "He taught us everything from the ground up, emphasizing the importance of understanding the numbers in our business."

A Leader Who Demanded Excellence

Javad was a tough mentor, but his expectations pushed the team to excel. "He was brilliantly fast and would question you in such a way that he was really evaluating whether you knew your business. If you walked into a meeting unprepared, he would tear you apart," Richard explains. This rigorous approach ensured that only the most capable individuals could thrive at NeST.

Embracing Fearlessness And Innovation

Javad's fearless approach to market opportunities set him apart. "He was always three steps ahead of everyone," Richard notes. Javad's strategy involved building competencies that could be redirected to attack new market opportunities as they arose. This forward-thinking approach allowed NeST to adapt and grow in a rapidly changing industry.

Navigating Early Challenges

In the early days, NeST faced numerous challenges. "India was just getting started from an engineering perspective," Richard recalls. "The first time we brought a major client to India, we had more people sitting at desks than we had engineers." Despite these initial hurdles, Javad's strategic vision and Richard's business acumen helped secure long-term relationships that were crucial for the company's growth.

Balancing Technical Excellence And Business Acumen

Richard and Robert's differing approaches eventually found harmony. "Robert wanted to focus on interesting project work, while I looked for long-term relationships. Over time, he saw the benefits of these relationships," Richard says.

This balance between technical excellence and business acumen became a defining characteristic of NeST Technology.

The Mentor's Final Word

Javad's mentorship left an indelible mark on Richard. "He taught us to never fear making mistakes, as long as they weren't fatal. He was always there to support us, but he demanded excellence."

This combination of freedom, clear objectives, and unwavering support created an environment where Richard and his colleagues could thrive.

Legacy Of A Visionary Leader

Today, Richard looks back on his time with Javad Hassan as the most significant learning experience of his life. "He was a person of integrity and humility, and he inspired those qualities in us," Richard reflects.

Javad's fearless approach to business and his unwavering commitment to excellence continue to influence Richard's career and the success of NeST Technology.

An Interview With Saju Thomas

Saju is Javad Hassan's Head of Finance and has accompanied him through his entrepreneurial journey.

The Genius Of Javad Hassan:
Insights From Saju Thomas Empowering Leadership:
Freedom To Innovate

Saju Thomas, the finance head of Javad Hassan's company, paints a vivid picture of a leader who thrives on empowering his team. Javad's leadership style is rooted in granting freedom and opportunities, allowing his employees to explore new avenues and ideas. Saju recalls a time when he felt the monotony of his role, but Javad's support inspired him to take on new challenges. "One plus point for Chairman working with him is ready to give us freedom and opportunity to try something new," Saju mentions. This empowerment is not just about trust but also about fostering an environment where innovation can flourish. Javad's backing gave Saju the confidence to delve into complex financial markets and derivatives, leading to significant achievements in fund management.

Mastering Finance With Calculated Risks

Javad Hassan's approach to risk management is both bold and calculated. Saju recounts how Javad's confidence in his abilities allowed him to manage high-risk financial structures that yielded impressive returns. "I give all the credit to Mr. Hassan," Saju says, emphasizing how Javad's willingness to take calculated risks has been a cornerstone of his business philosophy. This approach not only empowers his team but also drives exceptional performance. Saju manages a portion of the company's fund and consistently outperforms benchmarks, attributing this success to Javad's strategic risk-taking and trust in his team.

Financial Independence: A Debt-Free Visionary

One of the most striking aspects of Javad's business approach is his aversion to debt. "He knocks on cash," Saju explains, highlighting Javad's preference for funding operations through generated revenue rather than borrowing. This principle ensures financial stability and reflects Javad's desire to maintain control and independence in his business dealings. Unlike many companies that rely heavily on loans, Javad's company operates debt-free, demonstrating a unique financial discipline. This independence allows Javad to make decisions free from external pressures and obligations, a rare and commendable trait in today's business world.

Personal Integrity: A Clear Separation Of Roles

Saju admires Javad's ability to separate personal and professional matters. Despite managing Javad's personal and company finances, Saju maintains a clear boundary, focusing solely on financial aspects. Javad's reluctance to mix personal issues with business decisions exemplifies his integrity and professional discipline. Saju shares, "I always kept a different distance from his personal affairs I manage his personal finance I manage his company's finance but I never got involved is personal stuff." This clear demarcation ensures that personal biases do not influence business decisions, fostering a professional and transparent work environment.

Trust and Autonomy:
Building Confidence Through Empowerment

Javad's trust in his team's capabilities is evident in his approach to management. Saju describes how Javad gradually reduced oversight as he gained confidence in Saju's financial strategies.

"He added more funds... and he actually not interfering anything with that," Saju shares. This autonomy fosters a sense of ownership and responsibility, driving team members to perform at their best. Javad's approach is not just about delegation but about empowering his team to take initiative and make decisions. This trust and autonomy create a dynamic and motivated workforce, capable of achieving outstanding results.

Simple Living, High Thinking: A Humble Lifestyle

Despite his immense success, Javad's lifestyle remains simple and unpretentious. Saju notes, "He lives in a very simple house," indicating that Javad values substance over showmanship. This humility, combined with his financial acumen, sets him apart as a grounded and pragmatic leader. Javad's choice to live modestly despite his wealth reflects a deep understanding of what truly matters. His focus is on meaningful achievements and contributions rather than material possessions, a philosophy that resonates deeply with his team and admirers.

Ethical Leadership: Prioritizing People And Integrity

Javad's people-centric approach is highlighted by his willingness to give second chances and support his team. Saju reflects on Javad's reluctance to dismiss employees at the first sign of trouble, instead providing opportunities for redemption.

"He gives multiple chances. That to be frank with you. I don't really understand why he's doing that," Saju admits. This compassionate leadership style, however, does not compromise on integrity, as Javad remains firm against those who repeatedly breach trust. Javad's ability to balance compassion with firm principles creates a supportive yet accountable work environment.

Shrewd Business Acumen: Unique Validation Methods

Javad's unique approach to validating financial decisions is a testament to his innovative thinking. Saju recounts how Javad often bypasses conventional financial analyses, relying instead on practical outcomes and cash flow assessments. This ability to simplify complex financial data and focus on results underscores Javad's sharp business acumen. Saju shares, "He has his own way of validating all statements or whatever coming in front of him to take a decision or study or understand whatever it is."

This practical, result-oriented approach enables Javad to make informed and effective business decisions quickly and confidently.

Investing In People: Recognizing And Rewarding Talent

Javad's recognition of Saju's contributions through financial incentives illustrates his belief in rewarding merit and hard work. Saju recalls how Javad offered him a percentage of investment profits, a gesture that motivated Saju to strive for excellence.

"He offered me every time. And even though he was not very easy to get money from him," Saju notes. This investment in people is a hallmark of Javad's leadership style, fostering loyalty and dedication within his team.

By recognizing and rewarding talent, Javad ensures that his team remains motivated and committed to achieving their best.

Legacy of Independence: A Self-Made Visionary

Javad's journey from a self-made entrepreneur to a successful business leader is marked by his unwavering commitment to independence and self-reliance. Saju highlights how Javad's avoidance of external funding and his preference for internal growth reflect a deep-seated belief in creating and sustaining success through one's own efforts.

This principle of self-reliance is not just a business strategy but a core value that defines Javad's approach to life and work.

His legacy is one of resilience, innovation, and unwavering independence, inspiring countless others to pursue their dreams with the same determination and integrity.

Conclusion

In summary, Javad Hassan's leadership is characterized by empowerment, integrity, simplicity, and shrewd business practices. His ability to inspire and trust his team, combined with his commitment to financial independence and ethical conduct, makes him a remarkable entrepreneur and a role model for future business leaders. Through the eyes of Saju Thomas, we see a portrait of a leader who is not only successful but deeply principled and profoundly human.

Javad's journey is a testament to the power of trust, integrity, and the relentless pursuit of excellence.

An Interview With Dennis Hayes

Dennis heads up finance for Ashling, one of Javad Hassan's companies.
He has supported Javad on many projects and initiatives.

Javad Hassan: A Visionary Entrepreneur With A Keen Eye For Innovation A Journey Of Acquisitions And Growth

Dennis Hayes, the finance head of Ashling Microsystems, speaks highly of Javad Hassan, an entrepreneur with a remarkable ability to turn businesses around. Dennis first met Javad in 2006 when Javad acquired Ashling Microsystems, where Dennis had been working since 2002. Over the years, Dennis has observed Javad's business acumen and unique leadership style across various companies in Europe and beyond. This journey has not only showcased Javad's business prowess but also his commitment to growth and innovation.

The Master Of Financial Acumen

One of the most striking aspects of Javad's leadership is his exceptional financial insight. Dennis recounts how Javad could assess a company's health with just a few key financial metrics. Javad's ability to cut through complex financial reports and focus on essential numbers like cash flow, payroll costs, and gross margin is a testament to his sharp business mind. This skill has enabled him to make swift, strategic decisions that have driven the success of many ventures.

His financial acumen is not just about understanding numbers but about seeing the bigger picture and making informed decisions that propel the company forward.

A Global Entrepreneur With A Local Touch

Javad's business activities are not confined to a single region. He has expanded his enterprises across Europe, including ventures in Sweden, Germany, Tunisia, Dubai, India, and France. Dennis highlights how Javad managed to grow a small company in Milton Keynes into a multinational entity, eventually packaging and selling it profitably. This global perspective, combined with his attention to local details, has made Javad a formidable force in the business world.

His ability to navigate different markets, understand local business environments, and adapt strategies accordingly has been crucial to his success.

An Eye For Innovation And Sizzle

Javad's passion for innovation is evident in his approach to acquisitions. He seeks out companies that offer something unique and exciting. For instance, his purchase of a Swedish company involved in cutting-edge laser technology was driven by the impressive, high-tech environment of the company's cleanrooms. Javad believes that a company's sizzle—the impressive, tangible aspects of its operations—can be a significant draw for potential partners and customers.

This focus on innovation and the 'wow' factor sets Javad apart from many entrepreneurs who might only look at the bottom line.

A Risk-Taker With A Strategic Vision

Dennis describes Javad as a fearless risk-taker who is willing to invest in new and innovative ideas. Whether it's fiber optics, embedded software, or other high-tech industries, Javad's willingness to take calculated risks has paid off. His strategic vision allows him to see the potential in niche markets and unique technologies, making him a pioneer in various fields.

Javad's risk-taking is not about reckless gambles but about informed, strategic moves that align with his vision for the future.

The Personal Touch In Business

Despite his business success, Javad values personal relationships and trust. Dennis shares anecdotes of traveling with Javad, including memorable trips to France and Italy, where they stayed in luxurious hotels and enjoyed fine dining. These personal interactions have strengthened their professional bond, highlighting Javad's ability to balance business with genuine human connection.

His approachability and the genuine interest he takes in people around him make him a beloved figure among his colleagues and partners.

The Charismatic Leader

Javad's charisma extends beyond boardrooms and business meetings. Dennis recounts how Javad's friendly and disarming nature makes him approachable to strangers, from fellow travelers on the Eurostar to waitstaff in cafes. This ability to connect with people on a personal level is a key part of his leadership style, fostering loyalty and trust among his colleagues and business partners. His charm and ease in social interactions help in building strong networks and alliances, which are invaluable in the business world.

Turning Challenges Into Opportunities

Javad's tenure with Ashling Microsystems showcases his resilience and strategic thinking. The company, founded in 1982 and struggling for many years, has seen a turnaround under Javad's guidance. By making tough decisions, such as downsizing and focusing on core competencies, Javad and his team have steadied the ship and positioned Ashling for future growth. His ability to navigate through crises, make difficult decisions, and steer the company towards stability and growth is a testament to his leadership.

A Legacy Of Success

Javad Hassan's journey as an entrepreneur is marked by his keen financial insight, innovative spirit, and ability to connect with people. His leadership has transformed numerous companies, turning challenges into opportunities and ensuring long-term success. As Dennis Hayes's accounts reveal, Javad's unique blend of strategic vision and personal touch makes him a truly remarkable figure in the world of business.

Inspirational Leadership And Human Connection

Javad's story is not just about business success but also about inspirational leadership. He inspires those around him to strive for excellence and to believe in their potential. His human touch, his ability to connect deeply with people, and his knack for recognizing talent and potential are integral parts of his success. Whether it's a casual conversation with a stranger or a strategic business meeting, Javad's genuine interest in people and his ability to inspire trust and loyalty make him an exceptional leader.

The Art Of Strategic Decision-Making

Another crucial aspect of Javad's leadership is his strategic decision-making. He has an innate ability to see the potential in businesses and make decisions that might seem risky to others but are based on a deep understanding of the market and the business environment. His decisions are not impulsive but are backed by thorough analysis and a clear vision of the future. This ability to make the right strategic moves at the right time has been a significant factor in his success.

Nurturing Innovation And Creativity

Javad fosters a culture of innovation and creativity within his companies. He encourages his teams to think outside the box and come up with innovative solutions to problems. His support for research and development, as seen in the Swedish laser technology company, reflects his belief in the power of innovation to drive business success. By creating an environment where creativity is valued and nurtured, Javad ensures that his companies stay ahead of the curve.

Commitment To Excellence

Javad's commitment to excellence is evident in everything he does. He sets high standards for himself and his teams and strives to achieve them.

This commitment is not just about achieving business goals but also about personal growth and development. Javad believes in continuous learning and improvement, and this philosophy is reflected in his approach to business and life.

Building A Lasting Legacy

Javad Hassan is building a legacy that goes beyond business success. He is creating a lasting impact on the people he works with, the industries he is involved in, and the communities he serves. His leadership style, which combines strategic vision, innovation, financial acumen, and a personal touch, is a model for aspiring entrepreneurs.

Javad's story is one of perseverance, ingenuity, and the power of human connection, and it will continue to inspire future generations of business leaders.

In summary, Javad Hassan's story is one of vision, innovation, and relentless pursuit of excellence.

His ability to see potential where others see problems, combined with his genuine interest in people, has cemented his legacy as a successful and respected entrepreneur. Through his journey, Javad has shown that with the right combination of skills, mindset, and heart, extraordinary success is achievable.

An Interview With Joseph Abraham

Joseph looks after strategic business advancement for Javad Hassan's group of companies.

The Multifaceted Brilliance Of Javad K Hassan: Insights From Joseph Abraham
An Unforgettable First Encounter

Joseph Abraham first met Javad Hassan in September 2000 at a dinner party. Over glasses of wine, Javad mesmerized the guests with stories of his ventures after leaving IBM and AMP. His knack for quickly understanding how Joseph could assist in his business expansion was both impressive and memorable. This initial meeting was the beginning of a deep and insightful relationship.

A Master Of Strategy And Intelligence

Javad's intelligence is striking, and his strategic brilliance shines in every interaction. Joseph recalls how Javad assesses people quickly, making them feel like they are leaders of their own domains.

Javad's knowledge covers politics, science, religion, arts, and business, making him a formidable figure in any conversation.

Anecdote: The Sharp Evaluator

Joseph shared a story about a business presentation where Javad's sharp evaluation skills were on full display. During a pitch, Javad asked pointed questions that quickly revealed the presenter's lack of depth. The presenter, thinking they were impressing Javad with new information, didn't realize that Javad already knew more about the topic. This ability to stay several steps ahead is a hallmark of Javad's strategic acumen.

Compassionate Yet Calculated

Javad's compassion extends to both his personal and professional life. He often loans money to those in need and supports his team members during tough times. However, this compassion is balanced with sharp business acumen. Joseph describes Javad as someone who can be positively manipulative, ensuring the best outcomes for his ventures.

Anecdote: Strategic Investment in Cybersecurity

A notable example of Javad's calculated compassion is his approach to investing in a cybersecurity company. Instead of pouring in large sums directly, Javad offered the company office space in exchange for shares. This strategic move ensured he had a stake in the company's success without risking significant capital. This anecdote highlights Javad's ability to combine generosity with shrewd business decisions.

A Family Man At Heart

Despite an outward appearance that might suggest otherwise, Javad is deeply committed to his family. His love for his daughters, grandchildren, and siblings is profound. Joseph notes that Javad often speaks fondly of his family and is generous with his wealth, donating properties to family members and ensuring their well-being.

Anecdote: Generosity Towards Family

Joseph recounts an instance where Javad offered prime properties to his nephews. This act of generosity underscores his commitment to family and his desire to share his success with loved ones. Despite his immense wealth, Javad remains grounded and focused on the well-being of his family.

An Aesthetic Frugality

Javad's appreciation for the finer things in life is evident in his exquisite taste for décor and fine whiskey. However, he practices an aesthetic frugality, despising wastefulness and ensuring maximum use of resources. This practical approach is a hallmark of his personality, blending luxury with sensible living.

Anecdote: The Frugal Businessman

Joseph shares a quirky yet telling detail about Javad's frugality. Javad is known to make full use of paper towels before discarding them. This small habit reflects his broader approach to life: appreciating quality while avoiding unnecessary waste. His ability to balance luxury with practicality is a defining characteristic.

A Reluctant Public Figure

Javad prefers to operate under the radar, avoiding the limelight despite his immense success. He enjoys intimate gatherings over crowded parties and values meaningful conversations on diverse topics. His extensive knowledge, drawn from reading multiple newspapers daily, keeps him well-informed and sharp.

Anecdote: The Private Intellectual

Joseph describes Javad as someone who thrives in intimate settings where deep, intellectual conversations can flourish. He avoids crowded parties, preferring the company of a few close friends with whom he can discuss politics, science, and the arts.

This preference for privacy and depth over public recognition is a key aspect of his personality.

Precision In Business

Javad's business acumen is precise and decisive. He quickly identifies bad ideas and is unafraid to admit mistakes, a rare quality among successful entrepreneurs. His willingness to gamble on high-return investments has led to both successes and failures, but his ability to pivot and learn from these experiences sets him apart.

Anecdote: The Decisive Leader

Joseph recalls a time when Javad made a swift decision to divest from a failing venture. Despite the potential backlash, Javad's ability to admit his mistake and take corrective action saved the company from further losses. This decisiveness, combined with his willingness to learn from failures, distinguishes him as a leader.

Leadership And Loyalty

Loyalty is paramount to Javad, and he seldom fires employees unless absolutely necessary. He values long-term relationships and is tolerant of unproductive periods, believing in the potential for improvement. His leadership style fosters a sense of ownership among his senior team, motivating them to act as leaders within their respective areas.

Anecdote: The Loyal Leader

Joseph shares an example of Javad's loyalty. Despite underperformance from certain team members, Javad chose to invest time and resources into their development rather than letting them go. This commitment to his team fosters a strong sense of loyalty and respect, encouraging employees to strive for excellence.

A Visionary With Foresight

Javad's visionary thinking allows him to anticipate future trends and act accordingly. His investments in IoT, media, and AI platforms demonstrate his ability to foresee technological advancements and capitalize on them. His decision-making process is thorough, often taking time to mull over information before reaching a conclusion.

Anecdote: Betting on IoT

One of the most telling examples of Javad's foresight is his investment in an IoT platform. Despite initial skepticism from his team, Javad's belief in the technology's potential led him to invest $3 million. This gamble paid off as the platform grew, showcasing his ability to see potential where others might not.

A Blend Of Tradition And Modernity

Javad's approach to life combines traditional values with modern thinking. He respects religious practices and is deeply spiritual, yet he keeps his faith private. He values good food, fine décor, and enjoys intellectual pursuits. His frugality and discipline are balanced by his appreciation for quality and comfort.

Anecdote: The Traditionalist

Joseph recounts how Javad yearns for his mother's cooking and enjoys traditional Kerala food. Despite his success and modern lifestyle, he remains connected to his roots. This blend of tradition and modernity is a testament to his balanced approach to life.

An Engaging Conversationalist

Javad is known for his ability to engage in meaningful conversations. He enjoys discussing a wide range of topics, from politics and business to arts and innovation. His ability to keep a conversation interesting and informative makes him a sought-after companion in social settings.

Anecdote: The Conversationalist

Joseph describes a typical evening with Javad, where discussions range from the latest political developments to technological innovations. Javad's ability to weave different topics into a cohesive and engaging conversation highlights his intellectual versatility and charm.

The Essence Of Javad K Hassan

In summary, Javad K Hassan is a complex yet remarkable individual. His blend of intelligence, compassion, frugality, and strategic thinking defines his unique approach to life and business. He is a man who processes thoughts at the speed of light and monetizes value at the speed of sound, embodying the essence of quick thinking, action, and returns.

His story, as told by Joseph Abraham, offers a window into the mind of a visionary leader who continues to inspire those around him.

Section 5

Sabiha

A Soul Mate And The Wind In My Sails

Sabiha

As I settled into my new job at AMP, little did I know that a simple dinner hosted by a colleague would lead to such profound and lasting connections. It was there that I was introduced to Dr. Ali and Sabiha Ahmed, a couple from Pakistan. Who could have guessed the impact that encounter would have on my life?

The richness of our diverse backgrounds laid the foundation for a friendship that blossomed beautifully.

I hailed from Kerala, driven by an entrepreneurial spirit that fueled my career as a business executive. On the other hand, the Ahmeds came from Karachi, Pakistan, bringing with them their own unique experiences and perspectives.

Our friendship was a tapestry woven with threads of vibrant discussions and mutual respect. Despite our contrasting personalities, our bond only grew stronger over time. Ali, with his serene demeanor akin to a tranquil lake, stood in stark contrast to my own energetic and determined nature, reminiscent of a rambunctious ocean. Yet, amidst these differences, a deep connection was forged.

Even after Ali's passing, I still hold him in the highest regard, remembering him fondly as a truly remarkable individual. He may have been quiet and gentle, but his presence left an indelible mark on my life.

I became a regular visitor at the Ahmed residence, finding solace and companionship within their circle of friends, predominantly comprised of doctors.

During times when I was on my own, this community became a sanctuary of social interaction and discovery, introducing me to new faces and forging lasting friendships. In their company, I found a sense of belonging and acceptance that I will always cherish.

It was during this time that I experienced both profound loss and newfound liberation

My parents, Nagoor Rowther and M.M. Khadeeju, were not just parental figures to me; they were my guiding lights, shaping my decisions and aspirations. Their passing, one after the other by 1991, left me utterly devastated. Despite achieving significant success in my professional life throughout the '70s and '80s, including reaching heights in corporate America that many immigrants only dream of, I remained deferential to their opinions. Their approval was paramount to me, and I carefully molded my path to align with their expectations.

The loss of my parents was a blow beyond measure, but amidst the grief, I also felt a subtle liberation. It was as if their departure granted me the freedom to pursue my passions and shape my destiny on my own terms.

Upon first arriving in Harrisburg, I was captivated by the city, envisioning it as the place where I might spend the rest of my days. For most of my decade-long residency in the region, I resided in a quaint townhome on Draymore Court. However, as my attachment to the area deepened, I decided to invest in a more permanent abode. I purchased land and enlisted the services of an architect to design an elaborate residence nestled near Hershey, Pennsylvania, atop a picturesque hill.

While my new home was undeniably comfortable, it lacked the opulence of the sprawling mansion that had characterized my tenure as an IBM executive in Arizona. Nevertheless, it was a testament to my determination and perseverance, qualities that defined not only my pursuit of material success but also my pursuit of love.

As the years passed, I found myself increasingly drawn to Sabiha. What began as a mere intrigue blossomed into a passionate infatuation. I was determined to win her heart, just as I had been determined to succeed in my professional endeavors.

My pursuit of Sabiha mirrored my approach to business – resolute and persistent. I knew what I wanted, and I was willing to work tirelessly to achieve it. Sabiha, however, viewed our relationship through a different lens. While she appreciated our deepening friendship and joyful meetings, she saw it as purely platonic.

Undeterred by her initial reservations, I continued to pursue Sabiha with unwavering determination. And slowly, over time, her fondness for me grew. Yet, despite her growing affection, she still viewed our relationship as purely friendly.

But I refused to be discouraged. My love for Sabiha only fueled my determination to win her heart completely. Just as I had navigated the complexities of my professional life, I was prepared to navigate the complexities of love.

In the tapestry of my life, each thread – from the loss of my parents to the pursuit of love – has woven together to shape the man I am today. And though the road may be fraught with challenges, I face each one with the same unwavering resolve that has guided me thus far.

The year 1998 marked a significant turning point in my professional and personal life. After departing from AMP and acquiring a substantial stake in Quakertown-based, AM Communications, I made the decision to bid farewell to Hummelstown. The daily commute spanning 90 miles from Hummelstown to Quakertown had become increasingly burdensome, prompting me to seek a residence closer to my growing enterprise.

The choice to leave Hummelstown wasn't solely driven by business pragmatism; it was equally motivated by personal aspirations. It presented an opportunity for both myself and Sabiha to embark on a new journey together in a fresh environment.

However, with my departure from AMP and Harrisburg, I found myself in urgent need of infrastructure and support as I transitioned from a corporate executive to an ambitious businessman. It was during this crucial moment that help arrived in the form of a retired Pakistani Air Force veteran, Durrar Aidrus.

Durrar, the son of Sabiha's maternal uncle, brought with him a wealth of experience shaped by his international upbringing. Born in Karachi, Durrar had traversed various professional endeavors before seeking a new challenge. When I extended the invitation for him to join me, he seamlessly assumed the role of my indispensable right-hand man.

I vested in Durrar an extraordinary level of trust and responsibility, involving him in every facet of my professional and personal life. From managing my meals to chauffeuring me around, handling my accounts, and even serving as a director for one of my companies, Durrar was a pillar of support during those early days.

Reflecting on our journey together, Durrar fondly recalls the myriad tasks he undertook for me. His dedication and unwavering support were instrumental in navigating the challenges of entrepreneurship and forging ahead in pursuit of our shared ambitions.

The turn of the millennium ushered in a significant shift in my life, both professionally and personally. After spending a few months in Blue Bell, Sabiha and I came to the conclusion that there were better places suited to our aspirations. Sabiha yearned for a more dynamic environment, and she proposed relocating to the Washington, DC area, where she had a network of friends and access to a vibrant South Asian cultural scene brimming with music, art, and poetry.

For me, the allure of DC lay in its status as the second-largest hub of the IT industry after Silicon Valley. Thus, in 1999, we made the move to McLean, where we have resided in the same house for the past 23 years. Despite engaging in various real estate ventures, including acquiring property along the banks of the Potomac in Mount Vernon, Virginia, and investing in a high-rise apartment in downtown Arlington, McLean remained our primary abode.

In McLean, Sabiha and I embarked on a new chapter of our lives.

The locality provided an ideal backdrop for the beginning of our shared journey. Sabiha, in particular, relished the vibrant South Asian American community that flourished in the region. She rekindled old friendships and forged new connections, rubbing shoulders with diplomats, high-ranking officials of international organizations such as the World Bank and IMF, and intellectuals from various think tanks.

For me, the Washington area presented an opportunity to elevate my corporate infrastructure and attract top talent.

I decided to relocate the corporate headquarters from a modest building in Quakertown to an upscale complex in Northern Virginia. This move wasn't just about changing physical locations; it symbolized a significant leap forward in the scale and prestige of my business operations. The sleek new building in Chantilly, Northern Virginia, served as a prestigious and centralized hub for my corporate endeavors, aligning perfectly with the thriving economic landscape of the Washington metropolitan area.

Throughout this transformative period, Durrar remained by my side, offering invaluable assistance in various capacities. He too relocated to a new apartment near McLean, seamlessly integrating himself into our evolving journey. Durrar's unwavering support and dedication were indispensable as we navigated the challenges and opportunities that lay ahead.

As time moved on I found myself drawn to Sabiha in a tale that epitomized the adage of opposites attracting. Our union was a fusion of two individuals from vastly different worlds, each molded by distinct upbringings that set us apart.

Though both of us hailed from affluent pre-Independent Indian Muslim families, the contrasts in our upbringing were unmistakable. Sabiha's nature, shaped by her lineage and upbringing, held an irresistible allure for me. Her father, a civil servant, and her mother, deeply immersed in Sufism, imparted a unique flavor to her childhood. Growing up amidst the bustling streets of Karachi, the commercial heart of nascent Pakistan, Sabiha's formative years were steeped in a rich tapestry of experiences.

For me, Sabiha exuded an old-world charm that resonated deeply. In her world, expressions of affection flowed effortlessly, reflecting the traditions of North Indian upper-class Muslim society. The nuances of etiquette, embodied in the customs of *aadaab* and *pehle aap*, were second nature to her, a graceful dance of politeness she navigated with ease. These customs were instilled in her by her parents, and discussions around the dinner table often revolved around literature and poetry in both English and Urdu. At the tender age of sixteen, she was gifted *'The Prophet'* by Khalil Gibran, and she was raised with the graceful principles of interaction and living according to elevated morals.

Aadaab, a term signifying respect and politeness, was more than just a greeting; it represented a cultural ethos of deference and courtesy. Saying *aadaab* was a gesture of conveying respect, while *pehle aap*, meaning *'after you'*, encapsulated the essence of humility.

Sabiha's cultured upbringing endowed her with the ability to seamlessly navigate diverse social circles. Whether rubbing shoulders with royalty at the opening of parliament in London or engaging in the humble task of sweeping the floor at the US President's inauguration, she exuded a versatility and humility that could only stem from a upbringing steeped in the highest moral values and life's lessons.

In Sabiha, I found not just a partner, but a reflection of the values and traditions that I held dear. Our differences only served to enrich our relationship, creating a bond that transcended the boundaries of culture and upbringing.

The juxtaposition of Sabiha's benevolent yet humble persona with my own rooted mercantile legacy formed the tapestry of our relationship, blending disparate threads into a harmonious whole.

Sabiha's compassionate nature led her to engage in numerous social welfare causes, from organizing Thanksgiving lunches for the less fortunate at the Church to volunteering at the pulmonary lab at the veterans hospital.

Her innate openness transcended religious boundaries, even leading her to be invited to speak about Islam at the Church in the aftermath of 9/11.

Influenced by her parents' teachings of unity and oneness, Sabiha orchestrated events such as the *'Peace, Love, and Unity in the World'* concert at the Warner Theatre in DC, attended by over 2,000 people. In these endeavors, I played a supportive role, standing by her side and bolstering her initiatives, thereby strengthening our bond.

In stark contrast, my upbringing was firmly rooted in a mercantile legacy entrenched within the confines of a traditional Kerala Muslim family. From an early age, I was groomed to shoulder the responsibilities of caring for my siblings and parents, following a life trajectory meticulously outlined even before my arrival into the world.

My childhood was devoid of overt displays of emotion, shaped by the towering presence of a business magnate grandfather and a police officer father. I embodied the archetype of resilience and unwavering commitment, reflecting the patriarchal legacy handed down through generations.

Within this cultural milieu, vulnerability and emotional expression were perceived as signs of weakness. The stoic environment that enveloped my formative years left little room for tender sentiments or displays of affection. Instead, I was steeped in a culture that prized strength and stoicism above all else.

Yet, despite these differences, Sabiha's compassionate spirit served as a beacon of light, illuminating the path forward.

Together, we navigated the complexities of life, finding solace and strength in our shared values and mutual support. Our union, forged amidst the convergence of disparate backgrounds, exemplified the beauty of harmony in diversity, proving that love knows no boundaries, cultural or otherwise. The intertwining of cultures and the exploration of new horizons marked a transformative chapter in my life, catalyzed by my relationship with Sabiha.

Meeting Sabiha's friends and relatives from Pakistan ignited within me a deep-seated curiosity and fascination for this novel culture. Eager to immerse myself further, I embarked on a journey with her in 1999, traversing the vibrant cities of Karachi, Lahore, and Islamabad. It was during this trip that I had the pleasure of meeting Sabiha's mother, an encounter marked by its warmth and dignity. The allure of Islamabad captivated me, prompting a desire to explore the famous Hunza Valley on my subsequent visit.

A few years later, accompanied by Durrar, I embarked on another voyage to Pakistan, delving deeper into its socio-cultural and economic realities. In the company of Durrar, I gained invaluable insights and had the privilege of meeting prominent figures, including Salman Taseer, the governor of Punjab.

Before bidding farewell to Karachi, I was graciously invited to lunch at Sabiha's mother's house. There, amidst the exchange of ideas and stories, I glimpsed into Sabiha's earlier life in India, a period she held dear. As I prepared to depart, Sabiha's upbringing manifested in her graceful expression of gratitude, moving me to a rare embrace, an act that was somewhat foreign to my accustomed demeanor.

During this period, I found myself profoundly influenced by the musical gatherings at Ali and Sabiha's home. These soirées served as a melting pot of cultures, where melodies from distant lands intertwined harmoniously. Occasionally, my daughter accompanied me, adding another layer of richness to the experience.

Before crossing paths with Sabiha, my interests in art were primarily confined to cinema. Throughout my adult life in the United States, I remained an avid enthusiast of Westerns and the legendary John Wayne. Yet, in the embrace of Sabiha's cultural tapestry, my appreciation for diverse forms of artistic expression blossomed, transcending the boundaries of familiarity and embracing the beauty of cultural exchange.

My journey into the rich tapestry of Indian classical and folk traditions was a gradual evolution, catalyzed by the entrance of Sabiha into my life.

In my youth, I remained relatively indifferent to the nuances of Indian classical music, favoring instead the lighter and more melodious strains of film music. Carnatic music, a staple in my father's repertoire, held little appeal for me, as I gravitated towards popular radio broadcasts like Binaca Geet Mala on Radio Ceylon.

However, with Sabiha, I embarked on a newfound appreciation for cultural dimensions previously unexplored. Sabiha, with her deep-rooted appreciation for North Indian folk, classical music, and the centuries-old Sufi tradition of *qawwali*, served as my musical guide. It was in her company that I first encountered the soul-stirring melodies of Hindustani classical music, including the haunting *dhrupad* and lyrical *ghazal*, not to mention the mesmerizing *qawwali*.

One pivotal moment occurred during a concert organized by Sabiha featuring the renowned Pakistani *ghazal* maestro Mehdi

Hassan in Harrisburg. As I sat in the front row, mesmerized by the performance, I felt a profound connection to the music that transcended language and cultural barriers.

During a subsequent trip to Kerala, I stumbled upon the *ghazals* of the late Malayalam singer Umbai, whose style echoed that of Mehdi Hassan and Ghulam Ali. Enthralled by Umbai's renditions, I eagerly acquired audio cassettes of his music for Sabiha, further deepening our shared appreciation for the art form.

Over time, my fascination with *qawwali* grew exponentially. Originating from the spiritual realms of Sufi shrines in India and Pakistan, *qawwali* captured my heart, particularly through the legendary maestro Nusrat Fateh Ali Khan. My introduction to the sons of Raziuddin, Farid Ayaz and Abu Muhammad, during a visit to Pakistan in the late 1990s further enriched my understanding of this soulful tradition.

Subsequent performances by Ayaz and Muhammad in the intimate setting of our home became cherished traditions, captivating our close circle of friends and family with their soul-stirring renditions. These gatherings transcended cultural and geographical boundaries, fostering a deep sense of connection and appreciation for the transformative power of music.

Today, as a devoted aficionado of *qawwali*, I am grateful for the journey that has led me to embrace the beauty and depth of Indian classical and folk traditions, enriching my life in ways I never imagined possible.

The intertwining of music, business, and profound personal experiences has shaped the journey of my relationship with Sabiha.

Among the musicians we patronize is Humayun Khan, an Afghan-American singer whose illustrious career spans collaborations with maestros such as Ustad Vilayat Khan and Fateh Ali Khan. Sabiha, recognizing his talent, commissioned a recording of Humayun Khan for Neestream, my media platform and first venture into the digital streaming world. With Sabiha's meticulous curation, the program featured the timeless poetry and music of Hazrat Amir Khusrau, the revered 13th-century Sufi poet. Humayun Khan's performances have become a staple at our home in McLean, gracing special occasions like New Year's Eve and other gatherings with his soul-stirring melodies.

As fate would have it, the winter of 2022 brought with it a profound loss with the passing of Dr. Ali Ahmed, Sabiha's husband of fifty years. Sabiha had been a devoted caregiver, providing unwavering support and companionship to Ali throughout his illness. Her weekly journeys from McLean to Lemoyne were a testament to her dedication and love.

Upon Ali's passing, I was there to offer solace and support to Sabiha, bidding farewell to our dear friend as we laid him to rest on a freezing morning. Our bond, forged through years of friendship and shared experiences, provided comfort in the face of grief.

In the summer of 2022, amidst the ebb and flow of life's trials, I made a heartfelt proposition to Sabiha, asking her to be my life companion through marriage. It was a moment imbued with vulnerability and sincerity, a culmination of our journey together and a testament to the enduring strength of our connection.

Section 6

The Early Days (Pre USA)

A Prelude: How My Early Life Emboldened My Leadership And Business Capabilities

This is a prelude and introduction to my early life story and how my family, culture, and strong individuals shaped and fortified me to make my mark in corporate leadership and business.

The Roots Of Resilience And Innovation

My journey in life and indeed to become a successful business man began in Aluva, India, through a fortuitous combination of heritage and repeatedly profound learning experiences. Within a family renowned for its lasting values of persistence and innovation, I was surrounded by examples of determination and leadership that would later influence my approach to business, and life itself, on this earth.

The influence of my parents and grandparents is particularly deep-rooted in the history and culture of Aluva. That influence laid the foundation for my career and prepared me to confront the trials and triumphs of entrepreneurship.

The Transformative Power Of Adaptability: 'The Art Of The Possible'

This is a philosophy that remains with me today. My father, Assanu Nagoor Rawther, learned the value of adaptability and determination after graduating from the police force to become a successful planter. From rule enforcer, he became a cultivator.

He encountered many setbacks, but his ability to reorient and succeed in alternate environments had a lasting impact on me. His entrepreneurial spirit was not so much about making a living as about creating value and seizing opportunity. This was a philosophy that forged my own thinking and awakened in me the spirit of *'The Art of The Possible'*.

My maternal grandfather was as important to my life as my father was in shaping it. Mackar Pillay's daring campaign to break the British-held global monopoly on lemongrass oil was an object lesson in both innovation and visionary thinking. His success was a beacon of what could be done with guts and a forward-looking mindset. Tales of his business triumphs have been passed down to me ever since I can remember." These lessons in how to think strategically and exploit available resources were more educational than mere family lore. He showed me that the key to success is not just hard work but of smart, innovative thinking having courage challenge the status quo.

The discipline in my family is reflected in high standards and meticulousness. This was the beginning of a lifetime habit.

Education was instrumental in my development. It provided the knowledge and critical thinking skills necessary for my future success. From the time I began school at Aluva Arabic School, where this academic discipline became clear to me, to my advanced studies in engineering, each step along the way of my schooling reinforced an important lesson: a good student never stops learning. It was in college that I first learned to appreciate independent thinking and self-reliance, two indispensable qualities for being an entrepreneur.

Serendipity And Strategic Connections

An important lesson for my future came from my childhood background. A chance encounter between my uncle and a judge educated at Yale on a long flight from the USA led to my marriage and, eventually, residency in America. This personal reflection underscores the focus on relationship-building and remaining open to new opportunities. It shows how our friends can help shape our destiny.

A Blueprint For Future Leaders

Summing up these early years, I see that successful entrepreneurship rests on resilience, creativity, discipline, and learning. Drawing on these early lessons, I've faced up to many different challenges and opportunities. They've shaped my corporate philosophy as well as my business strategy. My path into business leadership is a testament to the enduring power of these principles and how they can motivate success across a range of domains and sectors.

This project aims not only to record my own story but also with the hope that those who are to come after may be influenced by it. Persistent striving against setbacks, a tireless quest for new technology, adherence to high standards, and a never-ending desire for knowledge constitute entry into the realm of true ability. Abiding by these principles means that you can cut through the intricate world of business management and make a real mark. This is my entrepreneurial journey, and I hope that others will find inspiration and vital lessons but pursue them in their own way.

How My Early Life Emboldened My Leadership And Business Capabilities

A Heritage Steeped In History: The Roots Of My Upbringing

I entered the world on October 7th, 1940 in Aluva, a town along India's southwest coast rich with cultural significance. My parents, M.M. Khadijoo and Assanu Nagoor Rawther, welcomed me into Kattambli House, one of my maternal grandfather's homes.

Born into a lineage steeped in tradition, I was surrounded by reminders of family legacy from the beginning.

Aluva sat along the Periyar River, its banks bearing witness to eras of various rulers including the Zamorins of Calicut and the royal families of Kochi and Travancore. The town's historical importance and my family's local prominence created an environment steeped in tales of resilience, stewardship, and pioneering spirit.

These formative years, surrounded by a heritage of leadership and entrepreneurial daring instilled in me a profound respect for ancestry and the values it represents. The influence of my forebears' story shaped who I became, preparing me with a sense of duty and vision for what lay ahead.

Identity Through Custom

Several months after my birth, I was named Kuttikkaran Assanu Javad Hassan. This multifaceted title adhered to the conventions of that place and time. Kuttikkaran denoted the neighborhood in Pathanamthitta town where my father's lineage, the Rawthers, had resided through the generations. Assanu was the given name of my paternal grandparent. Hassan, as the surname, paid tribute to Arabic ancestry through a Tamil variation of that esteemed name, commemorating my grandparent.

At five years of age, when I entered the local Aluva Arabic School, the headmaster Achuthan Pillai inscribed my name erroneously as 'Javathu', as 'Javad' was uncommon then. Despite that minor inaccuracy, my formative education there instilled in me a passion for scholarship and shaped who I became.

To carry a name cemented in tradition and heritage connected me not only to predecessors but served constantly to remind me of the values and benchmarks expected. It reinforced the importance of upholding family legacy and honor and striving for excellence in everything I have done.

Foundations Of Knowledge And Humility

Aluva Arabic School was an elementary institution established by my maternal grandfather, Mackar Pillay. Housed in a small building of half a dozen chambers, the four-year curriculum spanned grades one through four. Despite its name, the language of tuition was Malayalam, not Arabic. Besides me, many other boys from my grandfather's (Mackar Pillay) extended clan attended the school. The headmaster, Gopalan Nair, was a tall, lanky teacher renowned for strict discipline. Even though the school was owned by our grandparent, my cousins and I received no preferential treatment from the headmaster or other educators.

Most girls in my village, such as my sister and cousins, went to the small school at the edge of town. It was founded by missionaries decades ago, even my mother had studied there as a young girl.

When I turned ten, I started at the larger academy in the nearby city. Run by foreign nuns. It was there that my English lessons truly began. School days passed unremarkably for the most part, except for the cherished rides into the city. My grandfather's driver, Kurian would ferry all the family children in the old car. The vehicle filled with shrieking kids both thrilled and daunted me. Kurian often imposed discipline in the car, trying to calm everyone down. If ever I stood up from my seat - seatbelts had yet to become mandatory – the driver would warm me loudly to sit straightaway, worried grease from my hair might ruin the upholstery.

Looking back, I see how those years formed who I am. Living under watchful eyes accustomed me to discipline, taught me duty, and showed me respect for authority. Growing up surrounded by such guidance ingrained in me a sense of propriety and determination to do well in all things. Unassuming as they were, that grounding era established the foundation and direction for all that was yet to come.

Shaping Ambition: The Influence Of Role Models

When I was young, I was more inclined to books than sports. Most of my friends would play football or catch in the coconut groves and paddy fields after harvests. I never joined them. Instead, when school was over for the day, I used to prefer spending time at home. Very nearly every day I would run errands or take up one of the many tasks that my mother had always told me needed doing.

On occasion, a friend and I would walk to the famed Marthanda

Varma Bridge which crossed the Periyar river as night fell. We would sit there for an hour or two chatting, watching the Periyar flow on majestically into the Arabian Sea.

My father's ambition for me was to join the Indian Administrative Service (IAS) or Indian Police Service (IPS), the country's two top civil service jobs. Failing that, he would be content if I got any government job that promised lifetime job security and a good pension. Most jobs in the government were within the state: there was no shortage of openings in different departments and offices. During those years, government employment had been the popular choice in our direct and extended families. Several men had high-paying, secure government jobs which meant that they were often seen as the benchmark for success.

At the same time my grandfather, Mackar Pillay, was a leading figure in my life. Often, I did not know which way to turn: should I seek to emulate my grandfather, or fulfil my father's expectations? This battle of ideas within me played a large part in what I became and thought of myself.

I was faced with a unique set of circumstances when my father and grandfather both gave me strong examples to follow in life. My father believed in the vision of civil service as a safe and respected field, while my grandfather had a bold, innovative spirit in trade and business. This dual influence spurred me to have the best of both worlds: the security and stability that comes from a profession while at the same time innovating and being courageous as an entrepreneur.

The Impact Of The Legacy:
Inherited Wisdom And Vision

The Pillays, who were prominent in the Travancore-Cochin region, were my mother's family. My maternal grandfather, Mackar Pillay, was a pioneering businessman and an important political figure. His entrepreneurial spirit and determination to break the British monopoly on trade in lemongrass oil were an inspiration. Such stories about family tradition and business skills deeply influenced my approach to life and gave me endless lessons in fortitude and innovation.

M. Pillay's influence went far beyond the business world, however. Born in 1885, he was junior only to his elder brother N. B. Pillay in a family believed to have descended from the Arab traders of centuries ago. His father, Manadath Kunju, was a planter and trader from Aluva (near Kochi), and his mother was Kunjupathu Manadath Pillai. Mackar Pillay was a well-known political leader from the Muslim community. In 1919, he became president of the Alwaye Panchayat Court, prior to its being absorbed into the Alwaye municipality as the town underwent rapid urbanization. When the Sree Moolam Praja Sabha (Popular Assembly) met in 1921 for one of its first experiments with legislative democracy under a new constitution, he was nominated at its first session. In 1924, he stood for election both to that assembly and its successor body, now known as the Legislative Council, which was transformed from bicameral into unicameral status in 1934. He won seats on both occasions.

Apart from his main concern, Mackar Pillay & Sons set up in the 1920s and chartered by 1941, M. Pillay ran several companies. One of them was the Bank of Alwaye, which he set up in 1942 and which became the leading financial institution of the region. It finally amalgamated with the State Bank of Travancore. (It should be noted that during British rule Aluva was spelled Alwaye.)

Khader Pillay, M. Pillay's elder brother, was born in 1880, and he too, commanded considerable authority. He became the first President of the new Aluva municipality. Khader Pillay was made 'Khan Sahib' by the Viceroy of India Lord Rufus Isaacs in 1925 in recognition of his leadership during the Great Flood of 1924. The flood, also known as the 'Great Flood of' 99' claimed over a thousand lives.

For three years from 1923 to 1926, Khan Sahib was also a member of the Travancore Legislative Council. He served as a member of the Sree Moolam Popular Assembly for 10 years. According to the "Hundred Years of Legislative Bodies in Kerala Centenary Souvenir," for example, he was the first Muslim to be honored with the title 'Khan Saheb' in Travancore Cochin.

Mackar Pillay had ten children with his first wife, Ishumma Tharackandathil. When Ishumma died, he married her younger sister Amina and had another nine children.

In stark contrast to most Muslims of the time, who were traders with a lack of interest in formal education, M. Pillay taught himself English through sheer hard work. He had an extensive library and was a great advocate of female education. He gave a donation to Aligarh Muslim University for the purpose of having women students study there. M. Pillay's first wife's two daughters, Khadijoo and Mariyumma, both went to Madras, then the largest city in southern India. Khadijoo did her matriculation at Madras Women's Christian College, traveling by herself all the way from Aluva to Madras on an overnight train which took about 12 hours. At this time, most conservative parents did not permit their daughters to live away from home or travel alone. This shows the progressive nature of my grandfather, who was willing to challenge the norms for his beliefs.

I imbibed many of these qualities, which have helped shape me and my values.

M. Pillay waited until his daughters reached the age of 18 before finding bridegrooms for them as mentees. And when it came to his future sons-in-law, he had a non-negotiable condition: he would only consider educated Muslim men with government jobs as suitors for Khadijoo and Mariyumma. Being a member of the Sree Moolam Popular Assembly, he was well-connected throughout the Travancore and Cochin regions. Khadijoo (my mother), was in her second year at the Women's Christian College in Madras when she married Assanu Nagoor Rawther (my father), an officer assigned to a police station in Vadakkan Paravoor, a small town close to Aluva. Mariyumma married Unni Mooppan, an officer in the Travancore forest department.

These stories of perseverance, vision, and strategic thinking come from my grandfather, which deeply affected me. They reinforced the importance of education, innovation and vision in achieving success. The Pillay legacy and my experience of their contribution inspired me to aspire to greatness and to make a positive difference in my own life journey.

Lessons in Resilience, Adaptability, And The Entrepreneurial Spirit

1946 was a turning point with the Punnappra-Vayalar uprising. My father, then a police inspector, met a moral dilemma between duty and family when my mother fell ill. The choice of family over duty meant suspension from office and a hard life for him with financial difficulties. My father's fall and subsequent resilience taught me the importance of adaptability and persistence in life.

This trouble originated in workers' movements and the growing dissatisfaction of people with the rule of Sir. C.P. Ramaswami Iyer, powerful Diwan of Travancore who proposed an independent Travancore.

In this conflict, with two villages at the epicenter, Punnapra, and Vayalar, in the vicinity of Cochin.

The government's efforts to suppress the rebellion killed hundreds.

My father was in an awkward position. My mother pregnant, desperately needed medical treatment. Unable to resolve the conflict between his duty as a police officer and his obligations as husband and father, my father chose the latter. He rushed to Thottumugham where my mother was living. This decision, although morally defensible, led to his cession suspended for failure of duty.

The financial difficulties that followed remained with me for a long time. Until that time my father had been someone with authority, a figure to whom people looked up. His sudden unemployment exposed life's weaknesses to me. It made me realize that any place, no matter how high or not humble is in reality impermanent. This experience taught me the importance of resilience and adaptability – assets which were indispensable later in my business career.

My father losing his work and the financial difficulties that ensued, made a strong impact on me. He bought farming land in Puliyanmala. These experiences deepened my understanding that seizing opportunities, despite adversity, leads to success. Every successful person has been diligent and hardworking no matter what the situation and kept a constructive mind, not giving up but finding a way.

Despite the setbacks, my father was not discouraged from reestablishing himself. He was a farmer at heart and able to see a future path. At the suggestion of a friend, Kasim, he invested in a vast tract of virgin forest twenty kilometers west Puliyanmal a. Though the land was largely uncultivated, it had the potential to be developed for profitable cardamom cultivation.

My father paid for the purchase of the estate with my mother's wedding jewelry as collateral. In honor of my mother, he named it Khadija Hill Estate. My father slowly transformed the estate by pursuing cardamom, rubber and coffee; his labor turned this once-forest land into a productive field.

My father's change from a police officer to a successful plantation owner showed his potential for entrepreneurship and survivor character. The ability to change direction when faced with adversity and road-blocks taught me the importance of adaptability and the value of hard work. These were the lessons which became the foundation of my own entrepreneurial journey, shaping my constructive and determined approach to challenges and opportunities.

These experiences made it quite clear to people that no challenge is too great when you put forth all your effort and determination. In the field of agriculture, my father's success was due completely to his perseverance; his strategic thinking always had an impact on me and inspired me to adopt a similar approach in all my business ventures.

The Hidden Will Of Perseverance
– New Horizons And Sheer Graft

My father's foray into agriculture, especially in the rocky, rugged Western Ghats, reflected a deep Wild West streak in him that later had a great impact on me. The success of turning wasteland into a profitable estate planted in me the power of persistence and innovation. He named the estate Khadija Hill Estate after my mother, out of dedication to her, strengthening my family values in life and regard for other people.

My whole approach towards entrepreneurship was shaped by these events.

The tight forests and challenging topography of the Western Ghats posed numerous difficulties. My father frequently made his way on foot through these primeval woods, facing threats from wild beasts and rough weather. Yet throughout all these challenges, he persevered in fulfilling his vision. He constructed a small house on the estate and stayed there for long periods of time to supervise cultivation work.

Love Your Work — Extraordinary Outcomes

This kind of labor of love soon began to yield profit and secure our family's financial position. The main crops grown here were cardamom, rubber and coffee. My father's success owed itself not only to his hard work but also to his spirit of innovation in farming and the sheer love for his work and these crops.

I remember when, many years later, full of my professional knowledge, I queried him on various practical business aspects such as the production costs, margins per square meter of the plantation etc. He asked me to come close to a cardamom plant, held a part of it gently in his hands, and said, "Just give this all your love, and don't worry about the rewards." This lesson has had a profound impact on me. As a result, my focus in my businesses has been the love of innovation and the creation of useful products and technologies that will be valuable to someone, rather than over concern of making money.

Perhaps that is what really made money for me.

Comfort Zones Stifle Progress: Smash Through – Welcome Change

Seeing my father's commitment and innovative spirit in the face of hardship made a deep impression upon me. It taught me that success often arises when one steps out of their comfort zone and welcomes change with open arms. This teaching naturally became part and parcel of my entrepreneurship philosophy, motivating me in turn to find innovative and effective measures for any challenge that came my way.

The Western Ghats experiences made it clear to me that perseverance and novelty are what conquer difficulties. My father's ability to adapt to new situations and find innovative solutions all served as inspiration for me in turning the corner and opening up some new doors in my own journey of life.

The Productive Power Of Collaboration: Building Character

In 1950, we moved to a larger home in Aluva, marking a fresh start. Our family was supposed to take care of a few coconut trees and some banana plants. This became my responsibility. These were further lessons in responsibility and cooperation, essential in any enterprise.

The new home, completed in the late 1930s by my grandfather, was very roomy. On the one-acre plot around it a small farm was established, with coconut trees, banana plants, and some other crops. We children were then assigned all manner of chores, such as cultivating and planting, taking care of cows and so forth.

From these duties, I gained the idea of duty and teamwork. Working together with my siblings to keep up the farm taught me how important it was to work in concert and that everybody could contribute according to their ability towards a common goal. These teachings were decisive indeed as I later shaped my attitude towards work, emphasizing cooperation as well as taking joint responsibility for tasks within a team.

Growing up on our small farm drove home to me the message that success is won by many hands. The traits of responsibility and teamwork that I learned here would prove invaluable in developing my leadership skills, since everyone needed to work together to bring valuable outputs every day for common aims.

Meticulousness And Method

My father's disciplined approach and fanatical dedication to his habits made a profound impression on me. His demand for basic 'cleanliness first' became my own approach to life both professionally and personally. I was brought up in a disciplined environment, and this, too, prepared me for the future.

I learned the art of meticulousness and a sense of method which are essential qualities in business.

My father's habits were precise. He liked eating meals alone and would always sit facing the walls at lunch. He would rest and take a nap after lunch and any interruption would upset him 'whether it be a leaf falling or a cat strolling by.'

I was educated in such a demanding environment of cleanliness and order that the necessity of organization became ingrained into my psyche. My father's high standards for cleanliness and order were transferred to me as part of my attitude towards both life and business. These attributes enabled me in the running of corporations, ensuring effectiveness and efficiency.

Living within such a disciplined framework teaches you the importance of attention to detail and meticulousness.

My father's example and system of living became the mold for my own approach to work, which particularly stressed precision and thoroughness as important elements in being outstanding.

Contribution To The Greater Good: The Importance Of Duty

My parents taught me the importance of duty and obligation. Helping with family chores, especially during the harvest season, taught me to be hardworking and loyal. These experiences strengthened in me the idea of contributing to a larger goal - a key element of successful leadership and business enterprises which I adopted and engendered in my career wholeheartedly.

During the harvest season, the whole family would gather at the fields. We would stay up until late at night, separating the grain from chaff and getting it ready for market. It was labor such as this that taught me to be serviceable and loyal.

I learned that commitment to the group and hard work are the necessary conditions for success. This sense of duty and obligation grew into a guiding principle as I set out on my own business ventures, leading me ultimately as it did to top echelons.

The concepts of duty and responsibility I learned from my parents taught me that real success means contributing to the greater good. These moral values became the cornerstone of my own modus operandi. I believe that dedication, teamwork, and a strong sense of responsibility are absolutely necessary for success.

The Path To Engineering: Developing Analytical Skills

I showed particular ability in mathematics and the sciences in middle school, and that path led me toward engineering. My father avidly read English newspapers and various magazines, which broadened my appreciation and knowledge of things. These early studies of science and mathematics provided me with a firm foundation on which to build my future understanding for computer programming.

I was drawn to engineering for my love of science and math. Finding my true level in these two areas while still in high school set the stage for subsequent studies and professional life. Success as a student reinforced the importance of continuous learning and mental development, two qualities which at the end of the day every successful businessman must possess.

Having a good foundation in science and math thanks to my early education was also the key to cultivating my powers of analysis. These subjects taught me to think critically, and to approach problems in a methodical way. This set the stage both for my eventual success as an engineer and businessman.

College Life And Independence: The Age Of Self-Reliance

Attending Union Christian College (UC College) in Aluva was a significant milestone for me. The relative freedom of college life allowed me to develop independence and self-reliance, virtues essential for every entrepreneur. This was also a time when I learned the links between networking and personal relationships.

UC College was the most illustrious educational institution in Aluva. Fortunately, the relative freedom of college life allowed me to pursue an array of activities and interests.

My political life began: I ran for class representative, and took part in various extracurriculars. Despite failure in the election, it was a priceless experience in developing my skills of communication and understanding leadership dynamics.

From these experiences, I learned the importance of networking and building relationships. The friendships and connections I made in college would prove to be significant assets in the years ahead. This period of self-discovery fostered confidence and self-reliance without which no entrepreneur could possibly hope to succeed.

Leadership training was one of the benefits of these college years spent in independence and self-reliance. Having the freedom to take action as well as responsibilities on my own prepared me for confident independence in my future foreign adventure. My keen advice to is to strive for autonomy and confidence as essential attributes in your journey to success.

Getting admission to the College of Engineering in Trivandrum in 1958 was a huge achievement. The move to Trivandrum, with its colonial buildings and wide promenades, was a liberating experience. Hostel life taught me the importance of independence and managing responsibilities away from home.

This new environment was both demanding and liberating. A challenging academic schedule and the necessity to juggle studies with daily duties prepared me for professional life's demands. These experiences drove home once again how critical it is to be able to fend for oneself: capabilities which are essential for entrepreneurs.

Innovation and adaptability were traits I strengthened in the challenging environment at the College of Engineering. Balancing academics and daily responsibilities prepared me for the complexities of the professional world. They emphasized the value of creative problem-solving and strategic thinking.

Mastering The Environment:
Strategic Planning/Optimizing Resources

When I was in college, I learned that by mastering your environment, you could make the most of both - academics and extracurricular activities.

This approach to mastering the environment became one of my guiding principles in business ventures: adapting to circumstances and taking the long view. The rigorous curriculum and competitiveness at the College of Engineering demanded strategic time and resource planning. Thus, I managed to balance academics with social activities, meeting my academic goals while also making valuable contacts.

Whether navigating market challenges or building teams, the ability to adapt and strategically plan became central to my success. These lessons were fundamental in my development into an entrepreneur.

Outsourcing And Innovation:
Leveraging Talent For Growth

To make the most of my demanding studies and devote time to social activities, I took to outsourcing various academic assignments to appropriate fellow students. This early-stage delegation showed me how to farm out work and optimize my work and life efficiency. Managing people is an art form. Many years later I would recognize this as a valuable lesson in the importance of leveraging talent and managing teams.

Years later, I understood such formative experiences subconsciously offered a lesson in innovation and resource management. The ability to delegate and leverage people's talents became part of my leadership approach.

These experiences showed the significance of strategic thinking and getting the most out of your resources, which can be called entrepreneurship. They were lessons in innovation and effective resource management taught through delegation and leveraging talent early on. These skills became indispensable for my entrepreneurial career, underscoring the importance of cooperation and delegation as strategy for growth.

First Job – Finding Direction And Passion

I found my first job as a graduate in 1962 at Fertilizers and Chemicals Travancore Limited (FACT). Although it was a government post, I found the work too easy.

This discovery prompted me to look for opportunities among private companies to make sure I was working in line with my passions and areas of competency. FACT was located just five miles from home. It was convenient but unfulfilling in a job that lacked the challenge and excitement I wanted. This early experience taught me that it is important to work in areas that fulfill both - your interests and capabilities. It also stressed pursuing challenges and new opportunities, a principle that would guide my career decisions in the future. As a guiding principle of my entrepreneurial pursuit, it highlighted the value of working on something both challenging and rewarding. That realization changed the course of my career.

Pursuing meaningful work that both inspires and challenges you. Which explains why I became an entrepreneur.

Open Minded Learning:
Hindustan Machine Tools (HMT)

Joining Hindustan Machine Tools (HMT) in Bangalore in 1963 was a turning point. Nine months of intensive training, exposure to all sorts of machine operations and their organization greatly broadened my technical skills and understanding of industrial processes. This period of continuous learning and training was essential for innovation-driven leadership.

At HMT I underwent an apprenticeship, which included learning to operate drilling machines, milling machines and lathe. By putting what I had learned to use in practice, this apprenticeship broadened my technical skills and deepened my understanding of industrial processes. Exposure to these advanced machines as well as knowledge of the production practice — derived from practice rather than book learning — were invaluable in shaping my frame of mind.

Continuous learning and skill development during that time taught me that curiosity and open-mindedness are crucial. Practice plays a more important part and practical application of knowledge is more valuable than anything else for a leader in an innovation-driven era. This became my whole approach to doing business: the value of technical expertise and the need for constant improvement.

It was through the experience at HMT I realized just how important technical expertise and continuous learning are. These then became the essential points in my leadership approach, emphasizing need for curiosity and continuous new knowledge acquisition which are the guiding principles of creativity and change.

The Transatlantic Match:
Power In Serendipity If You Act On It

In September 1962, while my uncle Abdul Hameed Pillay was on a flight from London to New York he met Noor Mohammed, a Yale-educated lawyer serving as a judge in the Somali Republic. During the journey, their conversation moved on to family subjects, and they exchanged ideas about possible matches for their children. In passing, my uncle said that he had a nephew who had just finished his studies at an engineering college. Noor Mohammed, in turn, said that he had a daughter, Meher Banu.

This meeting of pure chance led to our 1965 marriage. Meher was well educated with a family background. Who knew then that Noor Mohammed would be instrumental in my moving to the USA. That meeting on the flight underscored for me the need to build contacts and take opportunities that come by. Besides bringing home a lesson about the importance of serendipity in life overall, it also demonstrated that we should not close ourselves off from any chance. Meaningful relationships can help with mutual benefits - materially or emotionally.

A New Family And Responsibilities:
Balancing Aspirations And Commitments

Meher and I started our family at Aluva. The birth of our daughter Hafiza in Mogadishu in 1966 marked the beginning of an extremely important phase. Finding balance between family responsibilities and professional ambitions stressed the need for work-life balance.

After Meher became pregnant, we decided she should give birth in Mogadishu, following the tradition of daughters having their babies in their parents' home. Our daughter Hafiza was born in January 1966 in Mogadishu, delivered by her maternal grandmother.

A Burgeoning Entrepreneur From An Early Age

Reflecting on my childhood, a series of influential events and conditions have shaped my entrepreneurial mindset. The resilience and business acumen of my father, the spirit of entrepreneurship possessed by my grandfather, and the disciplined atmosphere created within my home together provide a solid foundation for all that I have achieved in business or want to achieve as a leader. People call it luck, but I know that these experiences have influenced me deeply.

Watching my father bounce back from setback time after time allowed me to understand the importance of resilience. His shift from a policeman to a successful agricultural entrepreneur demonstrated the value of adaptability and seizing opportunities. These lessons were key to my own life as an entrepreneur, reminding me to stick it out when things get tough.

Thanks to my grandfather's entrepreneurial success and hard work spirit, I was inspired for a lifetime. Breaking the British monopoly on the lemongrass oil business made him hugely successful. More importantly, it illustrated that with innovation and strategy, any venture can be fully capitalized upon. These lessons have always influenced my thinking in business management, causing me to seek out new brilliance and build strategic opportunities in my enterprises.

That was the family atmosphere in which I grew up. Early impressions were very important in shaping my attitude as an entrepreneur. They settled me on the principle of developing an enterprise step by step, beginning with little things and building them up into bigger ones. At the same time, these ideas formed into my head forever more. If anything went wrong, I blamed no one, not even the circumstances. Instead, I searched for new paths to better destinations.

Lessons In Resilience: Overcoming Adversity

My father's ability to come back from adversity has taught me first-hand the importance of resilience. Just as he had moved from being a police officer to a successful planter, so did the act of seizing chance and adapting to succeed in life. These were lessons which stuck with me all through my entrepreneurial career, and highlight that challenges must be faced and will not vanish without an effort made to conquer them.

My father's experience serves as an example of his determination and resilience. Even after losing the job of policeman, by embracing change he entered into agriculture which had been new to him. He turned a bad piece of barren land into prosperous estate: this success was all about perseverance and adaptability.

These experiences taught me that while setbacks are inevitable they also can be overcome by perseverance. This is what got me through. The most important characteristic in my entrepreneurial career has always been to be adaptable and persistent, with a mind like an antenna seeking out new possibilities (no matter what route they take you on). These lessons have hammered home the need for resilience and adaptability if one is to win out over long term.

The ability to fight back against adversity with grit and tenacity became the main tenets of my entrepreneurial mission. These lessons showed the value of perseverance through tough times, to stay on your course no matter what storm might blow up outside - and always inspired me in some way or other, however difficult it sometimes had been.

Innovation And Resourcefulness: Driving Success Through Creativity

My grandfather's skill in breaking the British monopoly on lemongrass oil drove home to me the importance of innovation and resourcefulness. Both his business success and his accomplishments in politics constantly reminded me what visionary leadership and strategic thinking can achieve.

Mackar Pillay's success in entrepreneurship was a storybook tale of how innovation combined with resourcefulness pays off. He successfully broke the lemongrass oil monopoly held by British companies. He was even nicknamed 'King of Lemongrass'. His ability to identify target markets and devise solutions totally from scratch was an exemplary model for success.

I was inspired by these stories of creativity and frugality to build my own business. They presented me with a new philosophy for doing business, stressing the importance of strategic thinking and how to spot opportunities. It became the essence of my entrepreneurial philosophy to learn from the above lessons, so I sought innovative answers and grasped opportunities where they presented themselves. This is when I honed my belief in *'The Art of the Possible'*.

Innovation and frugality thus became the theme tunes in my life. These served to remind me of the importance of creativity and strategic thinking in achieving success.

Visionary leadership was required to put these lessons to use creatively rather than continuing with old routines.

The Secret To Efficiency Is Discipline And Organisation

Optimization was practiced at home, especially by my father, so I learned the importance of discipline and organization. These qualities served me vitally in business practice and economic achievement: I needed organized operations and efficient management.

My father's models and his strict standards for cleanliness taught me many lessons. His disciplined way of life showed me the need for order and attention to detail. That became part of my own character and then my business ethos.

Discipline and organization proved very important for success in business. Organized operations and high efficiency were essential to achievement. These lessons taught me a lot about the importance of putting discipline and perfectionism into practice in business field of activities. It became a matter of course for me to have high standards and work efficiently. The importance of discipline and thoroughness in leadership was essential.

Empowering Leadership Is Based On Independence And Self-Reliance

Independence and self-reliance, both crucial in building a prosperous life, were the lessons college taught me. This period of self-discovery had to be experienced in order to gain the confidence needed to free oneself from a steady job and underpin later success as an entrepreneur. When in college, living away from home became a good chance to develop self-reliance and independence. The freedom that came with the arrival of life at university, with the opportunity to make one's own decisions and carry out your responsibilities as you wished, was a liberating experience.

These experiences helped me to realize confidence and independence are crucial in pursuing an entrepreneurial career. Making decisions and accepting responsibility were vital qualities during my journey along this path; these are lessons that have driven home the value of self-reliance and independence.

The power in being self-reliant and making one's own decisions was extremely formative for me to develop leadership. These lessons underscored the vital importance of confidence and independence in solving problems and achieving success by enterprise.

Strategic Networking: Developing Opportunities Through Relationships

My marriage resulted from a chance meeting, which later played a major role in my move to the USA, building a leadership career, and establishing my business ventures. It's called strategic networking.

For me, as I went along this journey it became clear that networking and building relationships are the order of life. They served me well as a student in college, and then in my career and business journey. The fortuitous meeting on a trans-Atlantic flight between my uncle and Noor Mohammed both led to marriage and highlighted the virtues of networking.

These experiences taught me that strategic networking is vital in expanding business ventures and opening up new markets to explore. Building and maintaining relationships is indispensable to achieving success and a critical element in the field of entrepreneurship.

Achieving Harmony And Fulfilment: Work-Life Balance

As I attempted to balance my family responsibilities with professional aspirations, I began to realize the importance of work-life balance. A supporting family environment and the ability to manage both personal and professional commitments well are essential for long-term performance.

Balancing the duties of a businessman and a family member was a challenge, but also rewarding. Happily, on both scores, I maintained an equilibrium and it has played a big role in my success

With that balance, I was able to achieve harmony and satisfaction in life. These remarks confirm the importance of the harmonizing function; they also underline just how complex this function is. Role balance is particularly vital to our growth and true success, symbiotically enriching our lives.

The Cornerstones of Future Success – Continuous Learning: To Embrace Open Knowledge For Growth

My experiences at various educational and professional stages of development served to reiterate the importance of lifelong learning. Personal experience also teaches that this is so - no matter where I was, in school or at work, the act of staying a learner became essential.

These experiences corroborated the argument for lifelong learning as the principal vehicle of innovation and advancement. Being capable of adjustment, adaptation, and, therefore, capitalization was a guiding principle in my corporate and business career. They underlined the importance of curiosity per se and of making sincere attempts to be better in all aspects. Knowledge is a continuous process, and those who can harness its power will always thrive.

The commitment to continuous learning is essential to promoting innovation and fostering growth. These observations underscore the importance of being curious and keeping up with new knowledge as well as the value of constant improvement in achieving success.

Leveraging Talent: Building Effective Teams

The early portions of my education included outsourcing some of my assignments to classmates. As a student, I learned the importance of team organization and getting things done effectively by leveraging talent. Building a capable and motivated team became one of my management goals, thus we were even more successful.

My experiences taught me the importance of strategic thinking and effective resource allocation. Excellent management of talent and people became a part of my leadership style. They also showed how teamwork and cooperation are essential to success.

Leveraging talent and building effective teams were crucial to greater success. That meant if you could get others to do your work, and they are amply able, you should go ahead and delegate. That way it will free up your capacity along with your abilities to concentrate on the things you are good at and as a result produce significantly greater results.

Visionary Leadership:
Pioneering Change And Innovation

My grandfather's entrepreneurship and vision also inspired a business approach that plans for the future. I work to keep up to date with change, to respond to market trends and above all else to innovate.

My grandfather, who was always an inspiration, encouraged me to develop a forward-looking vision. His talent was in finding opportunities and providing solutions that no one else would think of. He had a major influence in shaping my approach to business.

These lessons helped me realize the relationship between visionary leadership and strategic thinking within innovation. Welcoming novelty, looking to market trends, and constantly innovating were all key facets of my management philosophy. They showed me that forward-looking leadership is indispensable if we are going to achieve long-term success.

The pursuit of visionary leadership is necessary to bring change and innovation. The importance of strategic foresight, reading market trends and innovation while examining how changes in these areas provide brilliant opportunities is advanced thinking. It raises the odds of producing incredible results and heights of achievement.

Adjusting Course And Persevering When There Are Problems

In my entrepreneurial journey, the ability to adapt in the face of new and unexpected difficulties and stick to one's guns amidst downfalls have become two essentials. These two qualities enabled me to resolve dilemmas and snare opportunities, thus ensuring smooth resolutions and continuous growth. The early experiences of watching my father possess tenacity and flexibility made me aware that these characteristics were important.

These lessons not only symbolize the importance of tenacity but also show the ability to adapt to new circumstances when things suddenly change. They proved that, in entrepreneurial endeavors, tenacity and adaptability must be cultivated.

And every step of the way, the value of keeping your spirits up in adversity and facing up to changes is something you cannot put a price on in terms of progress or final success.

A Message For Aspiring Entrepreneurs And Future Leaders: Accept And Champion Your Journey

Reviewing the course of my career, many lessons learned from both past events and experiences that molded my thinking can encourage and guide future leaders as well as young businessmen. Perseverance, innovation, discipline, and constant pursuit of knowledge are always required to achieve success in whatever field we pursue.

When I think of my personal journey, what I find is that the valuable lessons and experiences that made me can also be instructive for future leaders or for those who are starting their own businesses. The spirit of perseverance, innovation, discipline, and the ability to keep learning continuously are paramount in reaching and even surpassing your goals.

The learnings display the importance of maintaining your curiosity even when young, that you should work in a way to maximize your time and productivity by utilizing the potential of people around you and also to keep a true balance between work and other areas of your life. Leverage successes and defeats, sailing into new waters. It is only with resilience and perseverance, that we can hope to achieve significant and durable success. These experiences are valuable references for aspiring entrepreneurs and future leaders.

The message that future business 'people' should take away is to be resilient and stick with it. Inculcate agility and think like a pioneer.

Creating A Long-Term Legacy:
Building Sustainable Influence

Specialized knowledge, a strong managerial strategy, and guts to face situations head on are factors from my life story. I hope that in sharing my own experiences, others can also find happiness, follow their dreams, and bring about a future that truly reflects their own heartfelt passions.

My journey serves as a testament to what impact family values, long-range planning, and visionary leadership can produce. By sharing my experiences, I hope that you will gain the strength to take off on your dreams and build a legacy with your own determination and love for what you do.

These lessons stress the importance of resilience, collaborative working and constant learning. How to adapt to changing circumstances and through perseverance overcome the problems that arise are all key elements in long-term success. These experiences will provide valuable guidance for the next great generation of entrepreneurs, and tomorrow's leaders.

Building a legacy is all about establishing a lasting impact and being inspired by your work that delivers this impact. These lessons highlight the criticality of strategic thinking and visionary leadership, highlighting the value of resilience and determination in achieving long-term success.

The Path Ahead – A Commitment To Excellence

As I work through the sometimes uncertain and ambiguous business world, my first concepts and early life education help put me right back on track. In any and all opportunities that present themselves, I see my path pushing through the chaos with the spirit of *'The Art of The Possible'*, and each time, I weather the storm and arrive at a brilliant destination of amazing business results. This story, applied to your own situations, can do that for you, too.

The path ahead is about remaining steadfastly committed to excellence and leadership driven by innovation. I can't emphasize enough - stay curious and adaptable, highlighting the value of continuous improvement and strategic thinking in achieving long-term success.

In previous chapters, I have charted my professional journey: how success was won through hardship – indeed, how bright the successes were despite tough situations.

These early lessons and principles have determined every step I've taken, imbuing me with an intense love for business innovation and entrepreneurship.

Section 7

The International Adventure

A Privilege With Opportunities, Risks, Decisions And Determination: Unexpected Plans – Goals Redefined

The idea of moving to America had never seriously crossed my mind before I married. While I admired America for its business successes, scientific achievements, and technological accomplishments, as well as on the sports field I always thought that I would make my life inside India. My earliest career thoughts had me pegged to two domains - going on to work for a reputable Indian company or in some fitting government job such as at FACT or Hindustan Machine Tools (HMT).

By marrying Meher Banu in early 1965, however, I gained new points of view. Meher's father, N.A. Noor Mohammed, thought that I could accomplish more than just having a job at HMT or a government service career.

For him, the world was a global village, and India, the epicentre of that village. He had studied in the United States and subsequently returned to India, where he entered a government career as director general of the newly established National Solid State Physics Laboratory in Madras. He had earned a Yale law Ph.D. in international law and was convinced that an American degree could greatly enhance my career prospects.

It was N. Mohammed's international experience and point of view that influenced him. He had grown up in India, got his degree in the United States and was involved in Africa. Now he felt that the U.S. represented a land of opportunity and that I would gain from education there. At that time, the US Congress had just enacted the Immigration and Nationality Act 1965 which abolished the discriminatory National Origins Formula operating since the past 108 years ago, making it more possible for foreign students like me to study and work in America.

The Turning Point: A Mentor's Encouragement

I was set up for a bright future thanks to N. Mohammed's vision for my future. Instead of planning to enter HMT or taking a government job that might not provide for lifelong career satisfaction, he suggested I ought to aim higher. According to him getting an international degree would be crucial for a full realization of my maximum potential. In his advice, my father-in-law was not only drawing on his U.S. education but also his working experience globally in different continents. There was great value in his guidance, and I could draw on his worldwide experience and contacts.

He knew that the easiest way to be accepted here in the United States was as a student: he had been a student here twice. Armed with a Ph.D. in law from Yale University, he shaped his career as an international judge. I, too, was looking forward to studying in America. Such a degree could get my career off the ground, just as an American degree launched his. I was enthused at the prospect but had no idea where to start – seeing this N. Mohammed enlisted Prof. Ernest E. 'Ernie' Hoffman, a friend of his from his days in New Haven and now a professor at New Haven College who was living in Bridgeport, Connecticut.

Hoffman, with links to the University of Bridgeport, a small private institution 20 miles south of Yale and sixty-five miles north of New York City, recommended it to me. Following Hoffman's lead, I applied for a master's degree in material science at the University of Bridgeport in Connecticut. After earning an undergraduate degree in mechanical engineering, the logical course of action was to go on to material science for graduate work. Hoffman counseled me through the admission process, and in the fall of 1965, I was accepted for the master's program.

The Admissions Process – A New Way Forward

The University of Bridgeport was no accident in the end.

The Hoffmans had always been there; having them nearby would be advantageous both for Meher and myself in the early days. Inside a few weeks, I got my I-20 document which the university had sent me, and which is necessary for a student to get into the United States. It was the start of a new adventure, full of anticipation and possibility.

But one severe obstacle loomed ahead: my father, Nagoor Rawther, was vehemently opposed to the idea of my going. He had two major concerns.

Firstly he was worried about the politics of and situation in America. It was the middle 1960s, a time when the civil rights movement and sporadic violence were rife. President John F. Kennedy's assassination in 1963 also affected him profoundly.

Secondly, my father wanted me to stay close by in order that I could continue my support for the family. As the eldest son, he expected me to take care of my brother and sisters and take on the family's responsibilities. Torn between the expectations of my father and the opportunities offered by my father-in-law, in the end I decided to postpone my admission for a year and keep working at HMT.

The Birth Of Our Daughter:
A Transformative Experience Of Fatherhood

Another important change in my life occurred in early 1966. On January 7, 1966, our daughter Hafiza was born to Meher in Mogadishu, at the house of her parents. The delivery was attended by a woman doctor from Russia, which showed the truly international environment in the United Nations compound where they lived. The birth of Hafiza was a source of great happiness for both our families.

In the seventh month of her pregnancy, she moved to Mogadishu to be with her parents for the delivery. This is a tradition, the daughter going back to her mother and father's house for her first delivery.

Broadening Horizons: New Experiences
Life In Mogadishu

Living in Mogadishu with my wife's parents was an enriching experience. Noor Mohammed dominated the legal sphere of Somalia, working as Vice-President of the Republic's Supreme Court and later becoming Legal Advisor to the Prime Minister. His accomplishments and the respect people felt for him were highly impressive. At a young age, in a Tamil Muslim family in Kottar near Nagercoil, he had to put up with many kinds of hardships, including a severe eye problem that had almost ruined his studies at Harvard. He showed great resilience, practicing yoga to improve his vision and later secured a scholarship at Yale. All of this displayed his determination and creative spirit.

These qualities were strongly present in his advice and guidance, which hugely influenced my decision to go for further education in the U.S.

For the next several months, our home was a big house belonging to my in-laws on the UN campus, overlooking the Indian Ocean. There were always people coming and going from the house. N. Mohammed's friends and UN people were always dropping by. This was my first major exposure to an international and mixed multi-ethnic community. This environment ushered in a fresh sense of life for me. Being a father and, at the same time, living in a multicultural atmosphere fermented new ideas and opened up my thinking on reaching for new horizons with confidence.

Reviving The U.S. Dream: A Strategic Decision

In Mogadishu, N. Mohammed revived the idea of pursuing a master's degree in the U.S. He reasoned that once my father saw how advantageous a U.S. degree could be, he would naturally change his mind. With his support and that of his UN colleagues, I decided to reinstate my admission to the University of Bridgeport.

This was not a decision I could take lightly. Although my father still disagreed, I was able to make an independent choice, especially helped by the geographical distance from him at the time. I explained my reasons to him calmly, stressing the long-term advantages that an American education would bring. Though my father was not happy, he finally came to accept my decision.

N. Mohammed hosted a farewell party for us with his friends and UN colleagues on the invitation list. A poignant moment on this elaborate occasion was when he asked me to speak. It was my first time speaking in public, and at first it felt difficult but then I enjoyed it as I thanked people for their good wishes.

It gave me a taste for speaking in public with ease.

A Difficult Goodbye

Leaving our daughter, Hafiza, in Mogadishu with her grandparents was a hard decision for us. As a student in the U.S., we would not have means to support her well. However, the knowledge that she would be well cared for by her grandparents was reassuring and ultimately proved a sound decision.

Two years after we were married, Meher and I left Mogadishu for New York in the fall of 1966. Our journey from Mogadishu took us first to London, courtesy of British Airways, then from London to New York on Pan American Airlines. My father-in-law had bought the tickets, a starting fund of $1,000

Starting In A New Culture From Scratch
- Arrival In The United States

As we arrived at Kennedy International Airport on a sunny day in September, Ernest and Betty Hoffman came out in their Volvo to greet us. They drove to the family house, where they had hosted my father-in-law when he was studying at Yale, and welcomed us to stay with them until I could find somewhere else.

Initially, living with the Hoffmans was also a pleasant introduction to American life, one with its own comforts and benefits.

Living with the Hoffmans was nothing short of a steep learning curve on the American ways. The individualist culture of America was so different from everything I knew in India. I remember one incident when I carelessly threw a shirt on the table without thinking anything of it. Betty immediately corrected me and emphasized the importance of cleanliness and doing things for oneself. This incident had a lasting effect on me, and cleanliness both at home and office, became a natural way.

Early Struggles – Finding Our Own Home

Within a few days, we set out to look for our own place near the school. Ernest made the rounds with me. But at the outset, we were hit by prejudice. A Polish immigrant landlord said he wouldn't rent me his property. Such was the prejudice and narrow thinking that he thought I was Puerto Rican. This was my first encounter with racial discrimination and was a stark reminder of the perceptions towards others in America.

Eventually, with the help of the Hoffmans, we secured living quarters in the attic of another Polish immigrant's home. Though the living conditions were humble, they were bearable. Independent and in our own place, I now turned my attention to think about future plans.

Managing Both – Work And Study: The University Of Bridgeport

The University of Bridgeport, located by the Long Island Sound, was a buzzing institution in a city with substantial industrial facilities. General Electric and Singer Sewing Machine Co. were among the industrial concerns located in Bridgeport, and the presence of major companies drew a diverse working-class population. But the city was also suffering from deindustrialization, which brought with it its own set of economic problems.

I signed up for evening classes and planned to find a job by day to support myself and pay my tuition and living expenses. Of the $1,000 we had with us, almost $600 went to cover the tuition fees for the first semester and one month's rent. My first job in America was with a small company, where the pay was low. However, a few months later, one of my teachers, who acted as a consultant for Bullard Machine Tools Co., helped me find a better job there.

Gaining Practical Experience
Working At Bullard Machine Tools

At Bullard Machine Tools Co, a leading manufacturer of machine tools, I obtained important practical experience. My work included studies of factory operations and observation of such operations as deburring gears. It's 'on-the-job' nature broadened my technical skills and also deepened my understanding of industrial processes.

Balancing work with the study was tough. I would take the 5 o'clock bus to work and get home in the late afternoon; grab a quick meal, then head over to college for evening classes. Meher also worked as a typist and secretary at the Red Cross office of Bridgeport Hospital, although her work was voluntary.

I just didn't care about the long hours and the demanding schedule. I was determined to succeed and willing to work hard. When I reflect on those days, what comes to mind is the simple pleasures we relished then, like having our regular Big Mac treat after work on payday or buying a black-and-white TV on an installment plan.

These small indulgences were signposts in our progress.

Resilience And Independence: Lessons Learned

- **Embracing Hard Work: Laying the Foundation.**
  The first year in the U.S. was tough going, but it was a time full of lessons for me in resilience and independence. Part-time study plus work was new to me, but it made me understand even more deeply the value of hard work and perseverance. At Bullard, I earned significantly more than my salary in India. I became a good saver and I began to build up reserves, savoring the increasing balances on my bank statements.

- **Remaining Strong and Resolved: Facing Prejudice.**
  In the first-year racism was tough and posed problems newcomers face. But it also had an impact on my own determination. By living through these complexities with toughness and determination I learned that the most important thing is to keep one's eye fixed firmly on goals and dreams.

- **Maintaining Ties: Staying Connected.**
  Although far from home, regular letters to my mother and the occasional telephone call kept me in touch with my roots. These connections gave me something to anchor myself upon and have emotional support at difficult moments.

- **Establishing Credit: Toward Stability.**
  One of the practical things I learned was the importance of credit history. Buying an installment-paid black-and-white TV set was all that was needed to get me started, and it was also an important step toward getting real stability in finance for migrants to the US.

Looking Forward: A Journey of Growth
Building A Firm Foundation
And The Importance Of Education

My decision to further my education in the United States was transformational. New horizons were reached, more opportunities appeared for which I was ready, and finally, a foundation was laid down. Without living through this period of experience, I could never have developed an entrepreneurial mindset of my own nor acquired the vital leadership skills from those successful entrepreneurs who surrounded me.

Embracing Change: The Power Of Adaptability

Adapting to a new culture and handling the difficulties of immigrant life was a lesson in adaptability. These experiences taught me to embrace change, to be resilient in the face of difficulty, and always have my eyes on the goal. Throughout the journey, Meher was an indispensable source of support. We mastered the challenges of a new country with its different pressures on work and study and family responsibilities.

The Future: A Vision For Success

As I continued my studies and took on practical work experience, I kept my long-term objectives in mind. The journey was just beginning, and the lessons of this period would stand me in good stead for future success. Decisions and actions on education, work and life built and displayed resilience in the face of adversity.

I was well prepared to meet the opportunities and challenges that lay ahead.

In Sections 1, 2, and 3 of this book, I develop on my professional journey and explore the obstacles faced as well as the achievements. The values and lessons learned in those early years supported or underpinned each step of my way forward, thereby contributing to an unwavering passion for entrepreneurship and leadership.

The Decision To Pursue Further Education Influencers And Motivations

Thinking back on my days in Mogadishu and the discussions with my father-in-law, Mohammed Noor, I saw just how important it was to have higher education. His experiences and accomplishments served to illustrate what a difference an advanced degree from an international institution could make. N. Mohammed himself was living proof that while opportunities may not be equal, education can still have transformative power. He thought that obtaining a degree from a U.S. university would open doors for me and bring great value and success to my career.

His help and advice had a lot to do with my decision. He talked about his time at Yale, the problems he encountered there, and how things turned out. Becoming a successful international judge was evidence that to persevere pays off, and it pays off more than you can imagine.

Winning Over Family To My Decision

It was no easy task to persuade my father to support my decision to pursue my studies in the United States. He worried about political stability in America and what form such uncertainty might take. Moreover, he was concerned with how I could reconcile my responsibilities as the eldest son to what he saw as a highly uncertain future in the United States and the effect on the family. However, I held firmly that the long-term advantages were more important than the potential risks. I explained this logic to my father, emphasizing possible career promotions and the opportunities offered by U.S. degrees.

My father gradually cast his doubts aside and gave my plans cautious support. He could see my drive and enthusiasm; he also saw financial success in what I was doing. This change of heart marked a major turning point in his attitude and enabled me to go ahead with confidence. My mother and brother offered great encouragement. Fortunately, with their support we could set sail on dreams to a bright future.

Preparing For The Voyage

Preparations got underway for the U.S. study. There were many technical details to be resolved, such as getting visas, organizing travel, and then finding a place to live. The network and contacts of my father-in-law were priceless in overcoming these obstacles. They filled me with encouragement and helped to make sure that I was fully prepared for this change.

Being parted from Hafiza in Mogadishu was a hard choice, but it was the only one suitable for us. We knew her grandparents would take good care of her, freeing us to concentrate on studying and later on building a firm foundation in the United States. Periods like this, so fraught with uncertainties and challenges, can also strengthen one's determination with the right attitude to come through. Recognizing these factors is the hallmark of someone who lifts themselves up to great heights of success.

Life In The United States Begins

After we arrived in the United States, a new life began. It was full of uncertainty and excitement.

Hoffman supported us as we adjusted to our new environment. His hospitality and help made those first few months feel stable and reassured us that we could settle well. It also allowed me to concentrate more on studies and the understanding of American culture

Living in America brought its own special challenges and opportunities. The emphasis on self-sufficiency and individualism required me to change my ways significantly. I learned the importance of personal responsibility and independence, which later would aid me in my entrepreneurial career. These experiences taught me to think more flexibly and to be resilient.

Academic Rigor And Practical Experience

Entering the master's program in material science at the University of Bridgeport was a big step forward. The classes were challenging, and the intellectual atmosphere there was exhilaratingly high quality. I had to combine study with part-time work for livelihood.

This called for a controlled timetable and will-power.

The practical experience that I obtained at Bullard Machine Tools Company was of great value. Working alongside specialists in their field, I learned about industrial processes and advanced production techniques. This practical experience (along with my academic study) gave me a complete picture of the engineering business. The skills and knowledge that I acquired during this period laid the solid foundation for my future career in business leadership.

A Support Network Matters

While at the University of Bridgeport, I realized the importance of a support network. Creating connections among teachers, fellow students, and co-workers gave a sense of togetherness and mutual help. These relationships gave me many useful hints and useful guidance in my development, both academic and professional.

The guidance and encouragement of one of my professors also made a huge difference. His guidance helped me to manage the balance between work and academics.

Managing Finances And Stability

Balancing the budget was a critical aspect of my journey. My education costs and living expenses had to be carefully balanced. Despite this, I was able to manage our expenses and also save well thanks to the fact that my salary at Bullard was significantly higher than what I earned in India. Being used to that lower amount we could live frugally. This financial stability provided a sense of security and enabled us to focus on our goals.

In the US, often your credit rating says more about you than your bank balance. Building my credit rating was another important milestone. A black-and-white TV purchased on installment helped to establish my credit history and it was a critical step toward financial stability in the US. This experience highlighted to me the importance of financial understanding and money management – lessons that have always served me in my entrepreneurial journey. I have built my companies debt-free yet highly profitable.

Cultural Adaptation And Personal Growth

The adjustment to life in the United States was a challenge and an education. American society's emphasis on individualism meant I had to make serious adjustments. On the other hand, the environment also provided opportunities for personal growth. As I gradually adapted to its cultural nuances, my communication skills improved, and my horizon broadened. Encountering racism and prejudice was a harsh reality, but it also stiffened my determination. I learned from such experiences to tackle difficulties with toughness, sticking to my goals and aspirations. The lessons learned during this period emphasized once again that persistence toward an objective is critical.

Forging Ahead: Embracing New Opportunities
The Value Of Perpetual Learning

The decision to undertake advanced study in the U.S. proved a turning point for me, providing new opportunities and widening my horizons. The lessons learned during this period affected my attitudes toward entrepreneurship and leadership. Making the approach to learning a habit slowly became my religion, infusing my spirit with light and energy. The combination of academic discipline, practical experience and adaptability to a new culture provided a solid base for my later successes. These experiences illustrated the value of pursuing knowledge and remaining open to new challenges. The journey was only starting, but the lessons learned during this period would provide an anchor for all future endeavors.

Strategic Connections And Mentorship

A support network and seeking out a mentor were essential to my journey. The connections made with professors, classmates and friends were invaluable sources of guidance and help. These relationships underscored how important it is to cooperate, how beneficial mutual aid can be in both professional and personal development.

Through strategic networking, new opportunities presented themselves widely, and my professional horizons broadened. The support of mentors, people like my professor who helped get me into Bullard has been a great help in confronting challenges and achieving success. These experiences reinforced the importance of forming and maintaining meaningful relationships in seeking to achieve my objectives.

Espousing Change

The process of entering a new culture and overcoming the difficulties encountered showed me that adaptability is the most important lesson. From my experiences I learned to follow change, withstand trouble, and keep my mind firmly on my goal. Overcoming cultural differences and surmounting difficulties became part of my understanding of the direction of enterprise.

Reflections And Future Aspirations
Looking Back: Insights For The Future

As I talk about my years at the University of Bridgeport and the experiences of coming to the States, it's dawned on me just how much this period is really a time full of transformation. The lessons picked up in areas such as resilience, adaptability, and self-study have greatly affected my thinking and approach to work. Living through many difficulties convinced of the significance of perseverance and determination.

Building a Legacy:
Inspirations For The New Generations

From family values and strategic thinking to a string of splendid ideas, that is what my life has been. You must hold firm to your dreams and not abandon them. You must reach out and leave something of value behind for future generations. Our experiences and our life lessons will become invaluable directions to newcomers in business and future leaders.

Committed to Excellence – Continuing the Journey

Although I continue to meet all sorts of trials in the business world, the values and lessons from my formative years keep me forever on track. Each challenge and opportunity further reinforce my firm commitment not only to innovation-driven entrepreneurship but also one that guarantees quality. Now we look at a new generation with possibilities lying before us like unopened flowers. The experiences and lessons learned during this period must continue to light our pathway ahead.

Epilogue

About Javad Hassan

The Art Of The Possible

As I sit here reflecting on my journey at the age of 84, I am filled with a profound sense of gratitude and fulfillment.

My life has been a testament to the belief that there are no limits to what we can achieve if we dare to dream and work relentlessly toward our goals.

This epilogue is not just a conclusion to my story, but a message of inspiration and encouragement to all aspiring entrepreneurs and future leaders. My journey from a junior engineer at IBM to a corporate vice president at AMP and then a serial entrepreneur embodies the essence of *'The Art of the Possible'*.

The Key Characteristics Of Success

1. Embrace Innovation

From my earliest days at IBM, I was fascinated by the transformative power of technology.

Innovation has always been the cornerstone of my success. Whether it was developing an automated wafer-handling system at IBM or pioneering new interconnection technologies at AMP, the drive to innovate kept me ahead of the curve. Innovation is not just about creating new products but about finding better ways to solve problems and improve processes.

For aspiring entrepreneurs, this means always looking for opportunities to do things differently and better.

2. Adaptability And Resilience

Life and business are filled with uncertainties.

My career has seen its fair share of challenges, from cultural adjustments at IBM to financial crises at AMP and beyond.

The ability to adapt to changing circumstances and remain resilient in the face of setbacks is crucial. Each challenge is an opportunity to learn and grow. When the market crash of 1997 impacted a significant portion of my business, resilience helped me rebuild and continue pursuing my vision. Resilience is about maintaining a positive outlook and persevering despite difficulties.

3. Value Mentorship And Relationships

Throughout my journey, mentors played a pivotal role in my development. Figures like George Micklus at IBM and Jim Marley at AMP provided invaluable guidance and support. Building strong relationships based on mutual respect and trust is essential. These connections not only provide support during challenging times but also open doors to new opportunities.

For future leaders, seeking mentorship and nurturing professional relationships should be a continuous endeavor.

4. Embrace Diversity And Inclusion

One of the most significant lessons I learned is the value of diversity. Working in different environments, from the United States to India and beyond, taught me the strength that comes from diverse perspectives. Building inclusive teams that respect and leverage individual differences leads to more innovative solutions and a collaborative culture.

As leaders, fostering an environment where everyone feels valued and included should be a top priority.

5. Follow Your Passion

Aligning your career with your true interests and strengths is essential for long-term success and fulfillment. My passion for technology and innovation drove me to take risks and pursue opportunities that others might have avoided. This passion was not just about personal achievement but about making a positive impact through my work. For aspiring entrepreneurs, finding and following your passion will fuel your motivation and drive you towards excellence.

A Message To Aspiring Entrepreneurs And Future Leaders

To the endeavoring aspirants and future leaders reading this, want to share a few thoughts that have guided me throughout my life:

Believe In The Art Of The Possible

Anything is possible if you believe in yourself and your vision. Do not be afraid to dream big and pursue those dreams with all your heart. Challenges will come, but each obstacle is an opportunity to innovate and grow.

Stay Curious And Keep Learning

Never stop learning. The world is constantly changing, and staying curious will help you adapt and thrive. Embrace new experiences, seek knowledge, and continuously improve yourself.

Be Persistent And Patient

Success does not come overnight. It requires patience and persistence. Stay committed to your goals, and do not be discouraged by setbacks. Each step, no matter how small, brings you closer to your destination.

Build And Nurture Your Network

Surround yourself with people who support and inspire you. Build a network of mentors, peers, and collaborators who can provide guidance, encouragement, and opportunities. Strong relationships are the foundation of a successful career.

Maintain Integrity And Respect

Conduct yourself with integrity and respect for others. These values will earn you trust and create lasting, meaningful connections. In the end, it is not just about what you achieve but how you achieve it.

Continuing The Journey Of Creativity And Innovation

At 84, my enthusiasm for creativity and innovation remains undiminished. I continue to explore new ideas and ventures, finding joy in the process of discovery and creation. The world of business and technology is ever-evolving, and there are always new challenges to tackle and opportunities to seize. My journey is an authentication of the fact that age needn't be a barrier to innovation and entrepreneurship and demonstrates that, ultimately, it is drive, passion, and belief that energize longevity and continued creativity.

Gratitude: A Foundation Of My Success

No journey is undertaken alone, and mine has been shaped by the incredible support, guidance, and contributions of many individuals. I owe a deep sense of gratitude to my colleagues, business associates, and exemplars who have influenced my path and enriched my professional and personal life.

Colleagues And Business Associates

At IBM, I was fortunate to work with some of the brightest minds in the industry. Their dedication and collaboration provided a fertile ground for innovation. In my entrepreneurial ventures, many partners and team members have contributed to the growth and success of our endeavors. Your hard work, creativity, and loyalty have been the backbone of our achievements.

Family: My Pillars Of Strength

My deepest gratitude goes to my family, whose love and support have been my guiding light.

My mother, MM Khadijoo, instilled in me the values of endurance, adaptability, and innovation. Her strength and wisdom have been a constant source of inspiration.

My father, Nagoor Rawther, taught me the importance of hard work and resilience. His transition from a police officer to a successful planter showed me the power of determination and adaptability.

Their teachings and sacrifices laid the foundation for my success, and I am eternally grateful for their influence on my life.

My wife Sabiha who has been a formidable energizing force and the wind in my sails. My daughters, who have been patient and encouraging, have made me proud of their own achievements.

To all aspiring entrepreneurs and future leaders, I leave you with this: *'The Art of the Possible'* lies within you.

Believe in yourself, stay curious, be resilient, and never stop dreaming. Your journey is just beginning, and the possibilities are limitless.

With gratitude and belief,

Javad Hassan

About Javad Hassan

A Mechanical Engineering graduate with a Master's Degree in Material Science, Javad Hassan's big dream was to work for the world's forerunning technology leader and US giant, IBM.

At IBM, he quickly distinguished himself by winning an Innovation Achievement Award and an Outstanding Innovation Award. He rapidly rose to Director of Corporate Engineering Technology Worldwide.

He then joined as a senior executive at AMP quickly rising to the role as Corporate VP of Technology and Strategic Products. Under AMP, he was at the fore of innovation, efficiency, and productivity, and increasingly, the successful driving force behind several key strategic acquisitions and mergers.

His entrepreneurial adventure had already started while at AMP, but the real odyssey began after resigning.

The NeST Group launched or acquired more than a dozen companies in fiber optics, software, system integration, IT infrastructure, healthcare IT, and digital media.

In recognition of his invaluable contribution to innovation and technology, Javad Hassan was awarded an Honorary Doctorate in Engineering from NJIT, New Jersey Institute of Technology.

www.ingramcontent.com/pod-product-compliance
Lightning Source LLC
LaVergne TN
LVHW092005050326
832904LV00018B/325/J